SEARCHING FOR TRUTH IN THE TRANSITIONAL JUSTICE MOVEMENT

Searching for Truth in the Transitional Justice Movement examines calls for a truth commission to redress the brutal war during the breakup of the former Yugoslavia, the decades-long armed conflict in Colombia, and US detention policies in the War on Terror. In so doing, it argues that transitional justice is an idea around which a loosely structured movement emerged and professionalized, making truth commissions a standard response to mass violence. By exploring how this movement developed, as well as efforts to make truth commissions in the Balkans, Colombia, and the US, this book explains different processes through which political actors translate new legal ideas such as transitional justice into political action. Further, it reveals how the malleability of transitional justice and truth commissions is both an asset and a liability for those hoping to ensure accountability, improve survivor well-being, and prevent future violence.

Jamie Rowen is Assistant Professor of Legal Studies and Political Science at the University of Massachusetts, Amherst. She received her doctorate from the Jurisprudence and Social Policy Program at the University of California, Berkeley, as well as a law degree from Berkeley School of Law. Dr. Rowen's work has been published in the *International Journal of Transitional Justice, Law and Social Inquiry, Human Rights Quarterly,* and numerous other outlets.

Searching for Truth in the Transitional Justice Movement

JAMIE ROWEN
University of Massachusetts, Amherst

CAMBRIDGE
UNIVERSITY PRESS

University Printing House, Cambridge CB2 8BS, United Kingdom

One Liberty Plaza, 20th Floor, New York, NY 10006, USA

477 Williamstown Road, Port Melbourne, VIC 3207, Australia

4843/24, 2nd Floor, Ansari Road, Daryaganj, Delhi - 110002, India

79 Anson Road, #06-04/06, Singapore 079906

Cambridge University Press is part of the University of Cambridge.

It furthers the University's mission by disseminating knowledge in the pursuit of education, learning and research at the highest international levels of excellence.

www.cambridge.org
Information on this title: www.cambridge.org/9781107108769
DOI: 10.1017/9781316258279

First published 2017

Printed in the United States of America by Sheridan Books, Inc.

A catalogue record for this publication is available from the British Library

ISBN 978-1-107-10876-9 Hardback
ISBN 978-1-107-51969-5 Paperback

To the Survivors

Contents

Acknowledgments

This book would not have been possible without the direct help of hundreds of people, and the indirect help of countless more. Doing a project that involved fieldwork in nine countries, four languages, survey research and analysis, hundreds of interviews, participant observation in dozens of conferences, and information documents from dozens of advocacy organizations, was a huge undertaking. This project would also not have been possible without the generous financial support of the National Science Foundation, the John L. Simpson Memorial Fellowship, the Foreign Language and Area Studies Fellowship, and support from iCourts Center of Excellence at the University of Copenhagen.

I might not have pursued graduate school, and certainly not a critical analysis of transitional justice, were it not for Professor Laura Nader. I decided to leave Swarthmore College and come to UC Berkeley as an undergraduate in 2000, hoping to work with Professor Nader and learn from her work on the anthropology of law. Soon, Professor Nader became my mentor, and remains my academic and intellectual conscience. Whenever I think of an argument I want to make, or how I want to pursue my career, I think of her and what she would say. Professor Nader would always cut right to the chase and say exactly what she thought. She taught me how to recognize when something that is wrong, and have the courage to say it.

Next, I would not have completed this book without my dissertation committee members at UC Berkeley. Lauren Edelman, Calvin Morrill, Daniel Rubinfeld, Rob MacCoun, and Laura Nader put their faith in me, which is no small feat when asked to get on board with a project of this scope. In particular, Lauren Edelman saw my potential and capabilities even when I felt convinced that I could not finish this project. Calvin Morrill was an incredible resource, always happy to give me new ideas and perspectives as we tried to make sense of the complexity of my case studies. His brilliance, and ability to translate that brilliance into effective mentorship, was invaluable through the latter stages of this project. Daniel Rubinfeld and Rob Maccoun were similarly inspiring mentors, and always believed in my ability to carry out this project and pursue my goals.

A number of other mentors at UC Berkeley, the American Bar Foundation, the University of Toronto also made this book possible. First, Laurel Fletcher modeled what it means to be an insightful academic and deeply caring advocate. Maria Echaveste's work and mentorship continue to inspire me. Roxanna Altholz is a similarly inspirational advocate, and gave me great guidance for my work on Colombia. Jamie O'Connell offered a course on transitional justice my first semester at law school and continued to thoughtfully mentor me as I developed my career. Michael Musheno helped me understand the importance of a well-designed study and passion for the subject material. He also helped me through the latter stages of the book writing process, and role modeled the kind of academic I want to be. Mariana Valverde similarly helped me think through the more difficult theoretical questions and implications. Jennifer Carlson was the most instrumental in helping me turn this project into a book, and motivated me with her drive and incredibly incisive analysis of complex social phenomena. At the ABF, Laura Beth Nielsen, Terry Halliday, and John Hagan generously welcomed me and helped me develop this project, as well as others.

Others helped me with more specific parts of this book, looking over chapters and different parts of the analysis. Su Li was a critical collaborator for the survey analysis, and Alexa Koenig has helped me numerous times with her thoughtful editing and perspectives on these issues that we both care so much about. Mark Massoud's remarkable work in Sudan inspired me to pursue a project focused on international and transnational law and society. Both Mark and Rachel Stern provided guidance on the book publishing process, and helped me think through various parts of my argument. I also thank Keramet Reiter, Brent Nakamura, Ming Chen, Gwyn Leachman, Ariel Meyerstein, Tamara Lave, Pamela Coukos, Lyn Chua, Hadar Aviram, Edi Kinney, Kerstin Carlsen, Crysanthi Leon, Ashley Rubin and many others whom I worked alongside with for years in the attic of the Jurisprudence and Social Science building at UC Berkeley, and shared insights about life with as we went through the tumult of being fresh academics.

The specific case studies in this book required a great amount of assistance. Of course, everyone that I interviewed deserves a special mention of gratitude, as do all those who helped me settle into places. In Morocco, Youssef Taleb showed me the meaning of generosity, and in South Africa, John Malherbe offered me great care and a lot of driving! I'll always remember and be grateful for Damir's couch in an old, Austrian-style flat, which was soon joined by Irina. I also smile to think of movie nights with Marija, Edin, and others on winter nights in Sarajevo. Tarik, Iman, and the rest of my Sarajevo community made me question whether I should just move to that gorgeous city. The strength of friendships there made me realize what I want for my life. My friends from Global Children's Organization, Ninja, Gogo, Adi, and others also reminded me of why I will always feel like I have a home in the Balkans.

Alma Elesovic, Feda Kulenovic, Karen Fagerstrom and Diana Malin, and the rest of my GCO family (Elisa Malin, David Glenn, and many others), inspired my love for the region and its people, and helped with logistics and insights when I needed them.

In Colombia, Pablo Rueda and Natalia Sarmiento treated me with generous hospitality. They helped me settle in and fall equally enamored with Bogota. When I returned to the city five years later, Maria Victoria Castro and Daniel Prieto were the best hosts I could ask for. With their bikes, I was able to traverse the frightening roadways in order to maximize the number of interviews that I could conduct in a day. Throughout my fieldwork in Colombia, I made great friends who made every day living as a foreigner feel far less challenging. The people I interviewed in Colombia, much like those who generously gave me their time in the Balkans, were unforgettable. I hope the stories that I share here do some justice to the incredible work that many people are doing to help heal the wounds of atrocity. Finally, my US case brought me to New York, where I was graciously hosted by Carlo Romero. I am also incredibly grateful to the dozens of individuals who took time from their important work to provide insights into their efforts to redress abuses committed during the War on Terror.

This book would also not have been possible without the support of my dear friends. Lara Hruska, Dalia Rotter Youngerwood, and Sarah Cohen were always near in my thoughts, while Leah Atwood and Erica Meta Smith were always near for an adventure or a hug. Peter Schorer served as an indefatigable support during my early years of graduate school. Towards the end of my time in Berkeley, Michael Schwarz helped me think through the nuances of my argument, and be able to argue. In Toronto, Christopher Miller, Mary Samplaski, Paulina Czajkowski, Matthew Light, and Gavin Slade helped keep me inspired to continue working even when I wasn't sure what I was working towards. In Amherst, my incredible community of wonderful scholars and caring friends made the last stages of this book far more enjoyable. Lauren McCarthy continues to read my work, give me great suggestions, and even simple copy edits. Charli Carpenter has been a mentor in every way possible. I am so grateful for her insights into the U.S. chapter, as well as to have found another academic and friend to emulate. Leila Kawar read parts of an earlier argument on the Colombia case. Paul Collins and Rebecca Hamlin have also provided me with great support, as have Justin Gross, Leah Wing, Deepika Marya, and the others whose presence makes me grateful to go to work every day.

Finally, my family continues to keep me afloat when I need that, and brings me back to the ground when I need that. My family members, however frustrating they can be, have modeled courage, dignity, and the dogged pursuit of meaning in our lives. My stepfather gave me my first Foreign Affairs magazine when I was twelve years old, well aware that I was going to pursue my passion for foreign countries, languages, and peoples. I'll always remember the sight of my mother's knee, which was at the same height as I was when she went back to graduate school, and the word "dissertation." Until graduate school, I thought dissertation translated to, "I cannot play with you right now, I'm working." I think the translation still fits. Watching a mostly single mother pursue a dissertation when one is knee height definitely gave me the work ethic I still have, and showed me that working hard can lead to the life we want. My father taught me to always question the underlying assumptions of any argument, and to fight when I see injustice. My older brother modeled the joy of learning a foreign language and making a life abroad, as well as asking sharp questions and devouring information. My little brother showed me how to appreciate the simple things, and treat everyone with kindness. I am incredibly grateful to my Aunt Wendy for chats at her kitchen table in Berkeley, to my loving Aunts Sheri and Lisa, to my grandparents whose generosity enabled me to visit my loved ones during graduate school, and to the rest of the fabulous families I am a part of.

The last two people I wish to thank are my life partners, my twin sister Tami and my love, Christopher Klimmek. Beginning with the latter, I am so grateful for Chris' unwavering affection and commitment. The foundation he provides makes the waves of uncertainty much easier to ride. Finally, it is difficult to express the gratitude I feel for my sister. I wouldn't even know who I was in the world without her. Since we were in the womb, wombmates as we like to call it, we have been supporting and pushing each other to grow. Her faith in me, and endless capacity to give emotional support, made this project possible.

EXPLANATORY NOTE ON THE COVER

The cover image is of an Ashura ritual in Turkey. The day of Ashura is marked by Muslims as a whole, but for Shia Muslims it is a major religious commemoration of the martyrdom at Karbala of Hussein, a grandson of the Prophet Muhammad. For Sunni Muslims, it celebrates the day Moses and his followers were rescued from the Pharoah. Jews also celebrate this event with the Passover ritual that recounts the journey from slavery to freedom. For some Muslims, the day also celebrates Noah leaving the Ark and Muhammed's arrival in Medina. Ashura is marked with mourning rituals and passion plays re-enacting the martyrdom. In a book about truth commissions, the image honors the myriad ways in which peoples throughout the world commemorate histories of violence, and forge collective identities through those practices.

1

Searching for Truth

Ah, now, a truth commission. Why do we need a truth commission? What did other truth commissions do – contribute to – what did they achieve? And you know I didn't know the answer to that question really. I suppose that they did achieve something. Otherwise why would so many commissions be established in the first place?

(Interview with Serbian scholar 2010)

In May 2011, a group of youths stood on the pedestrian thoroughfare in the center of Sarajevo, the capital of Bosnia and Herzegovina (BiH). They held clipboards in their hands, hoping to gather signatures on a petition to create a truth commission that would "establish facts" about the most recent war in the Balkans. Foreign donors were excited about this initiative and provided millions of dollars for the effort. Foreign consultants, including staff at the International Center for Transitional Justice, had mentored this campaign from the beginning. Watching these youths collect signatures, it was easy to see the disconnection between these foreign elites and the Bosnians they hoped to help. Dressed in purple shirts, these youths nervously asked fellow Bosnians, pedestrians hurriedly getting home from work or going out to a café, if they felt enough had been done to address war crimes during the dissolution of the former Yugoslavia. The war's violence in Bosnia left over 100,000 people dead, and 80% of the victims were Bosniaks (a postwar label for Bosnian Muslims). Few people in the Balkans would say yes to this question, and few did that afternoon in May. Despite this fact, few wanted to sign the petition. The coalition's leader, watching from the sidelines, struggled to understand why these Bosnians were so resistant to supporting their proposed commission. After all, who wouldn't want a truth commission?

On the other side of the Atlantic, also in 2011, the Colombian government was negotiating a new law on the creation of "transitional justice instruments," specifically a truth commission, in the event of a peace accord with guerrilla groups that had fomented violence in the country for nearly six decades. This was not the first so-called transitional justice law in Colombia, or the first bid for a truth commission. Six years before, in 2005, the government passed the Justice and Peace Law. This policy offered alternative judicial sanctions to demobilizing paramilitary groups and also created the National Commission on Reparation and Reconciliation (NCRR), which scholars referred to as a "sort of truth commission" (Laplante and Theidon 2006). At the time, critics of the Justice and Peace Law viewed "transitional justice" as a euphemism for impunity for paramilitaries and pointed out that a truth commission could only function effectively if the violence stopped. A decade later, those same "transitional justice instruments" became the key to a peace accord with guerrilla groups. Policy makers mandated that, as one of these transitional justice instruments, a truth commission must be created in the event of an accord.

Due north of Colombia, in Washington, DC, calls for a truth commission had come and gone by 2011. In 2008, President Barack Obama was elected amid public demands to investigate and prosecute those involved in torture and unlawful detentions in the seemingly unending War on Terror. For a brief window after the election, left-leaning scholars, advocates, and even legislators were calling for a truth commission to clarify the causes and consequences of military detention under the Bush administration. Some of these actors drew on the idea of transitional justice to explain their calls for a commission, but many resisted labeling their proposed investigative bodies this way, even if they were sympathetic to concerns about torture in detention centers. For them, truth commissions were useful only in countries where there had been a definitive political transition, or where courts were unable or unwilling to address the violence.

How can we explain these concurrent calls for truth commissions in such politically disparate settings? Depending on one's definition of "truth commission," there have been somewhere between forty and ninety of these quasi-judicial bodies, and the number is on the rise (see Dancy et al. 2010).[1] Scholars often suggest that truth commissions are appealing because they are practically and politically palatable (Chandler and Heins 2007). Bakiner (2015), for one, suggests that truth commissions

[1] The different numbers have to do with whether or not nongovernmental commissions qualify (most scholars leave these out) and whether the commissions actually completed their work and produced a report. For the purposes of this book, I rely on one of the first definitions of truth commissions, provided by Hayner, as investigative bodies that focus on a past history of violence, not a specific outcome, exist for a defined period of time, and usually have some sort of sponsor (Hayner 1994, p. 604) When the sponsor is the government, the truth commission is considered official; when created by a nongovernmental entity, it is unofficial. This book focuses on official truth commissions. Gready (2010, p. 3) identifies the "core characteristics" of "official" truth commissions as (1) a focus on the past; (2) their origins at the point of transition away from war or authoritarian rule; (3) the investigation of patterns of abuses and specific violations committed over a period of time, rather than a single event; (4) a focus on violations of human rights, and sometimes of humanitarian norms as well; (5) a temporary, short-term life-span, usually culminating in the production of a report with recommendations; (6) official status, as commissions are sanctioned, authorized or empowered by the state (and sometimes by armed opposition groups, in the context of a peace accord); and (7) a victim-centered approach (see also Hayner 2002).

are particularly useful because they provide political opportunities for new organizations to make political demands on their leaders, even when those leaders viewed creating a truth commission as simply convenient way to address past violence. Their appeal, in theory, lies in the fact that they do not prioritize punishment for perpetrators, as punishing perpetrators through court processes, in theory, could foment divisions (Minow 1998). Rather, truth commissions focus on creating an accurate historical record of the violence, enabling survivors to share their stories, and making recommendations for social and political change.

Despite these laudable goals, when truth commissions are actually implemented, they often disappoint their proponents. In particular, they often create very narrow explanations of violence, survivors do not necessarily benefit from participating, and commissions' findings and recommendations have little impact on government policies (Wilson 2001; Brahm 2007; Olsen, Payne, and Reiter 2010).

To understand their continuing appeal and disappointing outcomes, this book takes a distinct approach to examining why truth commissions are being promoted in such different contexts. I argue that we cannot understand the proliferation of truth commissions without first examining the phrase that is so commonly used to explain and legitimate them: transitional justice. This phrase emerged in the early 1990s, when scholars, policy makers, and advocates were considering how countries moving from authoritarianism or armed conflict toward democratic regimes were using law to address human rights abuses under former regimes (Arthur 2009). After the South Africa Truth and Reconciliation Commission (TRC) and the creation of the International Center for Transitional Justice, truth commissions became a signature intervention of transitional justice (Teitel 2003; Gready 2010).

While scholars usually write about transitional justice as a field (see Bell 2009b) or a discipline (see Andrieu 2010a) or even a theory (see Dukalskis 2011), and try to explain what it means and what different interventions do, this book takes a constructivist approach and argues transitional justice is better understood as an idea – meaning a thought, a plan, or a suggestion – about how to redress mass, often state-sponsored, violence and ensure democratic social and political change. The idea encompasses an identifiable vocabulary with words such as truth and reconciliation (Turner 2013; Robins 2012) and an associated set of interventions including tribunals, truth commissions, and reparations programs (Roht-Arriaza 2006).[2] This book also argues that a movement has emerged around the idea, with goals of ensuring accountability, improving survivor well-being, and preventing future violence.[3]

2 While most studies of transitional justice refer to these different bodies as mechanisms, approaches, or processes, I refer to them as interventions in order to emphasize that the default is doing nothing to redress mass violence. This is a strategy that many governments have taken, and is often called "forgetting" in the transitional justice literature (Vinjamuri and Snyder 2004). Creating new legal bodies or policies to redress mass violence is intervening in a transition.

3 Scholarly definitions of transitional justice's goals vary widely, often depending on whether the idea is being used descriptively or prescriptively (Subotić 2009). Teitel (2005, p. 838), for example,

Departing from studies on the meaning of transitional justice or the efficacy of its associated interventions, this book focuses on how transitional justice is translated into political action, which I refer to as instrumentalization. To this end, this book addresses the following three questions: (1) How do actors that mobilize around transitional justice understand their goals and strategies? (2) How do actors that mobilize around truth commissions understand their goals and strategies? (3) How do their mobilization strategies help them realize their goals? More narrowly, this inquiry provides insights into why truth commissions are being promoted around the world. More broadly, understanding the instrumentalization of transitional justice helps illustrate a broader law and society question: How, and why, do actors mobilize the law to redress mass, often state-sponsored, violence? This latter question is now largely taken for granted given the growth of international criminal law and creation of international criminal tribunals. Though law is a fundamentally limited tool to deal with the complexity of mass atrocity, many scholars, policy makers, and activists continue to promote trials and truth commissions in order to attain wide-ranging goals.

This book argues that the utility of transitional justice lies in its malleability, which includes both its aspirational qualities related to bridging social and political divides and its ambiguity with regard to the value of prosecutions to redress mass violence. The idea's malleability, which is the result of how the movement around the idea emerged and professionalized, means that transitional justice serves as a placeholder for actors to articulate their goals and strategies and to make claims against one another. Actors see truth commissions, too, as malleable, which means that actors in strikingly different political contexts see the utility of creating them. Within countries, individuals and organizations with complementary, competing, or even contradictory goals related to punishment, getting information about loved ones, and receiving financial compensation all promote truth commissions.

However, this book points out that the same quality of malleability that makes transitional justice and truth commissions appealing is also problematic. Actors interested in redressing mass violence often have contradictory goals for who should

defines the goals as "rule of law, legitimacy, liberalization, nation-building, reconciliation, and conflict resolution." The goals usually include some notion of accountability, but specify that accountability is not necessarily judicial accountability or prosecutions of perpetrators. The other goals often revolve around survivors of violence, including socioeconomic benefits and the chance for survivors to tell their stories, which have to do with survivor well-being. Finally, the goals of changing the structural factors that led to violence, creating an accurate historical record, and bridging social divides (e.g., reconciliation) all point toward preventing future violence. Likewise, Shaw's analysis of the Sierra Leone TRC says the goals are to establish individual accountability, foster reconciliation, and prevent a recurrence of violence (Shaw 2007, p. 185) Actors in Colombia, for example, use the phrase "truth, justice, and reparation" when describing transitional justice. "Truth, justice, and reparation" refer to a variety of claims, but one way to understand them is historical clarification of a conflict's causes and consequences (truth), judicial accountability including sanctions for perpetrators (justice), and financial compensation for victims (reparation).

be punished and how, as well as which narrative of violence is the most accurate. While it may be easy to support a truth commission, the support may be shallow, and mobilizing around one may actually reproduce the social and political divisions that actors seeking accountability, survivor well-being, and the prevention of future violence hope to alleviate.

To explain these findings, this book focuses on how, soon after the phrase "transitional justice" was coined, a loosely structured movement emerged around the idea and professionalized in a distinct way. While most analyses of professionalization focus on standardization – and early transitional justice proponents did create a uniform characterization of what interventions fall under the banner of transitional justice – the professionalization of transitional justice contributed to malleable understandings of the idea and, by association, malleable understandings of truth commissions.

Next, by comparing efforts to promote truth commissions in BiH, Colombia, and the United States, this book illustrates transitional justice's malleability by showing the different processes through which actors translate the idea into political action. I characterize the instrumentalization of transitional justice in the Balkans as disruptive – innovative and groundbreaking, but unmanageable. In Colombia, the process was transformative, as both understandings of the idea and policies changed as the idea was instrumentalized. In the United States, the instrumentalization was decoupled, meaning that actors used the same discourse and promoted the same interventions associated with transitional justice, but they did not want to associate their efforts with the growing movement. In each case, understandings of transitional justice and truth commissions echoed the work of the transnational actors that have promoted the idea and the intervention around the world. At the same time, these understandings differed in ways that reflected, and reinforced, the social and political dynamics in each country.

Finally, this book shows that, even where a truth commission is not created, mobilizing around transitional justice can have important social and political effects. In particular, the circulation of transitional justice into new settings created new sets of elites, fostered an idealistic discourse about what truth commissions can offer, and, perhaps counterintuitively, reaffirmed prosecutions for perpetrators as an important strategy to redress mass violence. Even where actors promoted truth commissions, they did so in ways that did not challenge the prevalent belief that retribution is important, if not necessary, to ensure accountability, improve survivor well-being, and prevent future violence.

This empirical analysis of how actors understand transitional justice and truth commissions reveals the importance of understanding *who* is promoting and appropriating transitional justice, *who* is mobilizing around truth commissions, and *why* they do so. In many places, calling for a truth commission became a default strategy – the "something" that many view as preferable to doing nothing – for redressing mass violence (see Fletcher et al. 2009). This book argues that, due to malleable understandings of the idea and intervention, transitional justice and truth commissions will continue to circulate through the loosely structured and growing movement that promotes them. However, this same quality also means that transitional justice may ultimately become yet another movement, like rule of law, law and development, and even human rights, that leads to disillusionment about the capacity of legal interventions to redress mass violence.

TRANSITIONAL JUSTICE AS A TRANSNATIONAL MOVEMENT

Given the variety of individuals and organizations that appropriate and promote the idea and its associated interventions, particularly truth commissions, characterizing collective action related to transitional justice is a challenge. At the same time, this exercise is useful to show the variety of actors who have contributed to the emergence and professionalization of the transitional justice movement. Understanding this variety also reveals why there are diverse understandings of what transitional justice means and what its interventions should do. As Cotterrell (1998, 191) notes, an inquiry that looks at individual understandings "cannot abolish disagreement as to what justice demands in any particular situation. But it can reveal the meaning of justice claims in a broader perspective by systematically analysing the empirical conditions . . . underlying these claims." Understandings of transitional justice are necessarily shaped by the social and political contexts where actors have promoted the idea.

My theoretical approach builds from the growing critiques of transitional justice, all of which point to the problem of seeing transitional justice as something separate from the individuals and organizations that utilize the idea. Bell, for example, explains the "battlefield" of actors that identify with and promote transitional justice, including the parties with a conflict of interest in controlling the outcomes: policy makers interested in "doing good" and academics arguing over disciplinary boundaries as they relate to human rights, conflict resolution, and international intervention (Bell 2009b, p. 29). Theidon suggests that transitional justice interventions and discourse have achieved a "global presence" and that transitional justice is now "an industry" with its own understandings of how to "do memory" (Theidon 2009, p. 1; see also Gready 2010). Taking an even more critical view, Madlingozi (2010) emphasizes the "entrepreneurs" who "produce" victims as they promote their agendas in places where violence has occurred. Vinjamuri and Snyder (2004), importantly, point to the fact that advocates have largely set the agenda for social science studies of transitional justice, which has contributed to normative assessments of the need to create transitional justice interventions rather than objective assessments about their benefits (see also Lefranc and Mouralis 2014).

Building from these disparate analyses, I refer to mobilization around the idea of transitional justice as a transnational movement in order to emphasize the distinct structural qualities of the collective action due to scholarship, policy making, and advocacy related to the idea. This characterization reveals how collective action around transitional justice is similar to, yet distinct from, transnational advocacy networks (TANs), epistemic communities, and social movements, three other typologies of transnational collective action. Understanding the theories of TANs, epistemic communities, and social movements helps illuminate how mobilization around transitional justice is structured in different ways in different places and how the movement's distinct blend of scholarship, policy making, and advocacy keeps the idea malleable and therefore useful to a variety of actors. Furthermore, given the variety of actors that draw on transitional justice in their work, and their different goals, looking at these different forms of collective action also provides initial insights into why the malleability of transitional justice and truth commissions can also be a liability for those hoping to use the idea and intervention to bridge social and political divides.

The individuals and organizations that mobilize around transitional justice often work as TANs, defined as sets of "relevant actors working internationally on an issue who are bound together by shared values, a common discourse and dense exchanges of information and services" (Keck and Sikkink 1998). By definition, TANs are more focused groups that tend to develop around issues that are unlikely to inspire mass mobilization. However, there are examples of mass mobilization in support of transitional justice in some places, such as the Balkans and Colombia, and simply information exchanges in others, such as the United States.

Some scholars refer to transitional justice as an epistemic community, which similarly denies a populist component of efforts to create truth commissions and other transitional justice interventions (Chandler and Heins 2007). Actors within epistemic communities often work as consultants or on advisory panels, making recommendations based on a shared set of internally validated processes and principles (Haas 2013).[4] A variety of individuals who identify with transitional justice play this consultative role and draw on standardized understandings of what transitional justice interventions are and what they offer. However, a variety of individuals who identify with transitional justice engage in claim-making in much the same way that more normative communities, such as social movements, do.

While one could analyze transitional justice as a social movement, actors who promote transitional justice often are elites, including well-resourced organizations, academics, and policy makers. While some scholars suggest that networks are less structured than social movements, the expansion, coordination and sophistication of coalitions have blurred the distinction between the two (Khagram et al. 2002; Sperling et al. 2001).[5] The truth commission in Morocco, for example, was the result of sit-ins and demonstrations by advocacy organizations. Still, as this book will

4 According to Haas (2013), epistemic communities have shared principled beliefs, shared causal beliefs, common notions of validity, and a common policy enterprise related to improving human welfare.

5 Della Porta points out that social movements are not necessarily formed by organizations, but rather "loosely linked networks of individuals who feel part of a collective effort" (Della Porta 2007, p. 7). Government actors can also be part of social movements, depending on their interests and approaches. Tilly and Tarrow emphasize that social movements "make claims bearing on someone else's interests,

show, the actors who promote and appropriate transitional justice around the world and in specific countries do not have the shared identity that characterizes social movements (Della Porta and Diani 2006). For example, all actors may share similar goals of accountability but view transitional justice as an idea that impedes this goal.

Looking at the limitations of these different labels, I use the broader category of a movement in order to emphasize the complex shared identity and loosely structured collective action around an idea.[6] Referring to transitional justice as a movement emphasizes that the idea is *in movement*, meaning that it is fluid and understandings of it change depending on who has appropriated it, how, and why they have done so. As the case studies of BiH, Colombia, and the United States illustrate, this movement is not unidirectional: Understandings of transitional justice do not flow from transnational actors to domestic actors, or simply get implanted, unchanged, across national boundaries. These understandings change as they circulate within domestic settings, as they flow from one setting to another, and as they are translated back to the transnational level.

A PROFESSIONALIZED MOVEMENT

By studying transitional justice as a movement, it is easier to understand why actors around the world are promoting truth commissions. This book's second chapter, which examines the idea's origins, shows how the movement professionalized in the wake of the South Africa TRC and the subsequent creation of the International Center for Transitional Justice (ICTJ). This organization helped formalize understandings of transitional justice as a distinct set of interventions and promoted the South African truth commission model around the world (Ancelovici and Jenson 2013). The ICTJ, through helping to standardize understandings of which interventions fall under the broad banner of transitional justice, promoted the idea and the intervention as malleable enough to apply to a wide range of conflicts and for actors with a wide range of goals.

As the movement grew, other actors found themselves appropriating and promoting the idea to explain and legitimate their work. In her study of how transitional

leading to coordinated efforts on behalf of shared interests or programs, in which governments are involved as targets, or initiators of claims, or as third parties" (Tilly and Tarrow 2007, p. 4).

6 Della Porta (2006) similarly analyzes disparate efforts aimed at social, environmental, and economic justice as part of a definable "global justice movement" comprising individuals and organizations working against corporate globalization. Likewise, in her work on *Social Movements for Global Democracy*, Smith (2008) characterizes loosely affiliated groups of individuals working toward human rights and economic sustainability as transnational networks of social activists. Kelsall's analysis of Sierra Leone's war crimes tribunal mentions the "global social movement" to ensure that perpetrators of human rights abuses are tried for war crimes (Kelsall 2009, p. 6). As part of this movement for judicial accountability, he identifies a number of organizations, including Human Rights Watch, Amnesty International, and the International Center for Transitional Justice (ICTJ), organizations that I study as part of transnational transitional justice movement (see also Subotić 2012).

justice and truth commissions circulated around the world, Lefranc identifies the importance of activists in the global North and the global South, the academics who work with them, international bureaucracies (including international financial institutions), governments that are not always recognized for their commitment to human rights, and a host of organizations called "civil society" in post-conflict countries (Lefranc 2008, p. 67). Her point is that ideas such as transitional justice do not spread because of the emancipatory goals of their proponents, or because they are effective. Rather, they spread because different political actors are aware of their utility for a wide range of goals. Financial incentives are obviously important in the professionalization of a movement, but the relationships between individuals, organizations, and funders were a more critical resource in the transitional justice movement (see Gamson 1975).

The professionalization of the transitional justice movement is still under way, and this book reveals that its trajectory is similar to yet distinct from those of other movements predicated on law as a tool of social and political change. In the human rights movement, for example, organizations such as Human Rights Watch and Amnesty International emerged as elites that helped shape understandings of human rights around the world, as well as what the human rights movement's strategies would be (Neier 2012). These strategies included the creation of treaties that codified human rights law, campaigns to name and shame violators of domestic and international human rights law, and courts to punish perpetrators. Proponents of human rights focused on constructing the idea as a universal good, with nonderogable standards of how states could treat their citizens. Most importantly, they advocated punishment for perpetrators of human rights violations (Neier 2012; Engle 2015).

The appeal of transitional justice, in contrast, lies not in its universality but in its malleability, particularly its ambiguity as to the value of prosecutions and its idealistic discourse about what its interventions can offer countries where mass violence has occurred. Furthermore, this book argues that the idea's malleability reflects the ways in which scholars, policy makers, and advocates utilize the idea to describe any number of conflicts and prescribe any number of solutions (see Subotić 2009). With circular logic, proponents of transitional justice point to existing tribunals and truth commissions to explain the idea's utility and draw on the idea to explain the need to create new interventions. At the same time, as the transitional justice movement has developed, actors with their own goals, strategies, and professional identities have developed their own understandings of the idea and utilized it in novel ways.

This book emphasizes how easy it is to appropriate and promote a malleable idea such as transitional justice, but also shows that the same malleability can be a liability. Professionalization in unstructured areas, such as international criminal law, often involves competition over which domestically located norms will prevail (Zald and McCarthy 1987; Fourcade 2006). Looking at understandings of transitional justice, both at the international and domestic levels, reveals that there is ongoing contestation of the centrality and utility of criminal prosecution in efforts to redress mass violence, as well as of the utility of the idea more generally, given that political actors draw on it to realize contradictory goals. Examining how different actors understand transitional justice and truth commissions reveals not only why this intervention is so appealing, but also why prosecutions are still seen as an important, if not necessary, strategy for redressing mass violence.

WHY TRUTH COMMISSIONS IN THESE SETTINGS?

Returning to the original question of why actors promote truth commissions in such disparate settings, this book compares initiatives to create truth commissions in three distinct settings and, in so doing, shows how their appeal lies in the fact that proponents see truth commissions as capable of helping them realize a wide range of goals, including documenting abuses, punishing perpetrators, letting survivors tell their stories in a public forum, and getting other types of compensation from the state.

While comparative analyses of truth commissions often focus on the factors that shape whether a truth commission will be successful, these studies do not point out the goals and strategies of actors that promote them (Roper and Barria 2009; Olsen, Payne, and Reiter 2010; Dancy et al. 2010). Case studies, in contrast, provide more information on the social and political context in which a truth commission is created, but it is difficult to make generalizations from them (Chapman, Baxter, and van der Merwe 2009). Looking at the effort to create a truth commission in South Korea, for example, Kim (2012) argues that domestic demands – not international pressures – for information and accountability about government massacres created the political opportunity for a truth commission to be established. Similarly, analyzing the genesis of a truth commission in Canada, Nagy (2014) reveals the influence of transnational organizations such as the ICTJ in helping the Canadian policy makers design their commission, but emphasizes how domestic actors translated their understandings of transitional justice to meet their specific social and political goals. These case studies, among others, are useful to show the interaction between domestic and transnational proponents of truth commissions, yet they only reveal the social and political dynamics in one country.

In looking at ongoing mobilization efforts to create truth commissions in three different countries, this book provides insights into both the specificity of truth commission initiatives and some of their generalities. It similarly suggests that the demand for a truth commission is domestically driven, but domestic actors are drawing from foreign models in their mobilization campaigns. Moreover, the same transnational actors, notably the ICTJ, were present in all three cases, providing guidance on truth commission development, design, and implementation. Domestic actors mobilize around truth commissions according to their own hopes and desires about what this intervention can do for them, but their understandings reflect the work of the transnational movement.

Beyond these findings, the book argues that the same qualities that make truth commissions appealing in such diverse settings also make mobilizing around a truth commission a problematic strategy. Proponents view truth commissions as tools for getting information about loved ones, public recognition for their suffering, financial compensation, judicial accountability for perpetrators, or some other symbolic or practical benefit. The result is that it may be easy for actors with contradictory goals to support a truth commission but, at some point, whether in the design or implementation of a truth commission, these contradictions will come to the fore. These differences may entrench social and political divides, not resolve them. In addition, the comparative analysis offered here reveals that, even though some actors see truth commissions as a tool for getting some form of accountability, others see them as offering a lesser form of justice than what a court might offer. Thus, there is a limit to their malleability, as proponents of prosecutions may simply reject calls for a truth commission altogether.

Finally, this book also points out that a truth commission's quasi-judicial nature is central to its appeal. In comparison with museums, memorials, or even locally based "truth-telling" mechanisms, formal truth commissions carry with them the legitimacy of state law. Thus, beliefs about law, and specifically law's power to sanction wrongdoing, play a crucial role in how individuals understand truth commissions. Their perspectives on law influence the reason why they want one, or do not want one, to redress mass violence in their country. Given that some actors understand truth commissions as a precursor or complement to a judicial process, promoting truth commissions can be a way to reaffirm the importance of prosecuting perpetrators of mass violence. Whether promoted as a complement or as a substitute for a court process, the malleability of the intervention, like the idea used to explain and legitimate it, makes mobilizing around a truth commission a politically potent and problematic strategy for actors seeking accountability, survivor well-being, and the prevention of future violence.

TOWARD A THEORY OF INSTRUMENTALIZATION(S): FRAMING, ORGANIZATIONAL DYNAMICS, AND POLITICAL OPPORTUNITIES

After explaining how a movement emerged and professionalized around transitional justice at the transnational level, the analysis turns to three different places – BiH, Colombia, and the United States – where different political actors mobilized around a truth commissions to order to redress state-sponsored violence. In studying these efforts, this book develops a theory of instrumentalization that emphasizes the different ways in which actors translate ideas into political action, and how social and political dynamics shape the translation process.

My approach to instrumentalization, or rather instrumentalizations, draws on theoretical concepts such as diffusion, brokerage, indigenization, and globalization (Tilly and Tarrow 2007; Nader 1999; Goodale and Merry 2007; Acharya 2004; de

Sousa Santos and Rodríguez-Garavito 2005). These concepts are useful for the study of transitional justice and truth commissions because they point to the importance of understanding the actors who appropriate and promote new ideas and new strategies (Levitt and Merry 2009). In particular, scholars who refer to the circulation of new ideas as vernacularization emphasize how key individuals, called translators or intermediaries, mediate the spread of foreign ideas related to law (Merry 2006; Merry and Stern 2005). In the process of vernacularization, new ideas become decontextualized and recontextualized in ways that, while unpredictable, reflect existing social structures and local meanings (Clarke and Goodale 2009, p. 7).

As the transitional justice movement became professionalized, transnational actors tried to standardize understandings of transitional justice and truth commissions and promote them to others. As Ancelovici and Jenson (2013) point out, these actors decontextualized the South African model of a truth commission and promoted it as a model that could conform to any number of settings. While law and society scholars often suggest that this translation process can deny local agency, this study reveals the dynamic processes through which domestic and transnational actors co-create understandings of transitional justice and truth commissions in order to make them appear useful for a wide range of conflicts, and for actors with a wide range of goals (Clarke 2009; Massoud 2011).

The idea's malleability means it is even more important to study how recipients of the idea understand it, and how they translate it into political action. For example, Andrieu (2016) argues that the phrase "facing the past," which she articulates as part of transitional justice discourse, was instrumentalized in Tunisia in order to promote certain types of victims and certain types of reparations. In contrast to Clarke's findings (Clarke 2009) about the lack of local agency that can occur in the transition process, Andrieu highlights that domestic political actors were well aware of what they were doing as they used seemingly apolitical discourse to make politicized claims that would have important repercussions in Tunisia's transition. This book similarly suggests that political actors in different settings were aware of how to translate transitional justice to achieve their particular goals. In addition, just as Andrieu's study points to a shallow, self-serving commitment to creating interventions under the banner of facing the past, my study offers warning signs about shallow, self-serving commitments to creating truth commissions under the banner of transitional justice.

Reflecting on these different understandings of transitional justice and truth commissions, my analysis builds upon Acharya's theory of localization, which helps explain how foreign ideas are "actively constructed" to align with "cognitive priors and identities" (Acharya 2004, p. 239). Since transnational movements have fluid structures and work in diverse settings, movement actors will actively construct ideas in different ways in different places. Moreover, individual beliefs and practices do not, by themselves, explain how, why, or to what effect actors around the world promote truth commissions. Institutional support, repeated exposure, and/or active instruction are required for an idea or strategy to take hold in new settings (Appadurai

1996; Bhabha 1994). In each of this book's cases, for example, the ICTJ educated advocates who were interested in redressing violence about the idea of transitional justice, but recipients of this training had very different perspectives on what the idea meant, what it did, and whether promoting a truth commission would be useful for them.

Thinking of transitional justice as an idea around which a movement emerged, it is easier to see that both transitional justice and truth commissions can serve as frames that actors draw on to inspire others and legitimate their goals and strategies (Benford and Snow 2000; Goffman 1974). Framing one's goal as the creation of a truth commission can name, interpret, and dramatize issues as ones in need of a novel strategy to resolve (Finnemore and Sikkink 1998). Framing strategies are especially important in emergent transnational movements such as transitional justice because proponents of new ideas and interventions must find frames that resonate with their audiences (Resnick 2009). Resonance depends on two key features: (1) salience, which refers to the importance of the issue to people's lives, and (2) credibility, which refers to the existence of empirical evidence and the reputation of the claim makers (Benford and Snow 2000). To ensure credibility and salience, actors must make use of the symbols and ideas that already exist within the society's political culture (Resnick 2009; Tarrow 1994; McAdam et al. 1996). As the following case studies show, actors can make transitional justice salient in a variety of places because of its malleability. However, understandings of the idea often reflect who has promoted it and how they have done so. As a result, the idea can easily become a placeholder for actors to make competing claims; and actors that promote truth commissions often want to name, interpret, and dramatize different aspects of the violence.

In addition to studying framing, this analysis of instrumentalizations also focuses on how organizational dynamics and political opportunities shape the translation process. I refer to organizational dynamics as the ways in which actors identify their goals and strategies, as well as relationships among actors working to ensure accountability, improve survivor well-being, and prevent future violence. Studying organizational dynamics requires a focus on resource mobilization, including the role of leadership and incentives in participation in a movement (Davis 2005). Building from neoinstitutional theories of organizations, I redirect attention from the financial incentives within organizations to internal social dynamics and external influences that shape organizational behavior (McAdam and Scott 2005; Meyer and Rowan 1977). Rather than increasing efficacy, many organizational practices, such as appropriating and promoting a new idea such as transitional justice, try to confer legitimacy, smooth interactions, and ensure the survival of the organization (Ingram and Clay 2000). In this study, it was important to look at professional identities and personal relationships, as well as financial resources, in order to understand the organizational dynamics at both the transnational and domestic levels.

Finally, understandings of transitional justice and truth commissions necessarily reflect whether governments are willing or able to redress mass violence, and how they choose to do so. That dilemma relates to political opportunities, a concept that refers to the degree to which formal political institutions are open or closed to change, and the degree to which a movement may be able to influence and change the status quo of the political system (see Brockett 1991). The political opportunities for the transitional justice movement are more complex because policy makers are often the ones drawing on transitional justice to explain their goals and strategies. In addition, the violence that these actors are addressing is often state-sponsored, and representatives of the state and advocacy organizations may have contradictory goals for who should be punished, and how. The challenge of state responsibility is particularly relevant in places where there has not been a regime change, yet actors have appropriated and promoted transitional justice as an idea that can help redress ongoing violence.

STUDYING INSTRUMENTALIZATION ACROSS TIME AND SPACE

Studying how actors around the world understand transitional justice and truth commissions required an innovative approach to data collection and analysis. For this book, I followed Nader's approach of looking at the horizontal as well as vertical relationships between political actors (Nader 1991), as well as Merry's approach of "de-territorialized ethnography," which emphasizes the need to examine a variety of sites where local and transnational understandings intersect (Merry 2006). In particular, Merry points out the challenge of tracing the circulation of ideas and practices across different sites while retaining the power of ethnography to examine power relations, social linkages, and information exchanges. While multisited ethnography allows important comparisons between different locales, the deterritorialized approach enables an examination of how ideas circulate. To trace the impact of foreign ideas, the deterritorialized approach encourages an examination of temporary sites of action, such as conferences, as well as of more permanent sites within countries where the ideas are translated into action (Merry 2006).

Building from this deterritorialized approach, I also draw from other scholars of transnational phenomena who note that participant observation must take place alongside reading newspapers, analyzing government documents, observing the activities of governing elites, and tracking the internal logics of transnational organizations (Gupta and Ferguson 1997). More specifically, I draw on Tsing's ethnographic approach of examining the "practical successes and failures" of translating transitional justice into political action (Tsing 2005, p. 7). Moreover, using constructivist methodologies to study international relations, this study engages in focused comparisons of different countries in order to explore how ideas shape political action (see Haas 2014).

In developing my methodology, I also took into consideration critiques of the separation between "the home," where one resides, and "the field," where one conducts research, as this distinction can reinforce the United States as a standard bearer and discount the fact that practices in the United States are as culturally specific as practices in other countries (Gupta and Ferguson 1997). My approach to deterritorialized ethnography blurs the boundaries between the "home" and "field" by looking at individuals and organizations in the United States, where I reside, that were interested in creating a truth commission for detention policies and practices under the Bush regime.

The overall data include a web-based survey of the largest transitional justice research network in the world, interviews (in four languages and in nine countries) with over 200 individuals, collected from 2009 to 2016, who were engaged in transnational and domestic advocacy related to transitional justice. In addition to the survey and interviews, I analyzed hundreds of organizational documents, engaged in participant observation in over fifty conferences and seminars on transitional justice, and conducted archival research on the origins of the International Center for Transitional Justice at the Rockefeller Archives in New York.

This study began in 2005 and 2007 with pilot studies on truth commissions in Morocco and South Africa. That research revealed the need for further analysis as to why truth commissions are being *promoted* around the world, not simply why they were being *created* or what their effects were. The data were used to develop the theoretical approach of this book and the questions that guided subsequent case studies. To explain why truth commissions are being promoted, I had to search out the individuals and organizations that could help answer these questions both at the transnational and at the domestic level. I found that scholars, policy makers, and advocates all play a role in translating transitional justice into political action, and their roles are different in different countries.

For the first empirical chapter, which I call the "horizontal slice" of the movement, I interviewed approximately thirty individuals who worked or had worked for the ICTJ, the Centre for the Study of Violence and Reconciliation, Human Rights Watch, Amnesty International, and other so-called transnational transitional justice advocacy organizations (see Subotić 2012). I also sent a survey to individuals who self-identified as transitional justice researchers or advocates, people who signed up to be on the largest listserv associated with transitional justice, the Africa Transitional Justice Research Network.[7] Surveying this network enabled me to access individuals who identified with transitional justice but were not necessarily the elites that I accessed in the interviews. At the time of the survey, there were approximately 1000 subscribers who signed up voluntarily to receive messages on reports, scholarly publications, job opportunities, and current events related to transitional justice. I received 136 responses: 58 complete and 78 partial

7 The Africa Transitional Justice Research Network explains the listerv in the following way: "The TJNetwork listserv . . . networks individuals in the transitional justice field globally to facilitate dialogue and the sharing of research, opportunities, and knowledge." Africa Transitional Justice Research Network, http://www.transitionaljustice.org.za/ (accessed October 18, 2010).

surveys on opinions about what the goals and strategies of transitional justice are and should be.

Next, taking "vertical slices" of the movement, I examined how the idea of transitional justice is translated into political action in three distinct places. Having studied opinions of truth commissions that had already been created in South Africa and Morocco, I did not want to study cases where a truth commission had been established, as this would bias understandings of transitional justice and truth commissions with post hoc reasoning based on the perceived success or failure of the efforts. Drawing on the comparative method of agreement (Ragin 1989), I looked for places with distinct political contexts but where, in 2009, actors were in the process of promoting truth commissions. I also decided to study three cases where, in 2009, the transitions were ambiguous. By analyzing cases where there was no clear break from armed conflict or an authoritarian toward a democratizing regime, as transitional justice was originally conceived, I was able to glean additional insights into how and why understandings of transitional justice have shifted along with the movement's professionalization. In interviews, I asked actors to explain their opinions of how the idea applied to their particular contexts.

Within cases, my analysis draws on process tracing techniques, engaging in careful description to explain processes of change in order to reveal novel political and social phenomena (Mahoney 2012; Collier 2011). This case method approach uses a detailed examination of a historical episode to develop explanations that may be generalizable to other events, such as movements around similarly malleable ideas (George and Bennet 2005, p. 5). My principal data for each case were interviews, gathered through a snowball-and-niche sampling technique. I focused primarily on scholars, policy makers, and advocates working in nationally based organizations related to transitional justice. While this focus on national organizations limited perspectives from those with less social and political power in a country, it helped limit the sample size and enabled me to compare across cases more effectively. For future studies, examining more localized variation would help illuminate additional important dynamics in the circulation of transitional justice in domestic settings.

When I began fieldwork for my first case – BiH – fifteen years had passed since the initial period of political transition after the end of a brutal war. In this case, I focused on an effort to make a truth commission for the former Yugoslavia, known as the Coalition for RECOM, as well as Sarajevo-based organizations that drew on the idea of transitional justice in their work. My fieldwork on understandings of transitional justice and truth commissions in BiH took place during five visits to the field between 2009 and 2014, and drew on knowledge from prior work experience in the Balkans, which was critical to establishing credibility and rapport with my interviewees.[8] The field visits took place for five days in September 2009, for

[8] I first traveled to BiH in 2002 with an organization engaged in cross-cultural educational programs for orphans from the war and returned in 2004 to help lead the organization's international group of

three weeks in November 2009, for seven weeks in April and May 2010, for two weeks in May 2011, and for one week in June 2014. The 2010 visit included fieldwork in Serbia and Croatia to interview advocates working on redressing the war's violence. The fieldwork yielded sixty-eight interviews with fifty-five interviewees working within domestic advocacy organizations, international organizations, and universities.[9]

I first heard about efforts to promote a truth commission in Colombia in 2008, when the country was still embroiled in its decades-long armed conflict. Scholars, policy makers, and advocates began discussing a truth commission under the banner of transitional justice as early as 2003, when the government was trying to develop its strategy to demobilize armed actors. The government promoted the 2005 Justice and Peace law as an example of transitional justice because it created an alternative penal process for demobilizing paramilitaries, as well as a "sort of truth commission" to provide reparations for victims (Laplante and Theidon 2006). In 2010, I conducted fieldwork in Colombia on understandings of transitional justice as they related to the Justice and Peace Law. That year, I conducted forty-six interviews in the cities of Bogotá, Medellin, Cartagena, and Barranquilla. By 2015, the government and the most notorious and longest lasting guerilla group, the FARC, were engaged in peace talks, and understandings of transitional justice had drastically changed. In 2015, I returned to Colombia and collected an additional thirty-two interviews in Bogotá, focusing on the scholars, policy makers, and advocates working on this peace process.

Finally, the United States, which is not typically studied by scholars of transitional justice, faced its own transition between the Bush and Obama administrations. For a brief period after Obama was elected, government and civil society leaders promoted a government-sponsored investigative commission on torture policies in the previous administration. Some called their proposed commission a truth commission, and some drew on transitional justice to explain and legitimate their strategy. Others rejected this label and, despite having similar goals, viewed their mobilization strategies as distinct from efforts to promote commissions in other countries. This case was particularly intriguing because some actors, notably the ICTJ, were arguing that transitional justice was a useful idea to help the United States address allegations of state-sponsored torture. Between 2009 and 2015, I collected approximately thirty

volunteers. For five semesters in graduate school at the University of California–Berkeley, I studied the language and the literature of the former Yugoslavia. I remained in contact with Sarajevo-based colleagues from my prior work and, when I returned to begin fieldwork in the fall of 2009, they helped provide initial contacts to begin my study on transitional justice. As domestic actors are inundated with requests by foreign researchers studying the war and postwar national relations, it was necessary to repeatedly contact potential interviewees and explain my prior work experience and language skills in order to gain access.

9 Five interviewees were interviewed twice, once in fall 2009 and again in spring 2010, and four of those five were interviewed a third time in spring 2011.

interviews with individuals who were working on these initiatives, which mostly fell by the wayside as Obama's presidency continued.

The transcripts were professionally transcribed and translated where necessary.[10] When coding the interviews and statements made during conferences, lectures, and symposia, I followed a grounded theory approach, looking for multiple layers of meanings as individuals described their actions, including (1) stated explanation, (2) unstated assumptions about action, (3) intentions to engage in it, (4) its effects on others, and (5) consequences for further action (Charmaz 1995). From this analysis, I derived my findings as to how transitional justice was instrumentalized at both the transnational and domestic levels.

REFLECTIONS ON STUDYING TRANSNATIONAL LEGAL MOBILIZATION

Conducting a study of an emergent transnational movement posed a number of important challenges and opportunities. Any researcher who works on issues related to mass violence must confront the distinct challenge of working with individuals who have suffered from years of traumatic experiences. Many researchers travel to foreign countries to explain phenomena that locals understand on an intimate level. Given their alternating disdain and deference to foreign academics, it was important to remain curious and treat all of my interviewees as the experts on their own countries. Moreover, I often felt that each case study would ideally have had its own anthropologist who could provide an in-depth analysis that I could not. To trace the circulation of transitional justice around the world, this study sacrifices depth for breadth.

Throughout the study, I tried to address these concerns in a variety of ways. First, my background in advocacy organizations was critical to establishing trust and rapport with my interviewees. Our interviews felt like conversations, which began with the same question, "Please tell me a little about your work," and always included a discussion of the same questions: "What is your understanding of transitional justice?" "What is your understanding of truth commissions?" The rest of the conversation flowed from what they wanted to discuss about their goals and strategies. The interviewees often expressed gratitude for the chance to talk about their goals and strategies. At the same time, rather than validating their beliefs and practices, it was important for me also to engage in dialogue that challenged their beliefs in ways that encouraged honest responses to my questions. Given the depth of our conversations, the presentation of results relies heavily on the interview data and is complemented by data gleaned from other sources.

As with any methodological approach, the findings will reflect the limits of the study design and execution. This is a study of meaning making, predicated on

[10] I translated four of the Spanish-language interviews and had the rest professionally translated. I identify individuals who wished to remain anonymous by professional affiliations.

the perspective that law, ideas, identities, and social and political action mutually constitute one another. My goal was to clarify understandings of transitional justice and how those understandings affect political action. In particular, I drew from ethnographic approaches that would enable me to "understand particular processes, events, ideas and practices in an informant's own terms rather than" my own (Shaw 2007, p. 188).

The insights from this qualitative approach helped reveal how actors utilize transitional justice for political ends, and why truth commissions continue to be promoted and created. This analysis, of course, cannot predict whether a truth commission will be created or be effective (let alone explaining how to measure effectiveness), but it can provide guidance on what questions truth commission proponents might ask when trying to create one in a new setting.

OUTLINE OF THE BOOK

Following this introduction on the theoretical and empirical underpinnings of my analysis, Chapter Two, *Building a Transnational Movement*, focuses on the emergence and professionalization of the transnational transitional justice movement. The chapter examines the origins of the ICTJ, an organization that helped standardize understandings of transitional justice while keeping the concept malleable enough to be promoted in a wide range of contexts. The chapter also focuses on the distinct blend of advocacy and scholarship in the movement, which both reflects and contributes to the idea's malleability. The chapter reveals how the emergence and professionalization of the movement created new sets of elites and an idealistic discourse and, given organizational dynamics at the transnational level, reaffirmed the belief that criminal prosecutions are an important, if not necessary, strategy to redress mass violence. In addition, this chapter reveals both ambivalence and skepticism about the idea of transitional justice on account of the ways in which the movement has professionalized.

Chapter Three, *Disruption: A Truth Commission in Bosnia and Herzegovina*, examines how, despite a clear lack of political opportunity, individuals and organizations decided to promote a regional truth commission in the Balkans. Mobilizing around a regional truth commission was innovative and groundbreaking, as well as unmanageable. This is a process that I call *disruptive instrumentalization*. The ambitious initiative by the Coalition for RECOM involved consultations with thousands of individuals in the region and a multimillion-dollar media and signature campaign. The chapter elucidates the organizational dynamics and political opportunities that stymied this Coalition's effort to promote a proposed truth commission in BiH, one of the countries where the Coalition was working. In addition to explaining the Coalition for RECOM, this chapter also addresses the UNDP's efforts to create a transitional justice strategy for BiH, and several other examples of how actors in BiH draw on transitional justice for wide-ranging goals. The analysis further shows how the malleability of transitional justice and truth commissions makes them easy to appropriate and promote, yet mobilizing around this idea and intervention can reproduce social and political divides that their proponents hope to alleviate.

Chapter Four, *Transformation: The Politics of Peace in Colombia*, focuses on a process I call *transformative instrumentalization*, meaning that the translation process changed both the political situation and understandings of the idea over time. Transitional justice first entered political discourse in Colombia during the Uribe administration in the early 2000s, when the government was developing demobilization policies for paramilitary groups. A variety of organizations appropriated the idea of transitional justice as a shorthand for victims' rights to truth, justice, and reparation. Over time, transitional justice became part of Colombia's laws, including its constitution, and a truth commission was mandated as part of the "transitional justice instruments" that would be created in the event of a peace accord with the guerilla groups. The instrumentalization of the idea paved the way for a peace accord with the FARC; yet there was little agreement on what the idea meant and what its associated interventions would do, particularly with regard to punishment for perpetrators. In particular, while most actors agree that a truth commission should be created, they have different opinions about what this intervention should prioritize. These problems, again, reveal how the malleability of transitional justice is both an asset and a liability.

Chapter Five, *Decoupled: Transitional Justice in the War on Terror*, examines the politics of mobilization around a truth commission in the United States. In 2009, during the transition between the Bush and Obama administrations, a variety of individuals and organizations promoted a truth commission to redress abuses in the War on Terror, particularly allegations of state-sponsored torture. This chapter provides insights into a country that would not usually be considered a case of transition and reveals both the malleability of transitional justice and the extent to which understandings of the idea have shifted since their origins. At the same time, the case also shows the limits of the idea's malleability, as many actors in the United States viewed it, and the interventions associated with it, as a lesser form of justice. Many actors believed that transitional justice is an idea that applies to countries with less political stability, and that a truth commission is unnecessary where courts can and should address violence. Despite promoting similar strategies and drawing on similar discourse, this instrumentalization process was *decoupled* from similar initiatives in other countries that were promoted under the banner of transitional justice. The chapter further reveals the extent to which transitional justice remains contested and viewed with ambivalence and skepticism about what the idea means and what its associated interventions do.

Drawing together the theoretical framework and the findings, the concluding chapter, *The Power of Legal Ideas*, rearticulates the theoretical and normative contributions of the study. First, to understand the appeal of truth commissions as tools to redress mass violence, the conclusion elaborates on the concept of the truth commission as a quasi-judicial medium, a body that serves to channel contradictory, competing, and complementary beliefs about law as a tool for social and political change. The concept helps explain why the malleability of the truth commission is both an asset and a liability for those who choose to mobilize around one. Next, the chapter explains how the professionalization of the movement has contributed to the idea's malleability, as well as skepticism about what its interventions offer. Third, the conclusion points to how the transitional justice movement and the idea's instrumentalization in different locales have contributed to the creation of new sets of elites, an idealistic discourse, and the anti-impunity turn in human rights advocacy campaigns (Engle, Miller, and Davis 2016). In this analysis, the chapter points to future areas of research that might further clarify why truth commissions continue to be created and what the effects of this mobilization strategy might be.

Finally, by focusing on the idea's malleability, the conclusion further elaborates on how the idea serves as a placeholder for actors to articulate their hopes and desires for the future, and for actors with contradictory agendas to make claims against one another. In this way, it emphasizes how new ideas shape legal politics (see Massoud 2013). More broadly, the conclusion points to the underlying dilemma of mobilizing the law to redress mass violence with the goal to ensure accountability, improve survivor well-being, and prevent future violence. Transitional justice is the latest in a long line of movements around ideas that are at once legal and political. These movements exalt law's influence on social and political relationships, but all of them have struggled in their efforts to use law to overcome entrenched structural dynamics that foment social and political divisions.

By reimagining transitional justice as an idea around which a loosely structured movement has emerged, this book encourages scholars to shift their focus from theoretical concerns about the meaning of transitional justice toward practical concerns about how different actors utilize the idea and mobilize around its associated interventions to ensure their goals. Such a shift will better clarify why transitional justice has circulated, why its associated interventions, particularly truth commissions, so often disappoint their proponents, and the effects of new ideas on domestic and international politics. Moreover, it provides broader insights into the appeal of malleable legal ideas and how mobilizing around them can be both an asset and a liability for those with concrete goals for social and political change.

2

Building a Transnational Movement

From the base of Central Park, one walks through midtown, Chinatown, and downtown, through the bankers and businessmen of Wall Street to arrive at the heart of the financial district. Turning left on Wall Street, one finds Hanover Square, the narrow street where the New York office of the International Center for Transitional Justice (ICTJ) is located. Entering the building, it is easy to sense the distance between individuals working for this transnational organization and the individuals they assist in war-torn countries.

I took this walk and handed my identification to the doorman before riding the elevator to the 24th floor. Looking out over the nearby skyscrapers from the organization's waiting room, I read reports about ICTJ's work with the truth commission in Liberia, an ambitious body that had been criticized for its lack of funding and the absence of adequate staff and technical support (de Ycaza 2013; Steinberg 2011). Listening to the hushed voices in the office, I contemplated the stark contrast between the luxury of this office and the truth commission's struggles in Liberia. For years, I'd heard about the ICTJ when asking scholars, policy makers, and advocates about their understandings of transitional justice. I wondered how staff might explain their understandings of transitional justice and truth commissions to me.

Starting from this skyscraper, this chapter provides a bird's eye view of influential individuals and organizations that shaped the transitional justice movement and promoted the idea around the world. It describes the idea's origins and presents a mini-case study of the ICTJ due to the important role that this organization played in the movement's professionalization. Looking at the emergence of the transitional justice movement through the development of this organization offers several important findings that are relevant to the rest of this book. First, this chapter explains how the truth commission became a signature intervention of transitional justice. Second, it points to the movement's blend of scholarship and advocacy related to the need to create interventions such as truth commissions, a blend that both reflects and contributes to the idea's malleability. Third, it reveals that this malleability is both an asset and a liability for those who promote and appropriate the idea. Actors hoping to ensure accountability, improve survivor well-being, and prevent future violence may draw on transitional justice to frame their work, but other with similar goals are unsure of what the idea means and are skeptical of others who utilize it and promote the associated interventions.

In addition, by looking at the movement's emergence and professionalization, this chapter provides a starting point to see how the transitional justice movement has helped create new elites, fostered an idealistic discourse about what truth commissions offer, and, despite its goal of broadening understandings of justice away from punishment, reaffirmed the belief that criminal prosecutions are an important, if not necessary, strategy for redressing mass violence. By analyzing the social processes through which the idea has spread, this analysis reveals not only why truth commissions have become a standard response to mass violence, but also how the malleability of transitional justice means that actors can draw on it to make competing claims.

THE ORIGINS OF A NEW IDEA

Although the idea is now ubiquitous in scholarship, policy making, and advocacy, transitional justice is a relatively young idea. Some scholars date the idea to interventions created in biblical times, classical Greece, or Reconstruction in the United States, but, more commonly, they refer to the post-WWII Nuremberg trials, which also represent the beginning of contemporary international criminal law (Teitel 2002; Teitel 2003; Elster 2004). However, at the time, no one referred to these interventions by the phrase "transitional justice." Where the phrase appeared in scholarship before the 1990s, it was usually in reference to Marxist understandings of social justice and the transition from capitalism to communism (Mouralis 2013, p. 86).

Transitional justice, as it is now understood, emerged in the late 1980s, and in reference to the democratic transitions of the communist regimes in Eastern Europe and the authoritarian regimes in Latin America. Hayner, a leading expert in truth commissions and a central figure in the development of the transitional justice movement, locates the idea's origins in a 1986 book entitled *Transitions from Authoritarian Rule* (Hayner 2010, p. 7). The book was the product of the Woodrow Wilson School's investment in a project titled "Transitions" and highlights the blend of scholarship and advocacy that characterized the transitional justice movement from the beginning. For this project, political scientists from around the world, with a "frank bias for democratic governance," met around conference tables to discuss the "causes, characteristics, and complexities in transitions from authoritarian rule" (O'Donnell and Schmitter 1986, p. vii). Their goal was not just to analyze transitions, but to make more "open, inclusionary, and accountable democratic governance" in Southern Europe and Latin America (O'Donnell and Schmitter

1986, p. vii). They noted that early commentators described their work on promoting democratic social and political change as "wishful thinking" based on Western legal liberalism (O'Donnell and Schmitter 1986, p. xiii). Through scholarship, they were able to blend their normative goals into questions about governance in democratic transitions.

Among the variety of issues that these so-called transitologists studied was democratic institution building through law, specifically the use of courts to punish past violence. They were interested in how, after the fall of communism in Eastern Europe, the new leadership in Czechoslovakia and Poland decided that, rather than putting individuals on trial, purging former party leaders from the new government was a politically palatable way to ensure accountability for past abuse. In South America, authoritarian military regimes killed thousands of political dissidents. The new, democratically elected regimes of Chile and Argentina were cautious with putting military leaders on trial, worried that they would cause more social and political upheaval. While Argentina held a few trials, both countries focused on documenting the abuse and providing reparations to victims (see Brito et al. 2001).

Looking at the common concerns and common strategies, scholars, particularly legal scholars, became interested in how new regimes were balancing calls to punish perpetrators of abuse with their interest in bridging social and political divides during political transitions. These scholars, as well as advocates working on similar issues, began meeting with some regularity, eventually developing a shared discourse related to justice during political transitions. For example, Arthur (2009) locates the origins of the idea at an Aspen Institute meeting in 1998 in Wye, Maryland. There, actors who were already in dialogue about questions of justice during political transitions discussed the dilemma between offering pardons and pursuing criminal accountability in countries emerging from authoritarian regimes.[11] The Aspen Institute, under the leadership of Alice Henkin, focused on these questions throughout the 1980s and 1990s, and helped produce books with titles such as *State Crimes: Punishment or Pardon*, *Honoring Human Rights and Keeping the Peace: Lessons from El Salvador, Cambodia and Haiti*, and *Honoring Human Rights: From Peace to Justice*. For actors working on these issues, the questions at stake were not merely about whom to punish, but about how punishment fit with other goals that scholars, policy makers, and advocates deemed necessary for democratic transition, namely the creation of legal systems that would protect individuals from human rights abuses.

In these meetings, actors began to conceptualize these questions about law as having to do with transition and with justice, but the phrase "transitional justice"

[11] Arthur points out that Jose Zalaquett, Jaime Malamud-Goti, Aryeh Neier, Juan E. Méndez, Diane Orentlicher, Lawrence Weschler, Alice Henkin, Tim Phillips, and Adam Michnik participated in several of these early meetings and helped create the conceptual foundations of transitional justice (Arthur 2009, p. 324).

was not part of these discussions. Ruti Teitel, a law professor at New York University, describes coining the phrase in 1991, when the Council on Foreign Relations commissioned her to write an advisory memorandum on challenges facing newly democratized societies (Teitel 2008). As a legal scholar, Teitel thought of justice in relation to criminal law. For her, transitional justice was a way to articulate new ways to think about "punishment" and the role of courts in the context of political transition:

> In the memorandum, I advocated a more expansive view of the question of punishment. I suggested that wherever the criminal justice response was compromised or otherwise limited, there were other ways to respond to the predecessor regime's repressive rule. And such alternatives could develop capacities for advancing the rule of law . . . in such hyperpoliticized moments, we learned that the law operates differently, and often is incapable of meeting all of the traditional values associated with the rule of law, such as general applicability, procedural due process, as well as more substantive values of fairness or analogous sources of legitimacy. (Teitel 2008, p. 1)

Although Teitel was thinking about justice as a question of punishment and liberal values associated with due process, actors began to utilize "transitional justice" in a broader way. Timothy Phillips claims to have "catalyzed the field of transitional justice"[12] as a result of a 1992 meeting in Salzburg, where Teitel was also a participant. In his account of the meeting, he describes talking with leaders from former Communist countries and reflecting on their similarities with leaders from South American countries dealing with political transitions. Phillips joined forces with Wendy Luers, then director of a foundation supporting the new Czechoslovakian government. The two looked for resources to bring together individuals who were interested in collaborating on democratic institution building in countries that were emerging from undemocratic regimes. Phillips was referred to George Soros for funding. Soros, the philanthropist behind the Open Society Institute, a major funder of democratization projects around the world, agreed to finance the travel of European participants (Phillips 2008).

In this meeting, conference leaders drew directly on the idea of transitional justice to explain the "legal, moral, and political issues" facing governments in transition and to develop a "new methodology" to address them (Mouralis 2013). The participants in the meeting underscore the distinct blend of scholars, policy makers, and advocates involved in this nascent movement. There were 85 participants, 30 of whom came from the United States, 34 from Eastern Europe, and 8 from Latin America. Thirty-three participants were government officials and 15 were professors, 9 of whom were law professors from the United States. Thirteen participants were human rights activists, 12 were journalists, and 9 were practicing attorneys (Mouralis 2013). While

[12] Beyond Conflict: History, www.beyondconflictint.org/history.

moral and political issues were part of the conversation, many participants were lawyers interested in questions of judicial accountability.

One of the participants was Neil Kritz, from the Rule of Law Program at the United States Institute of Peace (USIP). At USIP, Kritz had been working on law reform in countries emerging or at risk of violence since 1991 and saw transitional justice as a useful way to explain how different countries were dealing with issues of past violence. Drawing from its work at the Salzburg conference, Kritz edited a three-volume series on transitional justice in 1995. The title of USIP's series, "Transitional Justice: How Emerging Democracies Reckon with Former Regimes," illustrates how, from the beginning, the concept of transitional justice was ambiguously described by its proponents. The phrase "reckon with" can imply accountability, as in "the day of reckoning," but can also be understood more generally – and vaguely – as meaning "take into account" or "deal with."

These volumes helped define transitional justice and provided a foundation for how transitional justice is still understood. They describe transitional justice as a set of normative considerations, or goals, such as judicial accountability, documenting the former regime, and non-criminal sanctions, that could be operationalized through a number of practical options such as trials, truth commissions, and lustration programs that would facilitate the transition from authoritarianism to democracy. The first volume includes scholarly essays on issues related to accountability, documentation, criminal sanctions, non-criminal sanctions, and treatment of and compensation for survivors. The two other volumes provide case studies of countries shifting from authoritarian to democratic regimes, with examples of international and domestic laws and rulings related to these goals. By providing information on both the interventions and the reasons for creating them, these volumes became a reference for scholars, policy makers, and advocates who were interested in how to ensure accountability, improve survivor well-being, and prevent future violence.

USIP's volumes highlight how the idea's malleability, particularly its descriptive/prescriptive nature, made it useful to actors with different goals. By promoting transitional justice as an idea characterized by certain interventions, and with theoretical explanations for why these interventions are important, these early actors served as norm entrepreneurs – individuals who "alert people to the existence of a shared complaint and can suggest a collective solution" (Sunstein 1996, p. 926). Part of the collective solution was to develop tribunals, as well as complements or alternatives to court processes in countries that were trying to democratize after periods of violence or repressive rule. Judicial accountability remained an important strategy, but this emphasis on quasi-judicial and even non-judicial strategies distinguished transitional justice from related ideas such as rule of law and human rights. The idea was always predicated on liberal legality (Vinjamuri and Snyder 2004), but its focus was the contextual nature of justice and the importance of creating laws that would offer more than retributive justice.

A GROWING INTEREST IN TRUTH COMMISSIONS

Truth commissions were just one of several "options," in Kritz's volumes, and this intervention was not very well known before the 1990s.[13] Hayner (1994) refers to the 1974 Ugandan commission as the first contemporary truth commission, but this commission was titled the Commission of Inquiry into the Disappearance of People in Uganda, not a truth commission. Further, it was highly problematic for the way Uganda's ruthless dictator Idi Amin rejected its findings that his regime was responsible for deaths and disappearances. As early as 1978, the Ford Foundation provided financial support to organizations working on truth commissions and was particularly supportive of efforts in Latin America. In Argentina, these efforts led to the prosecution of military leaders and aided CONADEP, the presidential commission that documented the disappearance and execution of thousands of political dissidents and others swept up in violence. Ford's efforts intensified when it revamped its programmatic focus in 1981, putting "human rights and social justice" at the forefront of its agenda. The Foundation's leadership committed itself to the notion that rights, particularly civil and political rights, would lead to the reduction of poverty and justice (Carmichael 2001, p. 252).

Ford's focus on rights meant that it was interested in legal remedies to redress mass violence. By the mid 2000s, the Ford Foundation's assets exceeded $10 billion, with grant making nearing $60 million per year. Between 1976 and 2001, the organization spent approximately $200,000,000 on advocacy organizations working to promote human rights. For example, the Foundation provided $5 million to Human Rights Watch's (HRW's) endowment and $1,000,000 to its operating reserves, setting that organization up to be the international leader in shaping understandings of human rights around the world.

Ford was not the only donor interested in helping create new legal interventions. In 1988, less than $500,000 of OECD aid money went to countries under the title of "human rights" and "legal and judicial development." By 2002, it was $580 million (Oomen 2005, pp. 890–91).

While the Ford Foundation was interested in prosecutions, the Foundation's leadership also saw the value of culture in democratic institution building and viewed truth commissions as a tool in that endeavor (Korey 2007). In 1989, the Ford Foundation helped fund the creation of the Centre for the Study of Violence and Reconciliation in South Africa, where Paul van Zyl, who later became the Executive Secretary of the South African TRC and Vice-President of the ICTJ, began his work on truth commissions (Ancelovici and Jenson 2013, p. 300). The

13 The director of the Center for Civil and Human Rights at the University of Notre Dame emphasized this point when requesting $65,000 from the Ford Foundation to translate the report into English. In this proposal, dated January 30, 1992, the director noted that countries around the world would gain insights into how to redress gross violations of human rights if they had access to the final report from Chile's truth commission.

Foundation's Southern Cone Office decided to develop an initiative on Historical Memory in Chile.[14] This project helped collect personal accounts of the violence under the assumption that understanding the causes and consequences of violence might prevent its recurrence. Louis Bickford, who was later hired by the ICTJ, described his work with the Ford Foundation's Chilean office as a "movement to deal with the past."[15]

Part of this movement included the promotion of truth commissions, though few scholars used this label at the time (see Cassel 1993; Ensalaco 1995). In 1995, Popkin and Roht-Arriaza, for example, referred to these quasi-judicial bodies as "investigative commissions" created to develop an authoritative account of the past, vindicate victims, recommend legislative, structural, or other changes to avoid repetition of past abuses, and establish accountability or the identity of perpetrators (Popkin and Roht-Arriaza 1995, p. 79). Hayner, who became the world's foremost expert on truth commissions and later founded the ICTJ, was one of the first scholars to categorize the variety of investigative commissions created under the label truth commission. She had studied peace and global studies and psychology at Earlham College, and later global and international affairs at Columbia. During her studies, she completed an internship in El Salvador with its *Comisión de la Verdad Para El Salvador*, or the "Commission on the Truth," and this name stuck.

In 1994, Hayner published an article in *Human Rights Quarterly* that compared fifteen different commissions. In this article, she used the phrase "truth commission" as a generic term for the variety of commissions she investigated (Hayner 1994, p. 599). She defined these commissions as "official bodies set up to investigate a past period of human rights abuses or violations of international law" (Hayner 1994, p. 598). In particular, Hayner's interest was less in punishment and more in how commissions could help "heal wounds" from mass violence (Hayner 1994, p. 607).[16] Her definition of truth commissions was intentionally broad. She wanted to show the commonalities between what are now known as formal (government-sponsored) and informal (non-government-sponsored) commissions. She included commissions established by domestic governments, international governmental organizations (such as the El Salvador commission created by the United Nations), and a commission created by a nongovernmental organization in Rwanda.

These early commissions mainly focused on investigating human rights violations, which is why Kritz characterized this intervention as one that documents past abuses. In her article, Hayner mentions that South Africa was contemplating a truth commission "as a piece of the solution" to the transition from apartheid (Hayner 1994, p. 605). This observation was prescient, as proponents of the South Africa TRC

[14] Louis Bickford, *Memory and Justice: Confronting Past Atrocity and Human Rights Abuses*, International Center for Transitional Justice, 2008, on file with author.

[15] Ibid, p. 3.

[16] Hayner credits Juan Mendez with explaining how official acknowledgement might heal wounds. In turn, Juan Mendez attributes this articulation to Professor Thomas Nagel (Hayner 1994, p. 607, fn 12).

institutionalized a particular model of a truth commission as an intervention that would also be a public forum for individuals to voice their suffering.

THE SOUTH AFRICA MODEL

The South Africa TRC continues to influence perceptions of truth commissions as a malleable intervention that can bridge social and political divides in the wake of mass violence. This commission's focus on public hearings has contributed to understandings of truth commissions as interventions that focus on documentation, providing voice to survivors, as both an alternative and a precursor to prosecutions, and capable of meeting a variety of social and political goals. However, this was a very specific truth commission in a very specific transition, and it is often misunderstood both for how it dealt with the tricky issue of amnesty and what its effects in South Africa were. Understanding this truth commission provides initial insights into why, given their aspirational qualities, truth commissions are appealing, yet so often disappoint their proponents.

To begin with, the history of violence and injustice that confronted the South Africa TRC was dire, and the country's new leaders were hopeful that they could create a legal intervention that would minimize the bloodshed likely to occur in the transition. South Africa's overtly racist political system legalized racial discrimination. Blacks could not vote, were denied access to many jobs, could not marry whites, and needed government permission to enter parts of the country. The apartheid regime banned the African National Congress (ANC) and other opposition political parties and used the courts to maintain the oppressive political order. In responding to organized opposition to apartheid, the police force was brutal, with many officers committed to fighting what they saw as a terrorist, as well as communist, threat against their values. An estimated 135 political prisoners were killed between 1960 and 1990, 21,000 others died as a result of political violence, and hundreds more were disappeared.

The United Nations declared apartheid a crime against humanity in 1966, and individuals from around the world were invested in seeing South Africa become an inclusive democracy. Part of their campaign focused on the release of Nelson Mandela, a lawyer who founded the armed wing of the ANC after the 1960 massacre of nonviolent protesters in Sharpeville. In 1964, Mandela was found guilty of treason and sentenced to life in prison on Robben Island. There, he began to study Afrikaaner history and contemplate how the different racial groups might better understand one another. Under domestic and international pressure, in 1990, newly elected South African President F.W. de Klerk freed Nelson Mandela and unbanned the ANC. While under house arrest, Mandela met with de Klerk in secret talks about South Africa's political future.

For several years, South Africa's political party leaders tried to develop a new constitution that would allow equal participation in the political system. Part of this discussion revolved around how to redress the violence of the apartheid regime. Throughout the negotiations, there were many questions about how the new government might punish the architects and enforcers of the apartheid regime, particularly the secret police who were responsible for the deaths and disappearances of anti-apartheid activists. By 1993, violence had intensified and thousands of South Africans fled the country in what locals call the "chicken run." When senior ANC leader Chris Hani was assassinated in April 1993, few trusted that the political parties would actually come to a power-sharing agreement.

Finally, on November 18, 1993, the negotiators ended the deliberations on how to deal with perpetrators of violence, which paved the way for a new constitution. As an eleventh hour bargain, representatives of different political parties agreed to conditional amnesties for those who committed violence in furtherance of the apartheid regime. Following up on the agreement, the new government passed the National Unity and Reconciliation Act of 1995. The Act provided the legal framework for the now famous Truth and Reconciliation Commission. The Act states that "there is a need for understanding but not for revenge, a need for reparation but not for retaliation, a need for ubuntu, but not for victimisation. In order to advance such reconciliation and reconstruction, amnesty shall be granted in respect of acts, omissions and offences associated with political objectives and committed in the course of the conflicts of the past."

With their focus on "forgiveness, not vengeance," TRC proponents emphasized that trials for anyone but the most heinous human rights violators could undermine the country's unity. When a victim's organization, the Azanian Peoples Organization, challenged the law for violating the interim Constitution's guarantee to have disputes settled by a court or another independent forum, the South African Constitutional Court reiterated that the country should sacrifice retributive justice for truth and for peace. The Court asserted that individuals would be less forthcoming if they feared punishment, and that punishing individuals responsible for apartheid violence would lead to "continuous retaliation and revenge."[17]

There is ongoing confusion about the TRC's approach to amnesty, and this confusion means that opponents of truth commissions often cite South Africa as providing amnesty in exchange for truth. The Commission's conditional amnesty was not a blanket amnesty, or amnesty in exchange for divulging information about the violence. The Commission included three committees: one to decide on amnesties, one to decide on reparations, and one to take testimony from victims and perpetrators and publish a report on the history of apartheid violence. All three committees were conducted in a legalistic fashion, with a focus on direct acts of violence against victims as opposed to the structural violence that penetrated all levels of society. The amnesty committee evaluated whether the perpetrators were forthright in disclosing

[17] *Azanian Peoples Organization (AZAPO) v. President of the Republic of S. Afr.* 1996 (4) SA 671 (CC), para 19.

all of their acts, but a main concern was whether the violence was politically motivated and proportional to the political goals sought. Only 7112 individuals applied for amnesty. This is a small fraction of those who committed abuses, and 5392 of the applicants were denied. All but a handful received de facto amnesties, because the government did not pursue prosecutions. The commission, in theory, could have paved the way to prosecutions, and the specter of punishment might have encouraged actors to be forthright about the violence they committed. However, the small number of amnesty applications reveals that the Commission did not have its intended effect of encouraging perpetrators to fully disclose their violent activities.

In addition to the conditional amnesty policy, the TRC's focus on public hearings, in which victims shared their experiences of violence, made the commission the international spectacle that it became. By way of contrast, in Chile and Argentina, there were no public hearings in which people recounted their horrors. Rather, those commissions focused on finding how who was murdered, disappeared, or otherwise violated during the authoritarian regimes. The commissions' publications were widely circulated, but the victims and accused perpetrators remained largely anonymous (Chapman and Ball 2001). In South Africa, nightly news reports showed participants in emotional states as they described what they did or what was done to them.

Despite its laudable goals and international fame, various studies have shown that the TRC had a limited impact in reducing racism in the country or improving the mental and physical well-being of victims (Backer 2010; Gibson 2002). The TRC's historical report focused heavily on direct acts of violence and overlooked the variety of structural factors that continue to undermine social and political relationships in the country (Wilson 2001; Mamdani 2002). In particular, the Commission defined its start date as 1960, when the ANC moved from non-violent toward violent tactics. Clearly, the history of apartheid's violence began long before apartheid's resisters turned violent. Moreover, the reparations committee recommended a $21,000 payout to victims that never materialized, leaving many victims frustrated with the entire process. Violence continues to undermine political stability in South Africa, yet the South Africa TRC still serves as an influential example of how governments can create truth commissions to redress mass violence and promote democratic political transitions.

In the wake of the South Africa Truth and Reconciliation Commission, understandings of both truth commissions and transitional justice expanded (Teitel 2003). The Chilean commission of 1992, most notably, had already linked truth and reconciliation in calling itself a Commission on Truth and Reconciliation.[18] However, this commission did not have the same impact on the international community as the South African one did. As Kritz, the editor of USIP's volumes on transitional

[18] In describing the commission, one Chilean scholar even noted that the relationship between truth and reconciliation "is evident" (Sutil 1992, p. 1482).

justice, explained, truth commissions became "the favorite flavor" after the South Africa TRC. He suggested that donors, as well as other actors thinking about transition, decided that they "need to do something to facilitate transition." They were not sure what "works with respect to reconciliation," but believed that these truth commissions exist and "must play part of the solution" (interview with Neil Kritz 2010). Kritz later wrote about how, in the wake of the South Africa TRC, many countries decide to create truth commissions "usually based not on research but on instinct" (Kritz 2009, p. 17). Similarly, Teitel has suggested that the coupling of transitional justice with truth and reconciliation created "new language that had important juridical and political implications" (Teitel 2003, p. 83).

These observers were pointing to a growing belief among scholars, policy makers, and advocates that truth commissions are a useful, if not necessary, intervention to help depolarize societies and help them accept the violence that occurred (Sutil 1992). The South Africa TRC, with its public displays of victimization and religious overtones of healing and forgiveness, was akin to a new product or service, and soon a new group of professionals emerged to assist countries that were interested in creating one.

PROFESSIONALIZING TRUTH COMMISSIONS

As one of the few scholars who had written on truth commissions, the South Africa TRC created a slew of opportunities for Priscilla Hayner. She described being at "wits' end" to meet the demands of actors interested in what these quasi-judicial bodies might do in their countries. At the time, Hayner was finishing her book on truth commissions and working as a consultant for the Ford Foundation. She struggled with the logistics of travel, the logistics of funding, and other dilemmas associated with being an independent consultant. Alex Boraine, the vice chair of the South Africa Truth and Reconciliation Commission, was working near Hayner, teaching at New York University. He was finishing his book on the South Africa TRC, which celebrated the Commission's approach to amnesty, and was also flooded with requests to share his experience with others. Paul Van Zyl, the Executive Secretary of the TRC, was also eager to promote the South African experience.

Ford had been responsive to requests to fund truth commissions, but wanted to better understand what these interventions offer.[19] In 1997, Ford provided New York University, with Pricilla Hayner as the project coordinator, with a $100,000 grant to commission a set of academic papers on the truth commissions in South Africa and

19 In 1997, Christian Tomuschat, then director of Guatemala's Historical Clarification Commission, sent a request to program officer Christina Eguizabal. In the letter, he describes working in emergency mode with $3.2 million, 46.5% of what they needed. The letter requested $400,000 to help support a minimum of five field offices, extending contracts, going through the documents they gathered. Eguizabal sent the request to Anthony Romero. A month later, the program officers were able to commit $100,000 from different sources within the foundation.

Guatemala, hoping to develop a better understanding of what makes these commissions successful or not (Chapman and Ball 2001; Quinn and Freeman 2003). As Hayner, Boraine, and Van Zyl contemplated their growing number of requests for information on truth commissions, the Ford Foundation offered them a rare opportunity to better coordinate their ongoing consulting work with governments and advocates interested in truth commissions. In 2000, Anthony Romero, then director of the Human Rights Program, asked Hayner to put together a memo on what they called the growing "field" of transitional justice. He hoped her memo could inform the organization as to how to better finance efforts to help countries thinking about tribunals, truth commissions, and other interventions geared toward redressing past violence.

Hayner's memo highlights the varied understandings of transitional justice that existed at the time and the effort to professionalize the nascent movement. Her definition of transitional justice was purely descriptive, asking how countries emerging from conflict or repression respond to past human rights abuses. The memo was based on interviews with over fifty individuals who had worked on issues related to accountability, peace, and political transition around the world. Hayner emphasized the important role that courts, as well as truth commissions, played in transitional societies. She pointed out concerns about the fact that thousands of individuals are implicated in the crimes, that survivors need to be honored, and that social and political cultures must change in order to prevent the recurrence of violence. Most importantly for Ford, the memo articulated five needs to help coordinate the burgeoning requests for assistance on how to address requests from countries interested in legal interventions associated with transitional justice: (1) information clearinghouse/resource center/archive, (2) rapid response/technical assistance, (3) training and capacity building, (4) research, monitoring, and evaluation, and (5) network or consortium.

In response to the memo, Romero had recommended to Ford's president, Susan Berresford, that the Foundation fund a new international organization with over $10 million for five years. Berresford was enthusiastic, and Romero, Hayner, Boraine, and Van Zyl began contemplating how to create a new international organization that drew on their collective knowledge and experience.

DEBATING A TRANSITIONAL JUSTICE ORGANIZATION

Though Ford's leadership was already contemplating the creation of a new organization, Hayner's memo served as a background paper for a meeting on April 6, 2000 to discuss priorities for the Ford Foundation's new funding stream. The rapporteur's notes from the April meeting indicate that the goal was to discuss the emerging "field" of transitional justice and how to "institutionalize" it.[20] The participant list

[20] Rapporteur's Notes, Transitional Justice Meeting, FA 591, Rockefeller Archive Center, on file with the author.

included prominent leaders within U.S. think tanks and advocacy organizations, including Alice Henkin from the Aspen Institute, Marcie Mersky, who, at the time, was working at the Guatemalan Historical Commission and later joined the ICTJ in 2011, and Neil Kritz from USIP. Another contingent was academics who had written on truth commissions and criminal tribunals, including Doug Cassel and Naomi Roht-Arriaza. Others were familiar with issues related to transitional justice in their own countries, such as Graeme Simpson, from the Center for the Study of Violence and Reconciliation (CSVR), and Yasmin Sooka, who served on the South Africa Truth and Reconciliation Commission. Also in attendance were leaders in the human rights movement, such as Juan Mendez, who founded the Human Rights Watch Americas program, and Jeanne Sulzer, a French attorney with the Federation for Human Rights.

The question put forward to the group was "how to respond to political violence and whether and how to hold perpetrators accountable for their crimes?" This starting point reveals the normative assumption behind the transitional justice movement, which is that something must be done to ensure accountability for violence, particularly state-sponsored violence. The main question for the group revolved around accountability, an ambiguous phrase that could require any number of interventions. Larry Cox, then a senior program officer at the Ford Foundation, opened the meeting by explaining the importance of accountability in the human rights movement, and participants emphasized that governments do not have to choose between full-blown criminal accountability and amnesty. Their task, which they explained with transitional justice, was to think about the in-between space and how governments might create different interventions for the goals they choose.

While the group discussed their understandings of transitional justice, this meeting was far more about institutionalization than it was about conceptualization. However, on both issues, the discussion was contentious. With regards to institutionalization, there were two main attitudes about what to do with Ford's new funding stream. Some, particularly the leaders of the future ICTJ, emphasized the need for an organization that would serve as an international hub of research and advocacy, while others sought to fund organizations working within the countries undergoing transition. Paul Van Zyl, one of the ICTJ's founders (and now a high-end fashion designer), was excited about the opportunity to have a "rapid response" program that could provide technical assistance to countries. From his perspective, an international center would be the best way to meet the needs of societies undergoing political transition. Boraine also believed that an international center was necessary to provide a structure for training and capacity building in countries where violence had occurred.

Neil Kritz, in contrast, expressed concern that an international center might stifle the growing field, not consolidate it. Graeme Simpson, the founder of the Centre for the Study of Violence and Reconciliation in South Africa, emphasized that a regional approach might be beneficial, but noted that there would be contradictions between promoting a regional approach in places with great diversity and the challenge that many issues cross regions. He was also concerned about creating another hub for elites, leaving out individuals with less power in society. From his perspective, transitions are about changing power dynamics, and the proposed institution could end up reinforcing these dynamics. Ten years later, Simpson expressed concern that "what Ford was doing was creating an 800-pound gorilla when there were so many national and regional organizations that were doing this" (interview with Graeme Simpson 2010).

The main concern was that funding a new transnational justice organization might duplicate local efforts and ultimately replace the local organizations already working on similar issues. Roht-Arriaza also emphasized the need for better networking modalities, not just a new organization, while Cassel said that it might be better to create three different centers to provide networking, technical assistance, and research. Jeanne Sulzer offered the insight that organizations with mandates that are too broad usually fail. Moreover, Alice Henkin expressed the concern that locating a new organization in the United States could be problematic, as the United States' unilateralist approach to policy making may be unwelcome in countries undergoing a transition.

While the question of supporting a new international organization or existing domestic organizations was polarizing, there was also another division on the question of prosecutions for perpetrators of human rights abuses. For some, an organization predicated on the idea of transitional justice was worrisome because it was not clear whether the Ford Foundation was redirecting its resources away from the human rights movement's efforts to consolidate international criminal law. With the ratification of the Rome Statute in 1999, which created the International Criminal Court, many advocates working on accountability wanted to focus their full attention on strengthening international criminal law. While some participants emphasized the importance of prosecutions, others hoped that transitional justice would be conceptualized more broadly. Even in 2000, observers were concerned that little thought is given to what countries should do when a tribunal or truth commission finishes its work. In particular, Kritz emphasized that transitional justice was about far more than accountability and argued that the purposes should include reintegration and even development.

In the final wrap-up meeting on April 6, 2000, Anthony Romero tried to appease these concerns about siphoning attention from the human rights movement by emphasizing the differences between human rights and transitional justice, and suggesting that this new center would be a different type of organization. He reiterated that Ford would not be diverting funding from "future programming in the human rights field." Rather, the Foundation wanted to create something new, an "information clearing house and resource center, technical assistance, training and capacity building, research and monitoring, and the establishment of an active network of participants in the transitional justice field." This proposed center symbolized the blend of scholarship, policy making, and advocacy around transitional justice and the goal of developing an understanding of transitional justice that would be useful for actors with wide-ranging goals.

CREATING AN INTERNATIONAL CENTER FOR TRANSITIONAL JUSTICE

Looking at the different perspectives articulated at the April 6 meeting, it is clear that a new organization dedicated to transitional justice was entering a contested organizational field. With Ford's encouragement, Hayner, Van Zyl, and Boraine drafted a proposal for a new center in July 2000.[21] The proposal began by noting the "quickly expanding field of transitional justice and the many demands on those involved in the field." It explained that discussions had been going on for at least a year about the need for an "international center on transitional justice."[22] Ford approved the grant and provided $99,500 to pay Boraine, Hayner, and Van Zyl as consultants who would design an "International Center on Transitional Justice."[23]

While the initial grant was for an International Center *on* Transitional Justice, the organization that was created is called the International Center *for* Transitional Justice. The final grant report does not explain the change in preposition, but this shift is telling. The new center would not merely produce studies *on* transitional justice but, rather, vigorously advocate the use of transitional justice interventions in post-conflict states. ICTJ co-founder Priscilla Hayner recalls that the organization's name was decided in a couple of short conversations. "Transitional justice" was already a term of art; they settled quickly on "international center" and then addressed whether it should be a center "for" or "on" transitional justice. "That's the only discussion we really had on the subject, and it was short; I had no strong preference, but Alex Boraine said 'No, it's *for*, period. We're not founding something for an intellectual study, I'm here to do something *for*, I'm *for* transitional justice, we are here to promote good transitional justice, we are here as a center for transitional justice.'" That was the extent of the discussion, said Hayner (interview with Priscilla Hayner 2015).

[21] Years later, Boraine recounted how, after the April meeting, Susan Berresford asked the group to put together a memorandum so that the organization could help support this new center: "We were extraordinarily fortunate to have Ford's president, Susan Berresford, participate in the discussion. She called me the next day and said that Ford was ready for our proposal. The rest, thanks to her, is history." International Center for Transitional Justice, Annual Report 2006/7, p. 4, www.ictj.org/sites/default/files/ICTJ_Annual_Report_2006-2007.pdf.

[22] Ford Foundation Grant 1010-0270, on file with the author.

[23] The grant recipient was the Tides Foundation, a San Francisco based nonprofit that served as a financial go-between for individuals not yet set up as a 501(c)(3) nonprofit.

In this explanation of the organization's title, Hayner suggested that transitional justice was not a well-known phrase, but she saw it as an idea that could encompass their particular goals. Another early ICTJ staff member noted that Boraine wanted to create "an organization that would get its hands dirty" (interview with former ICTJ staff member 2016), meaning that the organization would help governments develop interventions that would meet their specific needs. This contrasted with organizations that identified with human rights, such as Amnesty International, which were increasingly promoting prosecutions as a nonderogable right for victims (Engle 2015). For the ICTJ, transitional justice was malleable enough to describe their less rigid approach of promoting prosecutions, limited amnesties, or whatever seemed most beneficial in post-conflict settings.

Boraine, a Methodist minister, believed that the South Africa TRC's approach of forgiveness would be helpful to other countries dealing with conflict. To observers, Boraine had a wisdom and charisma that made him very effective in inspiring others about South Africa's transition, and it was only natural that he headed this new organization (Korey 2007, p. 268). Anthony Romero also acknowledged the promotional aspect of the center, suggesting that the purpose of the new organization was to make the South African experience known to the world (interview with Anthony Romero 2015).

Boraine's leadership certainly helped the organization fundraise and grow at a rapid rate, and it also led the truth commission to become a signature intervention of the new movement. The ICTJ's three founders were already working full time on the organization in February 2001, and quickly began fundraising to show Ford their potential. Money slated for ongoing projects, such as Priscilla Hayner's project through NYU, now shifted to the ICTJ. The organization partnered not only with large donors such as the MacArthur Foundation and the Carnegie Corporation, but also with the UN High Commissioner for Human Rights, who provided the ICTJ with $50,000 for technical support on the East Timor truth commission. In March 2001, the Ford Foundation provided $4 million dollars to the ICTJ and pledged an additional $11 million for 2002–5. This donation was unprecedented, and meant that the ICTJ had the resources to develop into a highly influential transnational organization. Just six months after it opened, the ICTJ was consulting with governments and advocacy organizations in a dozen countries and growing at a rapid rate. By 2007, the organization had a $17 million budget and 100 employees and was working in over thirty countries on issues that fell under its broad mandate.

PROMOTING TRANSITIONAL JUSTICE

After the South Africa TRC, the idea of transitional justice was becoming mainstream, as were truth commissions. In 1992, transitional justice appeared once in an anglophone newspaper, in a report on the Salzburg Conference. In 2009, it appeared over 725 times (Mouralis 2013, p. 90). In 2002, a *Foreign Affairs* article suggested that "Unthinkable just a short time ago, such gestures [creating truth commissions] now accompany practically every transition from civil war or authoritarian rule." In explaining the prevalence of these commissions, the author referred to the ICTJ as the first "truth commission consulting firm."[24] Writing about donor-driven justice interventions in 2005, Oomen pointed out that "No post-conflict setting is complete these days without some form of Truth Commission set up under international tutelage" (Oomen 2005, p. 892). The ICTJ's most recent president, David Tolbert, suggested to me that, during this time, transitional justice and the ICTJ were "equated with one another," but then quickly suggested that transitional justice was now an "established field in and of itself" (interview with David Tolbert 2010).

As the idea circulated, the ICTJ's ambitions were clear: to become the go-to organization for information on truth commissions and other interventions that governments might create to address mass violence. For it to do so, its leaders had to promote an understanding of transitional justice that showed that they supported the creation of tribunals, as this strategy for promoting accountability was still dominant, but also to promote truth commissions as an important intervention that could be useful in a variety of contexts. To keep the idea malleable, the ICTJ defined the idea broadly: "Transitional justice refers to the set of judicial and non-judicial measures that have been implemented by different countries in order to redress the legacies of massive human rights abuses. These measures include criminal prosecutions, truth commissions, reparations programs, and various kinds of institutional reforms." At the time, the organization referred to these four measures as the "pillars" of transitional justice, which helped standardize understandings of the interventions associated with transitional justice. At the same time, in December 2001, the *New York Times Magazine* published an article on "designer truth commissions" in its "Year in Ideas" section. The article mentions Alex Boraine and the ICTJ, pointing out how the organization tries to help governments "tailor truth commissions to their specific needs."[25]

The ICTJ's influence on understandings of transitional justice will become clearer in the following chapters, but its work in promoting transitional justice at the transnational level had important effects on policy-making related to mass violence. In 2003, Kofi Annan invited the ICTJ to train UN officials on transitional justice and then followed up with an invitation for the organization to address the Security Council (Ancelovici and Jenson 2013, p. 302). In 2004, the United Nations Security Council published a report on the importance of transitional justice, defining transitional justice as "the full range of processes and mechanisms associated with a society's

[24] Jonathan Tepperman, "Truth and Consequences," *Foreign Affairs*, March/April 2002, www.foreignaffairs.com/articles/2002-03-01/truth-and-consequences.

[25] Tina Rosenberg, "Designer Truth Commissions," *New York Times Magazine*, December 9, 2001, www.nytimes.com/2001/12/09/magazine/the-year-in-ideas-a-to-z-designer-truth-commissions.html.

attempts to come to terms with a legacy of large-scale past abuses, in order to ensure accountability, serve justice, and achieve reconciliation. These may include both judicial and nonjudicial mechanisms with differing levels of international involvement (or none at all) and individual prosecutions, reparations, truth-seeking, institutional reform, vetting and dismissals, or a combination thereof."[26] After summarizing the importance of tribunals, the report emphasized the importance of truth commissions as a "complementary tool" to tribunals that have a "victim centered approach" to justice that can establish a "historical record and recommend remedial action." It goes on to describe reparations and lustration and the need to develop a roster of experts and technical tools to help with these interventions. The ICTJ and UN definitions are very broad and are based on an assumption that any one or a combination of these interventions will be able to ensure vaguely defined, idealistic goals of redress and reconciliation.

In addition, the UN, like the ICTJ, wanted to train individuals about their understandings of how and why to carry out these different interventions. To realize this goal, the ICTJ hired Louis Bickford, who had previously worked at Ford's Santiago, Chile office assisting the Historical Memory Initiative. Bickford helped organize training around the world, educating everyone from students to policy makers on the idea of transitional justice and its so-called "pillars." In 2002, the ICTJ launched its fellowship program, graduating ninety fellows from African, Middle Eastern, and Balkan countries over the course of three years. The program inspired the Latin American Fellowship program in partnership with the Center for Human Rights at the Law School at the University of Chile. Starting in 2006, the ICTJ offered a "transitional justice essentials" class, which the organization described in the following way:

> Aimed at European NGOs, universities, diplomatic staff, and graduate/law students, the course will cover the essential themes, mechanisms, and case studies in the field of transitional justice with the goal of imparting the knowledge required to develop and implement transitional justice policies based on international best practices.[27]

Through these workshops and this training, the ICTJ promoted a standardized understanding of "best practices," but also emphasized the malleability of these interventions in different settings. In doing so, they enhanced their professional status as experts in these best practices and encouraged leaders from around the world to create truth commissions or other interventions under the banner of transitional justice.

While these activities suggest that the ICTJ was an advocacy organization interested in promoting the idea and its associated interventions, staff did not see themselves as an advocacy organization. One emphatically said "no" when asked if the organization was an advocacy organization. Rather, he pointed to the role that the

[26] United Nations, *Report of the Secretary-General, the Rule of Law and Transitional Justice in Conflict and Post-conflict Societies*, UN 6/2004/616, August 23, 2004.

[27] International Center for Transitional Justice, *Annual Report* 2004/5, p. 16, www.ictj.org/sites/default/files/ICTJ_AnnualReport_2004-5.pdf.

organization played in helping design and implement these interventions. Just as they played a variety of professional roles, staff saw transitional justice as an idea that could help a variety of actors realize a variety of goals, yet they were ambivalent on which goals were most important.

MAKING TRANSITIONAL JUSTICE MALLEABLE

Early on, staff at the ICTJ recognized the importance of being *the* center for transitional justice, but they struggled to articulate what distinguished their organization from others engaged in similar work. The main challenge was how to articulate transitional justice, given that the ICTJ staff was promoting the idea to individuals with varied goals and strategies, particularly around the question of prosecutions for perpetrators of violence. The reflections of the organization's early staff show that, from the outset, understandings of transitional justice were unclear. Louis Bickford, for example, described ongoing discussions about "what exactly was this field?" He noted that "truth telling was the sexy new topic," but that they also had to consider prosecutions because "a lot of the human rights people" thought that was the "most important aspect of accountability." Bickford, who had worked on issues related to memory in Chile, also noted that "memory as a subfield got totally dumped by the wayside at that time." From his perspective, lawyers did not appreciate the "cultural side of dealing with the past" (interview with Louis Bickford 2015). In 2008, five of the ICTJ's board members were trained in international law, and nearly half of their New York staff was legally trained as well (Lefranc 2008, p. 68).

These diverse understandings of transitional justice within the movement kept the organization's approach in flux. Bickford's comments also indicate how the organization promoted the idea in a way that kept it malleable enough to encompass words such as truth and reconciliation without rejecting the use of tribunals. The ICTJ's president from 2004 to 2009 was Juan Mendez, who started Human Rights Watch's office in Latin America and was a well-known advocate for prosecutions of human rights abuses. When discussing his understandings of transitional justice, he explained how broadly he defined the idea, and how useful it could be in different settings:

> We are – transitional justice for us includes truth, justice, reparations, and institutional reform, and where applicable, reconciliation as well – all of it, right? But in terms of the tools and of the implementation of those principles, ICTJ was from the start and continues to be very deferential to what makes sense in each context. (Interview with Juan Mendez 2010)

With the ambiguity of the word transition, and the universal appeal of the word justice, those promoting transitional justice could claim that their idea encompassed the goals and strategies of related ideas, such as human rights, conflict resolution, peace building, and facing the past. It also meant that the organization could promote itself as offering practical interventions and provide practical assistance to actors interested in creating them.

Furthermore, the organization promoted the truth commission as a signature intervention of transitional justice and as malleable enough to be used in a wide range of settings and for a wide range of purposes. Paul van Zyl, for example, wrote in 2005 that truth commissions are more effective than other interventions because they "can make more effective and informed recommendations as to measures that can be taken to deal with these root causes or reduce the capacity of disruptive actors to perpetuate conflict" (Van Zyl in Ancelovici and Jenson 2013, p. 304). Part of making the intervention malleable was capitalizing on this idealistic discourse, exemplified by the term reconciliation, which is evident in efforts to promote truth commissions as well as in their mandates. The East Timor truth commission, called the Commission on Reception, Truth, and Reconciliation (CAVR), offers just one of many examples of how domestic actors appropriated this idealistic discourse:

> [O]ur mission was to establish accountability in order to deepen and strengthen the prospects for peace, democracy, the rule of law and human rights in our new nation. Central to this was the recognition that victims not only had a right to justice and the truth but that justice, truth and mutual understanding are essential for the healing and reconciliation of individuals and the nation. (CAVR Report December 2005)

The ICTJ worked closely in the design and implementation of this truth commission, even opening an office in the region. Promising peace, justice, rule of law, human rights, truth, mutual understanding, and reconciliation, this commission reflects the aspirations of Boraine, Van Zyl, and other transitional justice proponents who had high hopes for what truth commissions, explained and legitimated with the idea of transitional justice, could offer. They promoted truth commissions as adaptable and capable of realizing the aspirations of survivors seeking redress, as well as political leaders trying to consolidate their power.

THE DILEMMA OF MALLEABILITY

As the ICTJ grew in influence, the organization became a target for critique, as did the idea it promoted. Much of the concern about the ICTJ revolved around the ICTJ's consultation activities, particularly on truth commissions. Graeme Simpson, who worked for years to improve relations between civil society and the South Africa TRC, observed with disdain that the ICTJ appeared to be a "truth commission road show" (interview with Graeme Simpson 2010). Others suggested that the ICTJ's strategy was to decontextualize the South African experience, which was rooted in religious notions of reconciliation, and recontextualize it with secular language that would appeal to a wide range of actors (Ancelovici and Jenson 2013). Years later, at a conference panel in 2016, an expert on the South African TRC reflected a common perspective that the ICTJ promoted "IKEA truth commissions" that governments would just cut out of a box and construct.[28] The organization's original leaders, including Boraine, Van Zyl, and Mark Freeman, a U.S.- and Canadian-trained human rights lawyer who was hired soon after the organization formed, had all published articles and books on the importance of selective amnesties in political transitions. Their approach to amnesties drew skepticism from actors who wondered if governments were interested in truth commissions because these commissions might divert claims for justice and redress through courts.

One of the ICTJ's more involved projects was in Morocco, where the new king created the Equity and Reconciliation Commission (IER) to address the previous king's policies of detention and torture. During my fieldwork in 2007, individuals who worked with the IER referred to the ICTJ when talking about the commission's design, and former ICTJ staff emphasized the central role that the organization played in the IER's development and implementation. While it was notable for being the first such commission in the region, various human rights advocates in Morocco expressed to me that the truth commission was not designed to address their concerns about detention and torture in the previous regime but, rather, to silence them. These advocates complained that witnesses were limited in what they could say, and calls for further investigations and prosecutions were sidelined. The IER provided information on 742 individuals who were detained or disappeared, but it did not name perpetrators, and it even made witnesses sign away their rights to name perpetrators. There have been no trials for the violence, and alleged perpetrators continue to hold positions of power within the government, leading Slyomovics (2005) to refer to the commission as a "performance of human rights."

In another well-known example of the ICTJ's questionable consultations, Alex Boraine initially assisted Serbia's attempt to create a truth commission on its role in the violence during the dissolution of the former Yugoslavia. Serbia's President Kostunica had appointed commissioners from various regions, yet it was clear that the goal of the quasi-judicial body was to legitimate Serbia's perspective rather than investigate the causes and consequences of the violence (Dimitrijevic 2008). Boraine eventually withdrew his services, but this consultation confirmed skeptics' fears about how political leaders might use the organization to legitimize divisive policies.

Soon, donors also began to question whether or to what extent transitional justice interventions were having an impact in the countries where they were created. One ICTJ staff member relayed how she shifted her focus from program development to monitoring and evaluation in order to meet these growing concerns. During our interviews in 2010, staff at a variety of advocacy organizations offered different opinions about what they perceived as a new emphasis on measuring outcomes. Several expressed satisfaction, noting a need to better understand what tribunals,

[28] Richard Wilson, "Mass Violence and Human Rights: The Global Politics of Truth and Justice," University of Massachusetts, Amherst, Feb. 5 2016.

truth commissions, and other interventions entailed. At the same time, one staffer who had worked for years promoting accountability in war-torn countries wondered how goals such as "justice" could ever be measured (interview with ICTJ staffer 2010).

These concerns about transitional justice did not simply reflect the efficacy of its associated interventions, but how the movement professionalized. A former employee of the ICTJ stressed that the organization was too disconnected from the people and places it was trying to help:

> The one thing I learned here is that international organizations, particularly in the North, sometimes enjoy platforms that are the product of proximity – proximity to power and money – and not necessarily because they deserve it on the basis of what they do on the ground. (Interview with former ICTJ staffer 2010)

Throughout my research in Europe and South America, as well as in the United States, I heard concerns that actors promoting transitional justice, particularly the ICTJ, were stifling, coopting, or exploiting the important work being done around the world. A former staff member at the Center for the Study of Violence and Reconciliation in South Africa, for example, suggested that "because of where CSVR comes from, we're not a transitional justice organization. We are a peace-building, violence-prevention organization." She went on to say that the "danger of the transitional justice discourse is that, unfortunately, those who have the most weight and the loudest voices have certainly been the western NGO's, the United Nations, the larger inter-governmental or international NGO's, et cetera" (interview with CSVR staffer 2009).

Other actors described similar concerns, not necessarily about the ICTJ, but about how ubiquitous transitional justice became within the advocacy community. Observers came to see transitional justice as an idea that activists and professionals could draw upon in order to make their proposed interventions compatible with actors who prioritized prosecutions and those who promoted other strategies (see Lefranc 2008). As more organizations, and programs within organizations, began to label their work as transitional justice, actors who identified with ideas such as facing the past, peacebuilding, and even human rights found themselves having to explain their work in relation to transitional justice. As they appropriated the idea to describe both legalistic and nonlegalistic goals and strategies, understandings of the idea continued to evolve.

WRESTLING WITH AMNESTY

The idea's malleability and increasing ubiquity meant that actors with contradictory goals, particularly about the utility of prosecutions, found themselves needing to square their differences. The ICTJ, with its goals of promoting interventions to redress mass violence, had entered an organizational field that was dominated by advocates who were committed to making sure perpetrators did not forgo punishment

(Engle, Miller, and Davis 2016). Hayner explained to me that much of her early work was mollifying concerns that the organization's purpose was to undermine ongoing efforts to promote prosecution. Aryeh Neier, co-founder of HRW, was particularly concerned about the ICTJ and any approach to redressing mass violence that did not prioritize punishment for perpetrators. In his book, *The Human Rights Movement*, Neier mentions how the creation of the ICTJ raised alarm bells for him because he worried that the organization was promoting a model of justice that did not prioritize international criminal law, which he saw as a major success of the human rights movement. Hayner and another ICTJ leader mentioned an "infamous" meeting between HRW and the ICTJ's leadership to talk about the ICTJ's work. One of the participants mentioned that the conversation was so heated, meaning that the HRW staff was so critical of the ICTJ staff, that the ICTJ contingent could have walked out of the meeting.

The ICTJ's challenges from HRW had to do with more than individual beliefs about criminal prosecutions. The organization's remarkable start-up funds and its leaders' seemingly flexible approach to amnesty raised concerns from fellow organizations working on similar issues and taking money from the same funding sources. Recall that Ford had also provided the seed money to start HRW. However, the malleability of transitional justice meant that actors who promoted prosecutions could also draw on the idea. According to a senior researcher at HRW, the differences between the ideas of human rights and transitional justice relate mostly to the vocabulary that actors use articulate their goals and strategies, rather than the goals themselves. She suggested that HRW "uses the language of impunity, there's a problem of impunity and weak rule of law." Seeing how transitional justice was being promoted and appropriated around the world, she continued: "That's the way that we say it. I think that translates, in NGO speak, as we need transitional justice" (interview with HRW staffer 2009).

This researcher saw few differences between human rights and transitional justice, viewing the distinction as one of framing more than substantively different perspectives. For her, transitional justice was not an idea that undermined prosecutions, it just depended on how actors utilized it. By 2010, Amnesty International, also a well-known proponent of prosecutions for human rights violations, decided that it needed to directly address the circulation of transitional justice and, in particular, the growing number of truth commissions in countries where international crimes had taken place. The organization published a report on truth commissions in 2010 that concluded, "more than half of the thirty-eight truth commissions with relevant practice examined in this paper recommended and/or actively contributed to the prosecution of all crimes under international law."[29] As an Amnesty staffer explained in our interview, the organization saw transitional justice as "a question of label" but they there "is a policy or a deeper reason" for maintaining the label of

[29] Amnesty International, *Commissioning Justice: Truth Commissions and Criminal Justice*, Index: POL 30/004/2010, Apr. 26, 2010, p. 5, www.amnesty.org/en/library/info/POL30/004/2010/en.

international justice: "[W]e have seen that in some countries that the term transitional justice is used to basically justify a lower level of justice" (interview with Amnesty International researcher 2010).

From this Amnesty International researcher's perspective, like that of HRW, there was not necessarily a substantive difference between transitional justice and their preferred label of international justice. Moreover, they also believed they could promote truth commissions as part of a broader strategy to ensure prosecutions for perpetrators of human rights abuses. Given its malleability, human rights proponents could draw on transitional justice to reaffirm their commitment to international criminal law.

Given these broad understandings of transitional justice, transnational transitional justice advocacy came to include both actors who prioritize prosecutions for mass violence and those who do not. This reaffirmation of prosecutions within the transitional justice movement is evident in the ICTJ's changes over time. When its founding leaders left at the end of the 2000s, the ICTJ's interim president was Juan Mendez, a well-respected jurist from Argentina who, as noted, founded HRW's Americas program. The Center's next president, David Tolbert, had worked in the prosecutor's office at the International Criminal Tribunal for the Former Yugoslavia. His appointment as president was a signal to the advocacy community that the organization was committed to international criminal law and would promote judicial accountability in the countries where it worked.

Under Tolbert's leadership, the organization streamlined its definition of transitional justice. In 2008, the organization's definition included prosecutions, truth-seeking, institutional reform, gender justice, reparations, peace and justice, and memorials. By 2011, the organization defined criminal prosecutions as one of its four primary "approaches," the others being truth-seeking, reparations, and institutional reform. In 2015, the organization's overall "vision" of transitional justice included its first strategy for societies to "regain humanity in the wake of mass atrocity," which was for "impunity to be rejected."[30] This statement highlights how the ICTJ worked to rebrand itself from the days in which it was simply considered a truth commission consulting firm and the emphasis it decided to put on promoting prosecutions to redress mass violence. Though just one organization, the ICTJ reflects broader changes in the transitional justice movement toward an emphasis on prosecutions as an important, if not necessary strategy to redress mass violence (Subotić 2012).

ACADEMICS IN THE MOVEMENT

While the earlier discussion focuses on the ICTJ's role in promoting a malleable understanding of transitional justice, the transitional justice movement was professionalized through the work of many who may not see themselves as part of

[30] International Center for Transitional Justice, *Strategic Plan 2015-2018*, www.ictj.org/sites/default/files/ICTJ-Strategic-Plan-2015-EN.PDF.

a movement, particularly academics who continue to draw on the idea in their scholarly work. The overlapping professional communities within the movement reflect how malleable understandings of transitional justice make it useful to social scientists, to legal scholars, and to what Vinjamuri and Snyder (2004) refer to as advocate-scholars. In writing about expanding understandings of transitional justice, Bell (2009a, p. 9) describes how, whereas discussions of transitional justice were once confined to legal scholarship, "today, transitional justice scholarship is an ever-increasing set of inquiries that take place across a range of disciplines, including anthropology, cultural studies, development studies, economics, education, ethics, history, philosophy, political science, psychology, sociology and theology."

What makes these disciplinary approaches to transitional justice notable is how much of the scholarship on transitional justice has retained its normative edge. In part, the normativity reflects the distinct blend of scholarship and advocacy that characterizes the movement. One obvious example of this blend can be found in the ICTJ's research unit. Soon after its founding, the ICTJ developed an academic research program and offered three-month sabbaticals to staff so that they could catch up on related literature. By helping to define its understanding of transitional justice, the research program was fundamental to the organization's mission as a center dedicated to the promotion of transitional justice. The organization's staff did not see themselves as either a think tank or an advocacy organization but, rather, as an organization that blended different approaches to scholarship and advocacy in order to develop practical strategies for actors interested in transitional justice interventions. At the same time, the organization played an important role in shaping academic understandings of transitional justice. For example, working as ICTJ's deputy research director, Paige Arthur wrote a widely cited intellectual history of transitional justice for *Human Rights Quarterly*, and the research director, Pablo de Greiff, published academic articles on the meaning of transitional justice (see De Greiff 2012).

De Greiff, who now works as a Special Rapporteur for the United Nations, first worked as a professor of philosophy at SUNY Buffalo before moving to the ICTJ. In 2010, he explained the appeal of moving from a university setting to the ICTJ from his desire to do "empirically informed normative theory." He noted that he never considered the ICTJ "akin to a research think tank" but, rather, to be an "action oriented institution." This meant that the research on transitional justice was "normatively guided and very, very normatively reached – it was supposed to be useful both the institution and the field as a whole" (interview with Pablo de Greiff 2010).

De Greiff's explanation of the ICTJ's research as "normatively guided" is not the same as advocacy in the way that organizations such as HRW and Amnesty International engage in campaigns to lead to specific policy changes or actions. Rather, organizations engaged in so-called action-oriented research have both short-term goals for specific interventions and longer-term strategies for changing beliefs and practices through their research. At the same time, the ICTJ's research agenda, from focusing on specific interventions in different countries to developing thematic reports on children, women, and development, helped the organization explain and legitimate its position that governments need to create legal interventions to redress mass violence.

The ICTJ was not the only organization that worked in different professional communities. The Centre for Violence and Reconciliation in South Africa also engaged in what it called "action research" related to transitional justice issues, both in the country and in the region. While this organization primarily engaged in research, it also hosted a prominent victims' association that continued to press the government to fulfill the promises of the South Africa TRC, particularly for reparations. CSVR, along with the Centre for Good Governance in Sierra Leone, the Centre for Good Government in Ghana, and the Refugee Law Project in Uganda, managed the Africa Transitional Justice Research Network (ATJRN) to better connect scholars and practitioners around the world. Though the network's name might suggest that it is a scholarly network, its original goal was explicitly advocacy-oriented: to ensure that "the transitional justice agenda in Africa is locally informed and owned."[31] In addition to managing a listserv for members, the network has also hosted seminars, workshops, and conferences and even sponsored books on how to study transitional justice, as well as to improve the efficacy of transitional justice interventions (see Okello 2012).

In addition, the director of CSVR's transitional justice program, Hugo Van der Merwe, was the founding co-editor of the *International Journal of Transitional Justice* (*IJTJ*), the flagship journal on transitional justice. When the *IJTJ* was getting off the ground in the mid 2000s, the first co-editors (the other was Harvey Weinstein from the Human Rights Center at the University of California, Berkeley) did not want to create another global-North-centric academic journal. They included a "notes from the field" section and actively encouraged scholars as well as practitioners from the global South to submit articles. By 2010, the *IJTJ* became the premier journal for scholars interested in transitional justice, achieving an impact factor of 1.756 (eight out of seventy-eight) for journals in the study of international relations.

The wide range of articles show how scholars helped construct malleable understandings of transitional justice. The journal has published studies on historical legacies of violence against indigenous populations, such as in Australia (Balint et al. 2014) and Canada (Nagy 2013), on countries enmeshed in violence, such as Afghanistan (Nadery 2007; Sajjad 2013), and on countries where violence was episodic, such as Kenya (Musila 2009). It has had special issues on civil society and transitional justice, international criminal law and transitional justice, victims and transitional justice, transitional justice and gender, and transitional justice and

[31] See Africa Transitional Justice Research Network, www.transitionaljustice.org.za/ (accessed Feb. 15, 2012).

development. In other publications, scholars writing about topics ranging from security to peacebuilding to "traditional practices" utilize the phrase *transitional justice* to describe their studies (e.g., Horne 2014; Shaw et al. 2010; Hinton 2010). Scholarship that draws on the idea continues to grow in new directions, expanding understandings and usages of transitional justice along with it.

Similarly, by institutionalizing the idea within universities, academics helped construct an understanding of transitional justice as a part of academic inquiry in addition to a form of advocacy. Tim Phillips, who founded the Project for Justice in Times of Transition soon after the 1992 Salzburg Conference, decided to move the project to Harvard Law School in 1999 in order to take advantage of the research, teaching, and publishing opportunities at Harvard University.[32] Similarly, in 2005, several legal scholars who were active in the peace process in Northern Ireland created the Transitional Justice Institute at the University of Ulster. According to the founding director, they named the new institute as such "to explain their diverse strategies to secure the peace deal and consolidate democratic reforms for the future" (interview with Christine Bell 2010). The program offers master's degrees, PhD degrees, and postdocs, furthering understandings of transitional justice as an academic enterprise. In contrast to the intervention-focused definitions offered by the ICTJ and the UN, this Institute describes transitional justice as a field focused on "the study of law in societies emerging from conflict and repression" and states that its goal is to inform policy makers as well as building a theoretical understanding of the relationship between "justice and peace."[33]

Much like organizations such as the ICTJ, these academic institutes have played an important role in expanding understandings of the idea in terms of its goals as well as where it might be useful. They receive financial support from their universities as well as from foundations, such as Ford, that are interested in supporting scholarship that can further innovative strategies to promote democratic social and political change. For example, the time the Foundation provided the seed funds for the ICTJ, Ford also helped finance a sociologist at Florida International University to develop a research consortium on transitional justice in Cuba. In 2003, her "task force" published a report on Cuban National Reconciliation. Obviously, there was no transition in Cuba at the time, but the sociologist saw the utility of the idea to inform policy decisions on countries that were not in transition.

Years later, scholars regularly drew on the idea of transitional justice to describe tribunals, truth commissions, and other interventions in politically stable regimes. For example, in 2009, Canadian scholars at the Liu Institute for Global Studies at the University of British Columbia created their own Transitional Justice Network.

[32] John F. Kennedy School of Government, Policy Research Centers and Programs, www.hks.harvard.edu/research/publications/01pdfs_rschrpt/pjtt.pdf.

[33] Transitional Justice Institute, About Us, www.ulster.ac.uk/research-and-innovation/research-institutes/transitional-justice-institute/about.

The Network was a response to Canada's Truth and Reconciliation Commission on human rights violations against the country's indigenous population. The Commission focused on Canada's residential school policies, which separated indigenous children from their parents and have been called cultural genocide, and offered a new model of creating a South Africa-style truth commission in a stable democracy. One of the network's founders suggested that the Canadian experience reflects the ways in which the idea of transitional justice "outgrew" its original meaning as an idea only for countries undergoing regime change (interview with human rights advocate 2009).

This blend of professional communities kept the idea circulating, but it also contributed to a complex shared identity within the movement. Given how academics have shaped understandings of transitional justice, several interviewees were quick to identify as "practitioners" in our interviews. Practitioners differentiated their professional identities by saying that they "create" or "work on" tools rather than studying them. For some of these self-identified practitioners, this division was important because they saw a disconnection between theoretical understandings of transitional justice and the practicalities of implementing interventions on the ground. This disconnect will become clearer in the following chapters, but actors working transnationally also expressed reservations about how theoretical transitional justice proponents were. For example, Patrick Ball, a demographer who worked in academia for several years and now helps design the databases that truth commissions use to manage and analyze their data, was highly critical of scholars for being more "interested in tenure" than addressing violence (interview with Patrick Ball 2010). He referred to the various transitional justice conferences and presenters as the "blah, blah," suggesting that those who study transitional justice provide little useful information to those actually engaged in practical work.

At the same time, most interviewees who identified as scholars articulated goals similar to those of advocates with regard to the impact of their studies. Like the ATRJN, these institutes offer seminars, workshops, conferences, and publications geared to other scholars, as well as policy makers and advocates, who hope to improve the efficacy of transitional justice interventions. Leigh Payne, a political scientist at Oxford who is well known within the academic community for studying the impact of transitional justice mechanisms, was quick to identify herself as a scholar. As an academic with expertise in transitional justice, she was often called up to present her work to diverse groups, including policy makers, and expressed enthusiasm about being able to have real world impacts. Similarly, Christine Bell, a co-founder of the Transitional Justice Institute (TJI) at the University of Ulster, was explicit about the ways in which the organization oriented its research to help in the Northern Ireland peace processes, and the dual roles that individuals affiliated with the TJI played in providing both academic and policy-relevant research. Clara-Lucia Sandoval Villalba articulated her role as an intermediary in providing insights from the academy to individuals working on the ground, noting how she sees her work with the University of Essex Transitional Justice Network as enabling "knowledge transfer" from this transnational network to local NGOs working to redress survivors of violence (interview with Clara-Lucia Sandoval Villalba 2010).

The blend of scholarship and advocacy is not unique to the transitional justice movement, but it is distinct in that these scholars do not see themselves as part of a movement. Within the human rights movement, for example, there are "porous" borders between activism and scholarship, particularly scholars interested in culture, law, and politics (Merry 2005, p. 245). Scholars who promote human rights are less resistant to seeing themselves as part of a well established movement. In part, this is because the effort to define human rights is largely over now that the idea has been institutionalized in international and domestic legal institutions, and few would say it should not be understood as a movement.

Scholarship on transitional justice, in contrast, continues to focus on self-definition and legitimation as an academic enterprise. To some extent, the ongoing efforts to define the meaning of transitional justice have to do with longevity, as the idea of human rights has circulated for decades and *transitional justice* is a newer phrase. However, a better explanation of this ongoing self-definition, as well as the movement's blend of scholarship and advocacy, has to do with the idea's malleability. In particular, the fact that actors use the idea to describe interventions and prescribe goals for countries wrestling with violence means that academics can draw on it without appearing to have normative goals, while advocates and scholars with a more normative focus can draw on it to legitimize their normative goals. Furthermore, the idea's malleability means that scholars have played a distinct role in developing theories that have been put into practice in so many countries. Scholars not only are experts who explain to policy makers and advocates what the idea means but also provide advice on what policies and advocacy campaigns should prioritize.

A CONTESTED IDENTITY

The above discussion highlights that, as the movement professionalized, understandings of transitional justice shifted to encompass a wide range of transitions and interventions. These understandings, in turn, affected the shared identity of the movement. Even as different actors appropriate and promote transitional justice, they express concerns about what the idea means and what the interventions actually offer.

The results from my ATJRN anonymous online survey provide additional insights into these dynamics, and further show how the idea's malleability is both an asset and a liability for the emergent movement. As noted, the ATJRN was created and managed by the CSVR, and it exemplifies the blend of scholarship and advocacy that defines the transitional justice movement. In 2005, staff at CSVR sent individual invitations out to scholars, advocates, and others they had come in contact with over their many years of work on the South African TRC. By 2009 – when I conducted the survey – the network had grown to over 1000 members who sent out daily messages about publications, conferences, and other information the moderators deem relevant to the virtual community. Survey respondents were more diverse than the interviewees in terms of their countries of origin and their professional backgrounds, though all had university degrees. They spent their childhoods in countries including Australia, Sierra Leone, Colombia, the United States, Nepal, and Saudi Arabia. While the majority identified as scholars (62%), nearly half also wrote that have worked directly on transitional justice interventions or with civil society organizations.

The survey asked individuals who had signed up for this listserv about their opinions on the goals and strategies of transitional justice. The majority of survey respondents expressed concern about the actors promoting transitional justice, how, and why they have done so. When asked how strongly they agree with the statement that "funding plays a decisive role in deciding which transitional justice mechanism/approach is adopted for a particular country," 83% said they "agree" or "strongly agree." In response to a question about the influence of various actors on transitional justice processes – survivors of direct violence, international policy makers, domestic policy makers, international human rights organizations, domestic human rights organizations, transitional justice scholars, and funders – several comments were highly critical of the question. The most extreme comment revealed concern that transitional justice interventions are yet another colonial imposition:

> Oh come on! You have to ask that? Look at all the many economic mechanisms through which rich countries control the destinies of the peoples of poor countries! It's not just bilateral governmental aid; it's also access to World Bank and IMF facilities; access to markets; access to FDI . . . the whole ball of colonial wax! So the government of whatever violence-shattered country we're talking about has to jump through all these (highly politicized) hoops to gain access to those things.

Another respondent expressed similar concerns, albeit with less intensity, about the (perceived) elite nature of the movement, and the professionals, such as the ICTJ, who benefit from the creation of transitional justice interventions:

> Again, [transitional justice] agreements are generally bargained by elites, and it is they who have access to the massive UN/USAID/DFID funding streams required to make these efforts go. Those elites (ICTJ is one example) then become the international consultants who make huge salaries in these endeavors and the victims are generally left with no compensation.

His concern about elites was common in the survey, and even more common in the case studies on BiH and Colombia. In response to the same question about which actor is most influential over the ways in which a transitional justice process is realized, 32% of the respondents identified international policy makers, while only 3% said that international policy makers should be most influential. Twenty-eight percent said that survivors of direct violence should be most influential over the realization of a transitional justice process, while no respondents believed that survivors are most influential.

Although participants in this study expressed a variety of opinions about who is most influential and who should be most influential, they tended to note that each process must be context-specific. Many survey respondents recognized that there are no simple answers to questions about the goals and strategies of transitional justice, another indicator of the idea's malleability. At the same time, the survey participants were also concerned that the transitional justice movement reinforced the human rights advocates' position that prosecutions were crucial to redress mass violence. Most survey respondents believe that policy makers prioritize prosecutions, though they do not believe this should be the case. When choosing the top three goals of policy makers engaged in a transitional justice effort, the majority (58%) of the respondents perceive "punishing perpetrators of human rights abuses" as one of the top goals, while approximately one-fourth (26%) said this *should* be among the top three priorities.[34] A close second was "identify victims, incidents/cases, and perpetrators," selected by 51.56% of the respondents; interestingly, almost the same percentage (47.62%) said it should be among the most prioritized. Moreover, while only 10% believe that socioeconomic development is among the top three priorities, 37% believe it should be. Table 2.1 shows these differences.

The results of the analysis reveal several interesting findings related to the idea's malleability. First, the respondents believe that policy makers prioritize individual accountability more than they should, evidenced by the statistically significant difference on the question about whether policy makers do prioritize or should prioritize punishment, and whether they do prioritize identifying perpetrators or should prioritize identifying perpetrators. This means that on both an individual and a group level, measured by the t and chi^2 statistics respectively, these respondents believe that policy makers prioritize individual accountability more than they should. For all other choices, there is no statistically significant difference at a group level.[35] Moreover, the findings reveal that individuals think policy makers prioritize socio-economic development far less than they should. These findings suggest that the respondents believe that transitional justice interventions should not be focused on individual accountability as much as they are, and that interventions should be

[34] To determine which goals to list, I relied on the findings from my pilot studies on how transnational actors understand the goals and strategies of transitional justice, as well as the general definition of transitional justice provided by the International Center for Transitional Justice in 2008, when this survey was developed: "Transitional justice refers to the set of judicial and non-judicial measures that have been implemented by different countries in order to redress the legacies of massive human rights abuses. These measures include criminal prosecutions, truth commissions, reparations programs, and various kinds of institutional reforms."

[35] The lack of significance on any variable means that one cannot predict respondents' answers to what policy makers should prioritize based on their answers to what policy makers do prioritize.

TABLE 2.1. *Priorities for the Transitional Justice Movement, as They Are and as They Should Be*

	Punishment		Identifying perpetrators		Identifying V, I/C, P		Public Education		Compensation		Development		Institutional reform	
	Is	Should	Is	Should	Is	Should	Is	Should	Is	Should	Is	Should	Is	Should
Mean	0.571	0.301	.301	.046	0.524	0.492	0.413	0.571	0.206	0.3334	0.127	0.381	0.444	0.476
Chi^2 stat	3.040		10.961		0.790		2.641		1.211		0.001		0.115	
$P(r)$	0.081		.001		0.374		0.104		0.271		0.97		0.735	
t stat	3.562		4.251		0.375		2.008		1.733		3.389		0.363	
$P(T \leq t)$ two-tailed	0.001		7.2E-5		0.709		0.049		0.088		0.001		0.718	

created with the goal of improving socio-economic conditions in countries that have experienced mass violence.

To gain further insight into this data, I generated a Pajek graph to get a visual representation of the data and descriptively examine the relationships between the responses. The thickness of the line between the two variables indicates the frequency with which individuals thought both of the linked goals should be prioritized:

> People have different opinions about what the goals of transitional justice are. In your opinion, where there has been a transitional justice effort, what goal(s) is/are usually prioritized by policy makers? (Choose up to three)

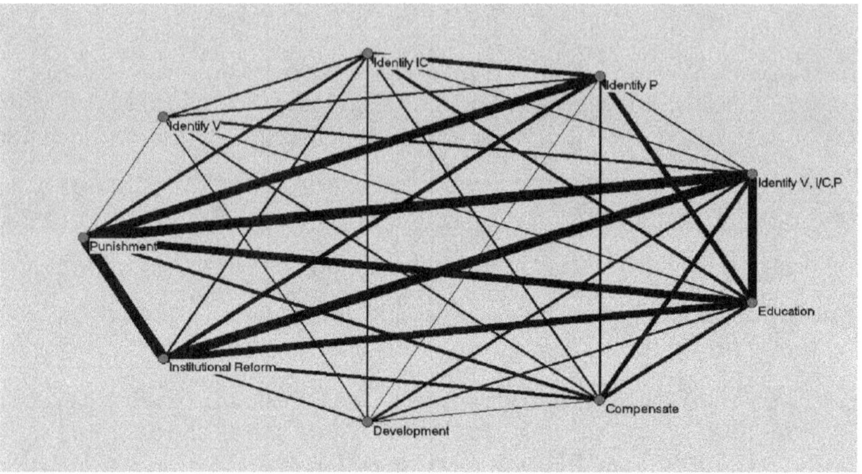

> People have different opinions about which goal(s) should be prioritized. In your opinion, which goal(s) of transitional justice should be prioritized by policy makers? (Choose up to three)

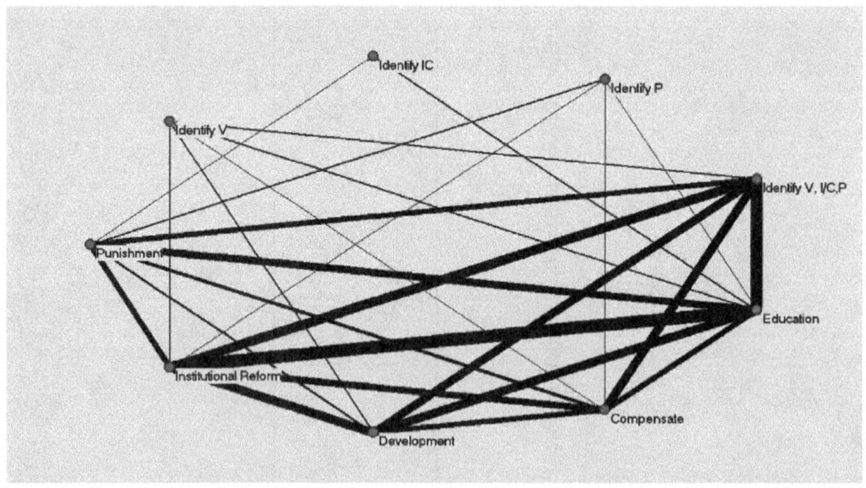

Looking at these two graphs, one sees little clustering in the first graph, meaning one cannot predict what respondents think about policy makers' top three priorities based on just one of their choices.[36] This latter graph, in contrast, shows a cluster on the choices that do not relate to individual accountability. This different clustering suggests that if a respondent believes that policy makers should prioritize identification of facts, public education, compensation, socio-economic development, or democratic institutional reform, he or she is also likely to believe that policy makers should prioritize another of these goals, which are distinct from goals of individual accountability. One inference from these findings is that these participants see transitional justice as an idea that should be geared toward broad goals of social and political change. Most importantly, the graphs reveal that the respondents see transitional justice as encompassing multiple goals.

This survey's findings shed additional light on the ongoing critiques of transitional justice as a "battlefield" of actors with contradictory beliefs and practices (Bell 2009b), as well as "entrepreneurs" who "produce victims" (Madlingozi 2010). The actors who participated in this survey reveal their varied understandings of what transitional justice means and what its associated interventions do. They critiqued what they saw as the emphasis on prosecutions, and the disconnection between those promoting interventions and their perceived beneficiaries. In short, the idea's malleability has led to different understandings about what the idea means and what is should mean.

CREATING A TRANSNATIONAL MOVEMENT

This chapter offers a number of findings about the emergence and professionalization of the transitional justice movement. First, it reveals that the idea circulated because of key individuals and organizations that appropriated and promoted it. Without these actors, transitional justice might have remained an academic term, like transitology, that did not outlive the specific time period in which it was coined. In particular, with the support of the Ford Foundation, the ICTJ helped popularize both the idea and, in particular, the truth commission as an intervention that can contribute to the idealistic goal of reconciliation. The ICTJ emerged as an elite in the transnational movement and fostered an idealistic discourse about what truth commissions can offer countries that are emerging from mass violence.

Next, by using the idea both descriptively and prescriptively, and applying it to a wide range of political contexts, this organization, along with the scholars and policy makers who also draw on the idea to explain and legitimize their work, have fostered a malleable understanding of the idea that is both an asset and a liability for those

[36] These graphs are limited in that they do not show the difference between the correlations in expectation and the actual correlations. For example, if 30% of all respondents choose variable A, one can expect that 30% of those who chose variable B would also have chosen variable A. The thickness of the lines could correlate to deviation from this expected value. Given the small number of respondents, the graphs show actual values to descriptively illustrate how these respondents understand the goals and strategies of transitional justice.

who appropriate and promote it. While scholars tend to critique these transitional justice proponents as standardizing the truth commission model, the story is more complicated. Although the ICTJ did popularize the South African model, they did so by promoting it as something that could be tailored to different contexts. While the following chapters reveal how this malleability means that actors translate the idea in different ways, particularly as they promote truth commissions, this chapter points to how this mix of standardization and malleability has fostered a complex shared identity within the movement. Actors, even those who promote the idea, have different opinions about what transitional justice means, does, or should do.

Ironically, even though I have argued that the professionalization of transitional justice has led to the coupling of transitional justice and truth commissions, this chapter also offers a new lens to understand the so-called "legalization of transitional justice," meaning the ways in which transnational transitional justice advocacy organizations promote prosecutions (Subotić 2012). Given the organizational field into which the ICTJ inserted itself, both the ICTJ and fellow organizations developed goals and strategies that blended their various perspectives on prosecutions. The malleability of transitional justice, and particularly its ambiguity with regards to prosecution, enabled these different actors to draw on it to explain and legitimize their goals with the idea whether they had complementary, competing, or contradictory understandings of it.

At the same time, given the idea's malleability, actors translate it in different ways in different places, particularly as they mobilize around truth commissions. The following chapters reveal that legal mobilization under the banner of a malleable idea can entrench social and political divisions, just as it can transform them.

3

Disruption

A Truth Commission in Bosnia and Herzegovina

Without [a truth commission], it's going to be in 50 or 40 years the same thing because every individual has his or her own story, his or her own pain, and then you need just one thing to bring all these things out in order to [re]produce the cruelty that actually happened.

(Interview with Bosnian civil society leader 2010)

In September of 2009, I arrived in Sarajevo, the capital of Bosnia and Herzegovina (BiH), to examine new initiatives being promoted under the banner of transitional justice. In cities and towns throughout the country, buildings remained in ruins, and survivors greeted visitors with the soft gaze of trauma. Decades after the war ended in 1995, the provisional government still struggles to bridge divides between the Serbs, Bosniaks (a postwar label for Bosnian Muslim), and Croats, the three main national groups in BiH.[37] Though scholars, policy makers, and advocates draw on transitional justice to explain various interventions in the Balkans, the words "transition" and "justice" seemed misplaced. With a stagnant economy and threats that Bosnia and Herzegovina might split into two entities, skeptical observers of Bosnian politics have long considered the "transition" to be war by political means (see Luttwak 1999; Chandler 2000). International and domestic tribunals have prosecuted hundreds among the hundreds of thousands of perpetrators, yet it is difficult to feel any sense of justice for the violence that occurred in the breakup of the former Yugoslavia.[38]

This chapter argues that actors promoting truth commissions, both domestically and transnationally, saw this intervention as so malleable that they proposed an ambitious model of a commission that would include all the countries, and one disputed territory, of the former Yugoslavia. It further shows how this effort, as well as others aimed at translating transitional justice into political action in the country,

37 These national groups are not to be confused with the citizens of Croatia and Serbia, the two countries where there is a majority population of Croats and Serbs respectively.

38 Portions of this chapter appear in my 2012 article in *Law and Social Inquiry*.

actually reproduced social and political divisions rather than ameliorating them. In this way, it shows how the malleability of both the idea and the intervention are an asset and a liability for those who choose to mobilize around them.

To make this argument, the chapter begins with an overview of the war and the peace accords. This section follows with information about efforts to use courts and create truth commissions to redress the violence. It then moves on to describe the Coalition for RECOM, the acronym for the proposed commission,[39] which tried to create a treaty-based commission for the six countries (Slovenia, Croatia, Macedonia, Bosnia and Herzegovina, Serbia, and Montenegro) and one disputed territory (Kosovo) of the former Yugoslavia. The chapter focuses on the rise of the Coalition as leaders received ample support, financial and otherwise, to promote a truth commission. It goes on to explain how, in promoting their initiative, the Coalition benefitted from letting individuals express their hopes and desires for a truth commission and focusing on how a future commission would enable them to tell their stories in a public forum. Proponents of a regional truth commission promoted it as something that would be able to ensure goals ranging from prosecutions to joining the European Union (EU).

The discussion of how the Coalition emerged provides insight into how, given the malleable understandings of a truth commission, it can be easy to get initial, shallow support for one. However, during my observations of this effort between 2009 and 2011, the Coalition's leadership in BiH unraveled and the effort faltered, leading one nationalist BiH newspaper to assert, "RECOM has inflicted enormous damage to reconciliation in the region."[40] In explaining how and why this initiative faltered, this chapter illustrates how the instrumentalization of transitional justice in BiH was disruptive – innovative and groundbreaking, but also unmanageable. The disruptive character of this instrumentalization in BiH reveals the dilemma of promoting a malleable intervention that may initially appeal to actors with complementary, competing, and even contradictory goals.

In addition to examining RECOM, the chapter also looks at how several other organizations attempted to translate transitional justice into political action. In so doing, the analysis further shows that the appeal of transitional justice lies in its malleability, both its aspirational qualities and its ambiguity with regards to the value of prosecutions. These initiatives helped spread the idea of transitional justice into BiH and, while doing so, helped create new sets of elites, an idealistic discourse, and a reaffirmation of prosecutions as an important, if not necessary strategy to redress mass violence. At the same time, a researcher from the United

[39] The acronym changed throughout the mobilization process as the leaders started to clarify what the commission would investigate. As of 2016, the acronym stood for "Regional commission for the establishment of facts about war crimes and other serious violations of human rights committed in the former Yugoslavia from January 1, 1991 until December 31, 2001."

[40] RECOM Has Inflicted Enormous Damage to Reconciliation in the Region (REKOM je nanio ogromneštete pomirenju u regionu), Dnevni Avaz, June 29, 2011.

States Institute of Peace summed up a common assessment in his observation that BiH "is a failed case of transitional justice" (interview with USIP researcher 2010).

THE LEGACY OF WAR

The ongoing divisions in BiH reflect a longer history of conflict in the region, extending beyond the rise and fall of the Ottoman Empire and the two world wars. Many Serbs reference the 1389 Battle of Kosovo as the start of the conflict, as this is the date when the Serbian army fell to the Ottoman Turks. With the fall of the Ottoman and Hapsburg Empires after WWI, Yugoslavia was unified as the Kingdom of Serbs, Croats, and Slovenes, and later as the Kingdom of Yugoslavia. During WWII, the Croatian Uštase aligned with the Axis powers and targeted Serbs as well as Jews. After the war, Marshall Tito established the Socialist Federal Republic of Yugoslavia, made up of the republics of Macedonia, Montenegro, Slovenia, Bosnia, Croatia, and Serbia. Until 1991, Yugoslavia was a socialist country that tried to suppress nationalist differences in order to promote unity. Tito, a Croat, put the capital of the country in Belgrade, Serbia, as a sign of equality. Laws prohibited discussion of the WWII violence, intermarriage was common, the middle class thrived, and the country's debt grew.

After Tito died in 1980, economic and political pressure mounted as the country struggled to recover from the oil crises of 1973 and 1979. As the federation weakened, nationalism reemerged and the republics sought independence. Slobodan Milošević rose to power in Serbia, and the rhetoric turned to violence. On June 25, 1991, both Slovenia and Croatia declared independence from Yugoslavia. These two territories were more economically prosperous and ethnically homogenous than BiH, and it took only ten days for Slovenia to win its brief war of independence. Croatia became an independent state in August 1991. In just one example of the war's complexity, Serbs in the Krajina region of Croatia declared independence. Even after the Vance Plan of 1992 set a ceasefire in place for the Krajina it was not until 1995 that Croatian forces took back the territory.

The war in Croatia was mild compared with the war in Bosnia, where the Serb population similarly feared being a minority in an independent country. Prior to the war, Bosnia was a multiethnic polity, 43.7% Muslim, 31.4% Serb, 17.3 % Croat, and the remaining 7.6% predominantly Jews and Roma. Bosnia's declaration of independence came in 1992, soon after Croatia and Slovenia's declarations. Bosnian Serbs boycotted the February 29 and March 1 referendum, meaning that although the referendum passed with 99.7% in favor, only 63.4% of Bosnians participated in it. Bosniak leaders believed the United States and European powers would recognize their right to independence, which they did on April 7, 1992. Bosniak leaders also assumed they would receive military support if their independence was contested, which did not come for many years.

On April 7, 1992, Bosnian Serb leaders, under the direction of Radovan Karadžić, declared the independence of the Republika Srpska, an area in the north and east of the country. The Bosnian Serb army fought a vicious war to create a Serb nation-state. Towns and villages were divided and destroyed through campaigns now known as ethnic cleansing. While there was fighting between Bosnian Muslims and Croats, much of the violence occurred between the Muslims and Serbs. An arms embargo left the beleaguered Bosnian Muslim army without the ability to defend themselves against the Bosnian Serb army, which received support from the Yugoslav National Army in Belgrade. The Bosnian Serb army mounted a three-year siege on the capital city of Sarajevo. As world powers sat on the sidelines, hundreds of thousands of individuals suffered human rights abuses including displacement, rape, and torture. Images circulated around the world of men being starved in concentration camps, harkening back to memories of WWII. On July 11, 2005, the Bosnian Serb army, led by Ratko Mladić, slaughtered thousands of Bosniak men and boys in Srebrenica, the largest massacre in Europe since WWII and now legally classified as genocide.[41]

After Srebrenica, the world powers intervened to stop the bloodshed. Led by United States negotiator Richard Holbrooke, the peace negotiations brought together Slobodan Milošević, who participated on behalf of Karadžić, Tudjman of Croatia, and Izetbegović from Bosnia. The three agreed to stop the violence and divide the country. The Dayton Peace Accords were signed in Paris in December 1995, and the new country of Bosnia and Herzegovina emerged.

JUSTICE IN TRANSITION

The Dayton Peace Accords ended the war, but created a political quagmire. The Accords served as the country's constitution and divided the country into the Federation, which is largely Bosniak and Croat, and the Republika Srpska (RS), which is largely Serb. Thus, an entity that never existed before the war, the RS, now had formal political status and its own leadership. Forty-nine out of 109 former municipalities were divided along the Inter-Entity Boundary Line. BiH's capital remained in Sarajevo, a city divided between the Federation and the RS. Dayton enabled the two entities to function independently but also required them to work together.

Dayton also legalized nationalist divisions that continue to affect BiH society. The country's presidency consists of a Croat, a Bosniak, and a Serb, with a rotating eight-month chairmanship between them. In *Sejdić and Finci vs. Bosnia and Herzegovina*, the European Court of Human Rights found that the Constitution violated the European Convention of Human Rights by denying the ability of Jews and Roma to participate in elections. The Accords have thus impeded the country's ability to join the European Union, which many see as the only chance for it to move forward economically. In another example of political dysfunction, given the need to form

[41] ICTY, Krstić Decision, IT-98-33-T, judgment rendered on August 21, 2001.

a majority parliamentary coalition, the Federation was without a government for nearly a year after the 2010 elections. With eight independent cantons within the Federation, and an independent district of Brčko that is not part of the RS or the Federation, there is little unity in the country, let alone functionality (see Moore 2013).

Beyond the structural problems created by Dayton, the issue of war crimes continues to stymie this ongoing transition. Annex 10 of the Dayton Accords created the Office of the High Representative (OHR), which was supposed to be a transitional governing body that would oversee civilian affairs. In 2008, the OHR made a closure plan known as the 5+2 plan, named for the five objectives and two conditions that would need to be fulfilled for the OHR to close and the BiH government to be independent. The last of these objectives is "Entrenchment of the Rule of Law," which would be demonstrated through adoption of a National War Crimes Strategy, passage of a Law on Aliens and Asylum, and adoption of a National Justice Sector Reform Strategy.[42] The National War Crimes Strategy included quotas for cases and a provision that required the courts to process the most complex cases within seven years and all cases within fifteen years. However, the backlog of cases continues to grow. Between 2008 and 2015, only 30% of the cases were resolved, and prosecutors have faced disciplinary procedures for pursuing easier cases or splitting up cases in order to meet quotas.[43]

In describing the closure plan in 2016, the OHR's website stated that "chronic disagreement among the main political parties has produced gridlock that has prevented the full implementation of the agenda."[44] The gridlock in the political system feeds nationalist divisions, and these divisions feed the gridlock. The education system in BiH fosters segregation, meaning the young are more divided than previous generations. Known as "two schools under one roof," the system was initially implemented in 2000 under the Organization for Security and Cooperation in Europe. The policy was part of their effort to encourage refugees to return to their homes. Since then, there have been different curricula, one for each national group, in the same schools. This education system has led to an entire generation of segregated youth who receive different history lessons about the recent war. This phenomenon has widespread effects in BiH society. Each national group has created its own version of the conflict's causes, and each portrays itself as victims in a defensive war.

This nationalist politics permeate social life in other ways. Efforts to bridge national divides, even for seemingly innocuous events, become politicized along

42 The other objectives are as follows: (1) Acceptable and Sustainable Resolution of the Issue of Apportionment of Property between State and Other Levels of Government; (2) Acceptable and Sustainable Resolution of Defence Property; (3) Completion of the Brcko Final Award; (4) Fiscal Sustainability (promoted through an Agreement on a Permanent ITA Co-efficient Methodology and establishment of a National Fiscal Council).

43 Marija Tausan, "Huge War Crimes Case Backlog Overwhelms Bosnia," BIRN BiH, Oct. 23, 2015, http://www.justice-report.com/en/articles/huge-war-crimes-case-backlog-overwhelms-bosnia.

44 Office of the High Representative, "Agenda 5+2," www.ohr.int/?page_id=1318.

those national divides. For example, in June 2014, tensions flared over commemorations for WWI, which began after the assassination of Archduke Franz Ferdinand in Sarajevo. RS politicians would not support public events, worried that Serbs would be cast as terrorists, given that a Serb was responsible for the assassination. Even an academic conference, which was supposed to focus exclusively on the history of WWI, became a site of contention when the French funding organization wanted to make the event another excuse to focus on reconciliation in the region. Serb academics boycotted the event, and the French organization withdrew its support.

Civil society also suffers under the nationalist pressures, which creates challenges for initiatives designed to bring the different groups together. Except for those few NGOs that have found ways to access foreign funds, the government decides which groups get the money. That means that many civil society organizations in BiH are not independent of the government. The organizations have faced criticism and have been investigated by the government for taking money and not spending it as they said they would.[45] Certain organizations, primarily those supporting combatants in the war, benefit most from the government's allocation.

Perhaps more problematic, BiH remains economically stagnant, which contributes to the general feeling of apathy and resentment about the war's legacy. While the touristic core of Sarajevo has boomed in recent years, public services are unreliable, and public servants' salaries often go unpaid. In 2010, the GDP per capita was $6600 – the lowest in the former Yugoslavia – and the unemployment rate was 43.1%. There was a brief respite from the apathy in 2014, when protests erupted over high unemployment and widespread corruption, but the activism was short-lived. Many youth see their futures as being outside of BiH and are trying to leave. In the 2000s, every country in the former Yugoslavia was seeking EU membership – and the resulting economic opportunities – which is also a reason that the government continues to tackle the issue of war crimes. The EU made clear that the countries of the former Yugoslavia must support the prosecution of international crimes in order to join (see Subotić 2009; Peskin 2008).

The instrumentalization of transitional justice in BiH reflects this difficult social, political, and economic situation. Adopting interventions aimed at ensuring accountability, improving survivor well-being, and preventing future violence is a monumental task.

TRANSITIONAL JUSTICE: GOING BEYOND THE COURTS

Scholars have been writing about BiH as a case of transitional justice for decades, mainly on account of the International Criminal Tribunal for the former Yugoslavia (ICTY). However, few scholars, policy makers, or advocates in the Balkans actually

45 Arnautovic, Maria, "Bosnia's War Victims Let Down by NGOs," *Institute for War and Peace Reporting*, Dec. 28, 2011, iwpr.net/global-voices/bosnias-war-victims-let-down-ngos.

use the phrase "transitional justice" to describe their work. Those who do promote transitional justice in the Balkans explain it as a way to think of complements, not replacements, to the ICTY. This judicial body has profoundly shaped understandings of justice for the war's violence, particularly in BiH (Nettelfield 2010). A 2010 United Nations Development Program (UNDP) survey on transitional justice in BiH exemplifies this understanding: "Transitional justice has its historical roots in the idea that the judiciary alone is incapable of coping with numerous and complex problems arising from massive and systematic violations of the fundamental human rights in totalitarian and authoritarian regimes or during armed conflicts. Judicial reactions, i.e. 'judicial justice' should be accompanied by appropriate non-judicial responses."[46] This definition affirms the importance of prosecutions, but articulates the need for "accompanying interventions."

The ICTY was the first international criminal tribunal since Nuremberg. It was created when, in an unprecedented action, the United Nations drew on its Chapter VII powers (which allow the UN to impinge on state sovereignty in order to maintain peace and security) in order to create an ad hoc criminal tribunal for an ongoing armed conflict. The tribunal was formed in 1993, in the midst of the war, and prosecutors went to work identifying high-level military leaders who could be held accountable for crimes against humanity, war crimes,[47] and genocide. The ICTY's questionable legal origins were challenged in early cases, but the tribunal quickly asserted itself as legitimate and competent to hear a range of cases not only from the wars in the early 1990s, but also from the war between Serbia and Kosovo at the end of the 1990s.[48]

Scholars of international criminal law often laud the ICTY for contributing the international jurisprudence on genocide, rape, joint criminal enterprise, and command responsibility.[49] After many years, the court was able to apprehend all

[46] Zoran Pajič and Dragan Popović, "Dealing with the Past and Access to Justice from the Public Perspective," Presentation from UNDP Conference on Transitional Justice, March 31, 2010 (on file with author). See also United Nations Development Program, "Access to Justice: Facing the Past and Building the Confidence for the Future," www.undp.ba/index.aspx?PID=21&RID=95 (accessed Dec. 17, 2011).

[47] There were actually two different crimes for war crimes, one being grave breaches of the Geneva Conventions of 1949, which can only be tried in the event of an international armed conflict, and the other being violations of the rules or customs of war, which can be tried regardless of whether the conflict is international or not. The ICTY did not want to address the question of whether this was an international armed conflict, as this requires stating whether Bosnia was actually an independent country or was still part of the former Yugoslavia. As a result, the prosecutors preferred charging individuals with violations of the rules or customs of war unless the acts were prohibited in all armed conflicts.

[48] Kosovo did not declare independence until 2008, and Serbia still does not recognize its independence. The war in 1998–1999 was between the Kosovo Liberation Army and Federal Republic of Yugoslavia forces in response to ongoing clashes between the Serb minority and the Albanian majority living within Kosovo.

[49] In particular, the court recast sexual violence during war, which was previously viewed as collateral damage during war, but is now understood as a crime that is now being successfully tried at the International Criminal Court. These latter two doctrines were developed after World War II and are

outstanding fugitives from its list of high-level perpetrators. By 2017, eighty-three individuals had been convicted and sentenced, while nineteen had been acquitted. The court has made information public to researchers and other interested parties around the world, and many articles and books have been written on the court's jurisprudence and how it implemented its ambitious mandate.

However, in the Balkans, disappointments with the ICTY abound. Its price tag of over $2 billion, approximately $14 million per individual trial, dwarfs BiH's GDP per capita, and the tribunal has done little to dispel divisive beliefs about the causes and consequences of the violence. Studies continue to show that Bosniaks, Serbs, and Croats express different opinions about whether the tribunal is fair and/or helpful to the region (Delpla 2007; Ivković and Hagan 2006; Nettelfield 2010). In spring 2013, after the notable acquittals of two famous Croatian generals responsible for reclaiming the Krajina, BiH civil society leaders drafted an open letter to the Secretary General of the United Nations. One hundred twelve individuals and organizations criticized the tribunals' acquittals and excoriated their leadership for allegations of tampering in decisions. The letter suggested that recent judgments were "eroding the credibility" of the ICTY.

In addition to the ICTY, the State Court of BiH established a War Crimes Chamber in 2005. This body has been trying cases of lower-level perpetrators for the past decade. The Chamber, like most of the BiH judiciary, is severely limited by its lack of resources. International and domestic NGOs, domestic media, and representatives from the ICTY criticized the tribunal for the time it has taken to process very few cases, as well as its lack of procedural safeguards for participants. Moreover, in 2013, the European Court of Human Rights overturned two of the Chamber's decisions, claiming that the defendants did not receive adequate due process given the gravity of the crimes and the fact that they were tried under the 2003 Criminal Code, which did not exist when the acts were committed. While courts may have shaped understandings of transitional justice, disappointments with these judicial bodies created the desire for new interventions.

EARLIER ATTEMPTS AT TRUTH COMMISSIONS

Since the war ended in 1995, domestic and transnational actors have tried to create a truth commission in the Balkans. These efforts reveal the multiple goals that actors have for truth commissions. Their different campaigns show how the malleability of the intervention make them appealing to actors interested in elucidating the

crucial in holding high-level leaders liable for violence that they did not directly commit. Generally speaking, joint criminal enterprise is similar to conspiracy, but casts an even wider net, at first holding perpetrators liable for crimes that were natural and foreseeable consequences of the criminal enterprise they joined. The doctrine of command responsibility enables individuals to be held accountable if one of their subordinates committed a crime and they knew or should have known of it (Danner and Martinez 2005).

numbers of individuals who were killed, and reveal broad aims related to accusing other groups of responsibility for the violence. For example, in 2004, the RS, under pressure from the Human Rights Chamber of the BiH government, created what many consider the only successful commission on the violence in Srebrenica, which clarified the number of boys and men killed in the 1995 attack. However, in March 2015, the president of the RS, Milorad Dodik, called for a new international commission to determine the "truth" about the violence.[50] Even counting those killed remains a divisive issue, particularly in Srebrenica, due to the ICTY's finding that the massacre was an act of genocide.

The Srebrenica Commission inspired Serb representatives to call for a truth commission to investigate what one leader referred to as the "genocide" of Serbs in Sarajevo at the start of the war, which could be "worse than that in Srebrenica" (Jouhanneau 2008, p. 170). In 2004, Serb representatives in the Sarajevo mayoralty proposed a commission to investigate the thousands of individuals who were killed in the siege, and in 2006, the BiH Council of Ministers approved the creation of a new commission designed "to determine the truth, establish a durable peace, and reinforce mutual trust in Bosnia." Their proposal asked for 3,300,000 KM, about $1,900,000 dollars, to fund seventy researchers over a two-year period. In addition to concerns about the cost (the Srebrenica commission, in contrast, cost 400,000 KM, or $231,000), some local leaders expressed concern that the commission was focusing on nationality rather than victimhood more generally. However, the original proponents of the commission wanted it to focus on nationality, particularly the suffering of Serbs, and were upset that the commissioners were trying to address the victimhood of all national groups.[51] Yet another critique centered on how much the commission proponents involved the family members of the disappeared, with some viewing it as an elite political institution that was dishonest and immoral (Jouhanneau 2008, p. 173).

Heavyweights in the transnational transitional justice movement also tried to promote a commission for BiH and faced similar dilemmas related to competing desires in relation to a truth commission. At the end of the 1990s, Neil Kritz from USIP worked with Jakob Finci, a well-respected Jewish civil society leader from BiH, to create a truth commission. That initiative ended when the ICTY prosecutor made clear that she would not support it. It was clear that a successful truth commission initiative could not challenge the ICTY's findings.

Finally, in 2005, eight leading political parties joined together to form a working group on creating a truth commission to "objectively examine the hostilities . . . in

[50] Denis Dzidic, Bosnian Serb Leader Urges Srebrenica Truth Commission, *Balkan Insight*, March 25, 2015 (accessed July 18, 2016).

[51] Mirna Buljugic, No Progress for Sarajevo Truth Commission, *Balkan Insight*, February 23, 2007, www.balkaninsight.com/en/article/birn-s-justice-report-no-progress-for-sarajevo-truth-commission (accessed July 18, 2016).

Bosnia and Herzegovina and the former Yugoslavia from 1990 to 1996."[52] The political leaders reached out to Kritz for consultation, and their objectives again reveal how malleable actors viewed a truth commission as being. They hoped to establish the number and identity of victims, including those killed, disappeared, raped, and tortured, the mass graves, and the demolition of religious and cultural monuments and private property. This commission was also to study what led to the ethnic distrust and misunderstanding, to establish the role and moral responsibility of individuals and organizations both in and outside of Bosnia, and to identify those who did not take part in the violence. As with other efforts to promote a truth commission, this ambitious effort slowly fizzled as deadline after deadline for next steps passed.

These initiatives reveal the ongoing desire to create a truth commission in BiH and the difficulty of actually creating one. In the 2010 UNDP survey, 70% of the Bosnian respondents agreed with the statement that "facts about the war have not yet been fully established." Only 60% of the population knew what a truth commission was, but among those who did, 90% responded that they wanted one in the country.[53] In theory, there was ample opportunity for yet another initiative to create a truth commission, particularly one that aimed at getting support from civil society as well as political elites. Creating one, however, was a far more complicated proposition.

A NEW INITIATIVE

The Coalition for RECOM had advantages that these previous initiatives for a truth commission did not. Its leaders were from different national groups as well as different countries, and were well connected with transnational elites, who provided funding and guidance every step of the way on how to conceptualize their goals and strategies. Their hope was that, by promoting an even more ambitious truth commission, one that would address all of the countries of the former Yugoslavia, and one that would include elites as well as the masses in developing the truth commission's design, they would be able to succeed where other efforts had failed.

An early staff member of the ICTJ, Mark Freeman, was working in the ICTJ's Brussels office when he began discussing the idea of a truth commission with Nataša Kandić, a prominent civil society leader from Serbia who had been working with other NGOs in the former Yugoslavia in order to better document the war's violence. As the director of the Humanitarian Law Center (HLC), Kandić was well known in BiH for assisting in the ICTY prosecutions against Bosnian Serbs. Those who know her often talk about her tenacity with a mix of admiration and fear.

At the time, the HLC was collaborating with Dokumenta, a Zagreb-based organization that tried to document Croatian abuses during the war. Its leader, Vesna

52 Nerma Jelacic and Nidzara Ahmetasevic, Truth Commission Divides Bosnia, *Balkan Insight*, March 31, 2006, www.balkaninsight.com/en/article/truth-commission-divides-bosnia (accessed July 18, 2016).

53 Pajič and Popović, supra note 9.

Terselić, is thoughtful and somewhat reserved and cautious with her words, a contrast to the outspoken Kandić. The two were also working with the Research and Documentation Center (RDC) in Sarajevo, which was well known for its efforts to calculate the number of people who died during the war. The RDC's leader was Mirsad Tokača, another prominent civil society leader whose efforts drew enmity from nationalist leaders who wanted to manipulate the numbers to reinforce their narratives of which national group was most victimized.

The Coalition's founding members reflected an impressive variety of experiences. However, as a prominent scholar from Croatia noted when discussing this Coalition, to lead one of these organizations one has to be "highly courageous and individualistic" and "asking these people to work together can be disastrous" (interview with Croatian scholar 2010). In addition, though the Coalition promoted itself as a local initiative that originated in a partnership between a Serbian, a Bosnian, and a Croatian organization, its leadership worked closely with the ICTJ and drew on the support of other transitional justice professionals. In a report on the Coalition's development from 2006 to 2011, for example, the authors noted that "ICTJ professionals gave their expert support to the entire process."[54]

In 2004, the three organizations signed an agreement to coordinate their efforts on documentation. While Freeman suggested to me that a truth commission was always the preferred strategy, another Coalition leader explained in our 2010 interview that a truth commission was not initially on their agenda:

> It was more mechanisms of truth finding or truth-telling. That could mean a lot of things. It could also mean writing newspaper articles about it . . . so no mention of the word "commission" at all . . . it was more like, "We think there's a need to do more in the area of truth-seeking and truth-telling. Let's discuss the possible mechanisms." (Interview with Coalition for RECOM leader 2010)

In Brussels, Freeman facilitated meetings with donors, who took an interest in a regional initiative. With his help, the organization received nearly 1,000,000 euros from the Dutch Embassy in Belgrade, more than 1,000,000 euros from the European Union, and more than 220,000 euros from a variety of donors, including USIP, in order to support their initiative.

To begin their campaign, the leaders held their first meeting with political elites, which they called a "regional forum," in May 2006 in Sarajevo. The forum was called "Determining Truth in Post Conflict Period: Initiatives and Perspectives in Western Balkans." At this first forum, participants from the ICTY, including then Chief Prosecutor Carla del Ponte, gave lectures on the need for a distinct mechanism that could address the ongoing needs of victims. In particular, Del Ponte emphasized

54 RECOM: The Consultation Process May 2006–February 2011 (July 19, 2011), p. 1, www.recom.link/the-consultation-process-on-the-establishment-of-the-facts-about-war-crimes-and-other-gross-violations-of-human-rights-committed-on-the-territory-of-the-former-yugoslavia/ (accessed July 14, 2016).

that while the ICTY had made significant contributions to understanding the crimes that occurred, the victims had not received sufficient opportunity to tell their stories. Her vision of a truth commission was clearly informed by the South Africa TRC, and she explained that such a commission would require genuine humility and forgiveness. Unclear whether those conditions existed, she supported the effort to help develop them. She acknowledged that the court had previously viewed a Truth and Reconciliation Commission as a problem for the ICTY, but she now viewed a truth commission as "logical."

What these various actors were proposing – a regional truth commission – was innovative and groundbreaking, and the Coalition worked to gain the support of as many people as it could. Most truth commissions, at least the formal ones (meaning those created by governments), are nationally based. Proponents of a regional truth commission believed that truth commissions that were locally or nationally based could entrench the divisive narratives, and could point to earlier attempts to create a truth commission in Serbia and the Sarajevo mayoralty as examples. In the first forum meeting, for example, Mark Freeman described the tensions in the region and the danger that a "nationally based truth" could set back reconciliation.

After this first regional forum, the Coalition labeled the subsequent meetings as Regional Forums on Transitional Justice. This label provided the group with a framing strategy that would last throughout the campaign. The forum's summary, which the Coalition for RECOM makes publicly available on its website, explains their approach to transitional justice as a way to explain and legitimize complements to judicial processes: "The participants supported the trials before the Hague Tribunal and the local war crimes trials aiming to establish individual liability of the war criminals, being aware that criminal trials are not sufficient for establishing truth about the recent past, bringing justice to victims, and preventing violence from reoccurring." Since they knew that many people in the Balkans think of justice in relation to the ICTY, a main focus of their strategy was to emphasize the need for a complement to judicial processes, and they drew on the idea of transitional justice to that end. They hoped that, by promoting transitional justice as an idea that could explain the need for new interventions, and by getting input on a truth commission from a wide range of actors, they could formulate a strategy that would overcome entrenched divisions about who is to blame, and how to redress victims of the war's violence.

PROMOTING A MALLEABLE INTERVENTION

The Forum's organizers were well aware of the need to mobilize support from the public, not just from foreign elites, in order to make their proposed intervention successful. They also knew that they would have to explain how their truth commission could meet the many goals, often contradictory, of actors who might be interested in creating it.

At the Second Regional Forum, entitled "Establishing the Truth about War Crimes and Conflicts," protesters came to the forum holding signs with names of Croatian towns where war crimes had occurred. They claimed that victims are the only rightful owners of the truth, and the organizers hoped that providing these survivors with the chance to participate in the campaign might mollify their concerns about yet another formal initiative to establish "the truth" about the war.

At the third regional forum in Belgrade, which took place in February 2008, the mobilization strategy, which emphasized the malleability of a truth commission, began to take form. The leaders decided to promote a regional body that would "establish facts" about war crimes and the conflict, but they would do so in a way that included a variety of constituencies. Aware that victims claim to be the "rightful owners of the truth," the leaders knew that they had to develop a mobilization strategy what would encourage survivors to participate throughout their campaign. The third forum had the first public meeting at which survivors could share their experiences of violence. Their hope was that, by presenting a truth commission as something that these constituencies could shape, they could get broad-based support and pressure recalcitrant political leaders who might be wary of creating a truth commission that would address all victims.

At the fourth regional forum in Kosovo, which took place in October 2008, the Coalition for RECOM was formally established. Over 300 representatives from the government and civil society, including 200 representatives from victims' groups, participated. More than 100 different civil society organizations and individuals throughout the region signed a charter for a formal coalition to promote a "Regional Commission for Identification and Public Disclosure of the Facts about War Crimes," the first official title of the commission. Nataša Kandić proposed the acronym "RECOM," and the Coalition for RECOM was born.

The Coalition's strategies were twofold: using the regional forums to get advice from transitional justice professionals and holding consultations with domestic actors in order both to promote their commission and to get ideas for how to design it. The result is that the goals of the commission continued to expand beyond the original fact-finding intentions. At the fourth regional forum, the Coalition further clarified its goals and strategies with regard to which countries and territories would be involved and which acts of violence it would focus on. In particular, rather than focusing on the period of time that earlier truth commission efforts had considered, namely the war that ended in 1995, RECOM's mandate would mirror the ICTY's and include the violence from 1991 through 2001 in order to include the violence between Kosovo and Serbia.

Beginning in 2009, the Coalition planned to spend two years engaged in consultations with victims' associations, clergy, public intellectuals, civil society leaders, and other constituencies. They would then hold a media and signature campaign in spring 2011. The goal was to gather one million signatures on a petition to create a government-sponsored regional commission. In addition, throughout this two-year period, a working group of experts familiar with truth commissions would draft a proposed mandate for the future commission. Including transnational professionals, domestic experts, and survivors in designing the truth commission shows just how adaptable they viewed this intervention as being, how ambitious their campaign was, and how they hoped this inclusive approach would help them succeed where others failed.

THE MULTIPLE GOALS OF A TRUTH COMMISSION

Throughout the effort, Coalition leaders received diverse feedback on what a truth commission could and should offer the region. Foreign donors, in particular, hoped that their money would contribute to social, political, and economic stability in the region. For example, at the sixth regional forum, held in March 2010 in Novi Sad, the opening speaker, Vincent Degert, who was the head of the EU delegation to Serbia, provided opening remarks, saying that "the EU backs this initiative," and mentioned the 1,200,000 euro investment.[55] Interestingly, he noted that the EU is most concerned with the creation of an independent judiciary, and saw RECOM as part of that goal. He emphasized the importance of civil society and a regional approach for the "establishment of jointly held facts at the regional level."[56] In addition, he made the incentives to create RECOM clear: "it is only with war crimes tackled that the EU integration process will end successfully."

One of the main concerns was whether a truth commission was malleable enough to affirm the ICTY while offering something that would appeal to this judicial body's critics. At the seventh regional forum in October 2010, the Coalition's leaders faced a question over whether RECOM's mandate should authorize an investigation into genocide. The group decided that the mandate should mention crimes against humanity and violations of international humanitarian law, as well as other forms of serious human rights abuses. Keeping the mandate focused on crimes against humanity and violations of international humanitarian law meant that RECOM's commissioners would have more independence in deciding whether to characterize the violence as genocide, which is a very contentious issue in the region. For those who do not see the violence at Srebrenica as genocide, the proposed commission would only appeal if it challenged the ICTY's findings. Ultimately, the Coalition leaders decided it would not challenge the ICTY's findings, reaffirming the finding of genocide and alienating Bosnian Serbs who might have otherwise been interested in this initiative.

55 RECOM, Sixth Regional Forum, transcripts, www.recom.link/wp-content/uploads/2010/03/Transcripts.pdf (accessed April 7, 2016).

56 RECOM, Sixth Regional Forum, transcripts, www.recom.link/wp-content/uploads/2010/03/Transcripts.pdf (accessed April 7, 2016).

Despite this challenge, the Coalition continued to promote RECOM as an intervention that would be able to meet the goals of diverse constituencies. One of the results of the seventh regional forum was the publication of a proposed statute that would define RECOM's authority and mandate. The preamble to the RECOM statute explains the group's assumptions about ongoing social and political divides in the region, and highlights the commission's wide-ranging objectives:

> Recognizing that this regional initiative, which is based on open dialogue, inquiry, and analysis of the facts, is the most efficient way to achieve a comprehensive historical record of the crimes committed in the period 1991–2001 and the role that national elites, institutions, and individuals played in those traumatic events; Resolved to help, to the best of their ability, to establish the fate of a large number of individuals who are still missing; Determined to jointly contribute to the process of dealing with the past by helping their citizens accept the facts about war crimes and other gross violations of human rights committed against all victims and by helping restore confidence between individuals, peoples, and states in the region.

This ambitious set of goals shows the aspirations of their campaign and how they tried to emphasize that the truth commission would meet the contradictory interests of different actors. The leaders promised a truth commission that would give individuals the opportunity to tell their stories, focus on creating an accurate historical record, contribute to judicial processes and more. The commission would not only create a comprehensive historical record, which is an objective and realizable goal, but also "help citizens accept the facts about war crimes" and create "the conditions necessary to achieve a lasting peace in the region."

Other parts of the mandate similarly show how the leaders tried to placate as many constituencies as possible, particularly Bosniaks, who were the primary victims, and Serbs, many of whom distrust the tribunals for prosecuting more Serbs than other national groups. They did this by focusing on inclusivity throughout the process of creating and implementing a truth commission. The mandate proposes to have the truth commission headquarters in Sarajevo, and five of the twenty commissioners come from BiH. Article 8 states that the Commission "shall make equal use of the Albanian, Bosnian, Croatian, Macedonian, Montenegrin, Serbian and Slovenian languages, and of the Cyrillic and Latin alphabets, as well as of sign languages, in accordance with the different persons and communities employing them." Article 17(5) provides that any witnesses who give statements will receive psychological and social support, something that many survivors need. Moreover, the initial statute included language that would enable the commission to make recommendations for pardons and sentence reductions from criminal tribunals. The mandate did not promise lighter sentences, which it could not do, but drafters clearly were trying to encourage participation in RECOM by suggesting that the ICTY and other tribunals should see such participation as a mitigating factor in sentencing.

This mandate also shows that RECOM's proponents were promoting an intervention so malleable that it was politically unfeasible. The group conceptualized RECOM as a treaty-based body that would be signed by the states that constituted the former Yugoslavia, including Kosovo, which is a territory with disputed statehood. This is just one example of the fundamental problems facing this proposed commission. Asking Serbian or BiH leaders to sign the treaty would require them to recognize Kosovo's independence, which they did not. For Federation leaders, Kosovo's declaration of independence represented what could happen if the RS decided it no longer wanted to be part of BiH. This bold initiative, exemplified by this large-scale mandate, was destined to be a difficult sell in BiH, the most important country in the initiative.

THE APPEAL OF PROCEDURAL JUSTICE

As the Coalition continued to promote the commission, they were well aware that they faced an uphill battle. As they listened to both foreign consultants and local stakeholders, it became clear to the Coalition leaders that "establishing facts" about the war would be a significant challenge. The Coalition's strategy reveals how promoting the process of this mobilization strategy, and particularly enabling survivors to share their stories, became a central component of their campaign and a way to channel disparate desires about what this commission could and should do. Engaging diverse groups in the process of creating a truth commission initially helped them overcome suspicion that this initiative was another top-down effort that would come and go.

Christian Correa, a consultant with the International Center on Transitional Justice, participated in the fifth regional forum in March 2010, almost a year and a half into the mobilization effort, and pointed to the monumental challenge of clarifying why the violence happened in the first place. In our interview, he explained the group's discussions on "how to deal with the past, how far back, or what's the role of a truth commission to investigate historical truth, the crimes committed, or the violence committed" and the benefits and drawbacks of more limited or broader objectives (interview with Christian Correa 2010). He described the dilemmas of focusing on the violence in the 1990s when some people see the problem as stemming from the 1389 Battle of Kosovo.

Mainly, the concerns involved how to characterize the violence in the 1990s, as some in the region viewed it as a war of aggression, while other saw it as preventing the violence caused by disintegration. He pointed out that "if you try to answer the last question, basically, you are trying to put the blame on one or on another for the whole violence" (interview with Christian Correa 2010). Like speakers at earlier regional forums who spoke about the difficulty of using truth commissions to establish an accurate historical record, Correa encouraged the group to focus on witness testimony rather than descending into the bottomless pit of disputes about the causes and consequences of the violence. From his perspective, the truth commission should focus more on changing social and political relationships for the future rather than focusing on the past, especially because narratives about the past are so contested.

Coalition leaders followed the advice of these consultants in several ways. As noted, they encouraged individual participants in the commission to clarify their hopes and desires for a future commission. As one former Coalition leader in BiH explained, they presented the commission as a vehicle for these survivors to have their desires heard:

> You say: this is why we want to do it. This is a completely open process. We are not coming with, like, prepared solutions and answers, but on the contrary, this is on the table, and we want to discuss with you. What do you think? How do you feel about it? What else would you like to see in this? What should be a mandate? (Interview with BiH Coalition leader 2009)

Through this process, Coalition leaders soon realized that the most important function of a truth commission would be to enable survivors to tell their stories:

> One thing that we are for sure 100 percent certain that throughout this process of consultations is that if [the] commission is established, there must be a public victims' hearing. This is absolutely something that people need and people want. (Interview with BiH Coalition leader 2009)

These comments underscore the utility of a truth commission as an intervention that actors can shape to their own desires. Coalition leaders promoted the truth commission as a body that would allow individuals to have a voice both in the process of creating a commission and in the proposed commission's work. Promising the chance to share their experiences in TC hearings was a way to engage individuals who might be skeptical of a truth commission, and it would also get them to join in the consultations. Their complementary, contradictory, or competing beliefs were voiced through a consultation process that focused on participation and individual needs, offering survivors of the war and the younger generations hope that a future truth commission might help them realize their many goals.

In the media campaign, one finds a more striking example of how Coalition leaders promoted the truth commission as malleable enough to ensure goals that had nothing to do with fact-finding. On the Coalition's 2010 website, for example, signing up to be part of the Coalition required writing one's name in a box above the statements: "For your own sake. So that everybody knows. So it doesn't happen again. To move on. To live better."[57] Media consultants decided it would be better to frame the commission as a way for individuals to learn about themselves and their current political challenges, rather than focus primarily on the past violence.

57 "Mandate for RECOM," *Coalition for RECOM*, www.recom.link/join-us-2/ (accessed Feb. 4, 2017).

Explaining the advice they received on the media campaign, one Coalition leader from the HLC noted,

> Well, they shifted a little bit the focus . . . Through this consultation process, we were trying to wake empathy in people for victims. We tried to explain how important to care about victims from our side and also from other sides. But the creative team shifted that focus from empathy to ourselves. (Interview with HLC staff member 2010)

The commercials broadcast around the region showed pictures of individuals and families saying statements exemplified by the following: "for me, so I know, for my future." This campaign touches on issues that have less to do with understanding shared victimhood and more to do with hopes for a better life. In the Balkans, part of moving on and living better means EU membership, and many in the region, including political leaders, have tried to speed up this integration process. Several interviewees explained that when people in BiH hear of transitional justice, they often think it has to do with the process of joining the EU, as joining the EU is often referred to as a transition. A former Coalition leader from Croatia explained that he was successful in getting adolescents to support RECOM by talking about visa liberalization and EU membership. When talking to young people, he would suggest that supporting the Coalition could help overcome the travel restrictions that were then placed on citizens of Croatia but not Slovenia, then the only EU member from the former Yugoslavia (interview with Croatian youth leader 2010).

Coalition leaders tried to show that a commission could help these different actors realize a variety of goals, yet they were careful about their framing strategy. In particular, although the leaders clearly drew inspiration from the South Africa TRC and developed its agenda with the support of the ICTJ, Coalition leaders mentioned to me that they tried to avoid the term "reconciliation." The Coalition leaders knew that many people in the Balkans view reconciliation with suspicion, as they see it as a term that implied both impunity and forgiveness. In the mandate, they instead chose to frame the commission's goals in terms of "establishing trust between the nations in the region, individuals, and the states." While they promoted the truth commission as adaptable to the regional context, they did not want it to be seen as an alternative to prosecutions.

Despite explaining their concerns about reconciliation, they still drew on the idea in their English language promotional materials. In its summary of the consultation processes, for example, the *RECOMmendations* booklet lists the second goal of the truth commission as reconciliation. The objective of reconciliation is elaborated as "essential in Bosnia and Herzegovina," something that will contribute to "healing and closure," requiring "the victim to forgive" and the aggressor to "admit his guilt and make reparation for his evil and violence." This articulation of reconciliation reflects the notion of "revealing is healing," the popular slogan from the South Africa Truth and Reconciliation Commission. Similarly, the HLC's 2011 grant from the Rockefeller Brothers Fund, which provided general support for the Coalition, was titled "Strengthening Constituencies for Reconciliation and Enduring Peace."

Figuring out how to frame their goals and strategies was just one of the many challenges the Coalition faced in trying to make their innovative proposal resonate with the diverse constituencies whose support they sought. This analysis reveals that one way to deal with the dilemmas of promoting a regional commission was to give voice, a central component of procedural justice, to a broad range of individuals, and to suggest that giving voice would help both individuals and groups rebuild fractured relationships (MacCoun 2005). Through enabling diverse constituencies to articulate their hopes and desires for a truth commission, Coalition leaders hoped to show political leaders that they had broad based support in the region. Given their ambitions, and the appeal of an initiative that might help bridge social and political divisions throughout the region, the Coalition received increasing domestic and international media attention for its efforts, even as its campaign in BiH faltered.

REJECTING A TRUTH COMMISSION: ORGANIZATIONAL DYNAMICS

With generous funding and a creative strategy of engaging in consultations throughout the region, the Coalition appeared to have distinct advantages over the many failed initiatives to create a truth commission in BiH. However, as the mobilization effort continued, these advantages all but evaporated. The Coalition's difficulties in BiH reveal how organizational dynamics, including professional identities, personal relationships, and financial resources, can make an innovative and groundbreaking campaign unmanageable. More importantly, they reveal how the ambitious nature of this campaign, which was predicated on creating a truth commission that could meet the hopes and desires of so many different constituencies, may have undermined its proponents' goals.

The problems in Bosnia and Herzegovina began even before the Coalition was formalized. Although Mirsad Tokača, then leader of the Research and Documentation Center in BiH, originally signed an agreement to work with his neighbors on fact-finding initiatives and had traveled to Brussels to learn about truth commissions from the ICTJ, he spoke out against a truth commission as early as 2006. He offered a general critique of truth commissions, as well as a specific critique about the viability of a commission in BiH:

> Unfortunately, a terrible confusion was created by offering (imposing) the idea and models (South African and other) of a truth commission which cannot satisfy the needs of the Bosnian society, due both to cultural differences and, particularly, to the nature, causes and consequences of the conflict... Furthermore, the management of the processes was left to politicians and hardened nationalists, or to completely incompetent people (with no measurable results in the field) who do

> not have enough knowledge about the problem, either in a theoretical or operational/organizational sense, to be able to maintain the efficiency and efficacy of such processes on a satisfactory level.[58]

Tokača's reference to South Africa reveals his concerns about creating an intervention that might offer conditional amnesties to perpetrators of mass violence. Many Bosniaks have expressed frustration that plea deals were possible at the ICTY, wondering how perpetrators of international crimes can get sentence reductions for divulging information or apologizing (Clark 2009). A truth commission predicated on any sort of conditional amnesty seemed out of the question. In addition, Tokača did not believe that either policy makers or civil society could manage a truth commission, and felt that promoting an idealized but unrealistic intervention would be a waste of time. In our 2010 interview, he explained that he was involved and withdrew "simply because three years of our very intensive work, there is no reaction from State." From his perspective, staying in the coalition would mean having "to travel like a circus around the region, to have every two, or one, or three months a consultation with somebody." He saw it as stopping his practical work for no reason:

> And then what will happen finally? Nothing. Why? Because there is no political atmosphere . . . This is not [the] time. And I have to reiterate. It is my moral act. I don't want to spend money, my dollars, and then to say, "Look, we failed." (Interview with Mirsad Tokača 2010)

While Tokača emphasized the lack of political opportunities, he was also concerned about the Coalition's structure and leadership. Coalition leaders presented the initiative as inclusive and participatory, but most interviewees referred to the HLC as the primary leader. Although many Serbs within BiH, as well as Serbia, questioned the HLC for its work in exposing atrocities committed by Serb leaders during the war, many Bosniaks, like Tokača, expressed concern that organizations in Belgrade and Zagreb "could not lead" the process. Tokača explained that he "will not allow that" because "all the problems came from Belgrade and Zagreb. This country is victim of Belgrade and Zagreb. Could you imagine that after Second World War Berlin will accommodate Jews? It's impossible" (interview with Mirsad Tokača 2010).

Tokača's actions matched his words. Soon after the Fourth Regional Forum in 2008, the RDC stepped out of the mobilization effort, though he still offered public support for it. Given the bitter feelings from the war, these actors in the region, who share goals and strategies, struggled to work together. Ongoing nationalist tensions make organizational solidarity, the kind of solidarity needed to effectively promote a regional or even a national truth commission, exceedingly challenging.

[58] Mirsad Tokača, "Truth and Reconciliation Commission III," *Puls Demokratije*, 2006, November 19, 2006, arhiva.pulsdemokratije.net/index.php?id=382&l=bs.

BRINGING IN NEW LEADERSHIP

With Tokača deciding not to lead the Coalition's efforts in BiH, the HLC asked another organization, the Helsinki Committee for Human Rights–Republika Srpska (RS), to coordinate the consultations in BiH. The Helsinki Committee worked in partnership with Izvor, a victims' association from Prijedor, the Citizens Forum from Tuzla, the Youth Initiative for Human Rights–Sarajevo, and the Center for Civic Cooperation from Livno.

The Helsinki Committee, the organization that was a precursor to Human Rights Watch, was particularly interested in the idea of transitional justice and what a truth commission might offer the divided country. The organization's deputy director in 2010, Aleksandra Letić, was a young woman of Serbian origin who grew up in Germany. Like others who left as children during the war, she returned with a desire to help the region. She was both a foreigner and a local, which gave her distinct advantages working in the region. It was difficult to accuse her of being loyal to her national group to the exclusion of others, yet she spoke the language and understood the culture.

Letić was familiar with the idea of transitional justice and was interested in a regional truth commission. By 2010, the Helsinki Committee was leading a "transitional justice school" program that educated youth in towns where international crimes documented by the ICTY were committed. When asked her definition of transitional justice and how it was taught in schools, Letić immediately related transitional justice to truth commissions and explained how few people in the Balkans utilize the idea "in accordance with the four mechanisms."[59] She noted that when talking about truth-telling initiatives, they usually talk about truth and reconciliation commissions in other countries. She added that part of her work is to point out that there is "transitional justice" in BiH, but "it's not recognized as this" (interview with Alexandra Letić 2010).

Notably, she immediately identified her understanding of transitional justice with the ICTJ's definition, as she, like many of her colleagues in the region, had attended trainings by ICTJ staff. Her comments about how few people know they even "have transitional justice in BiH" further highlight how the idea's malleability made it very useful in her efforts to promote the idea. Proponents of transitional justice could point to existing interventions to explain the idea's utility, in addition to using the idea to explain the need to create new interventions like truth commissions.

Initially, Letić wanted to help lead the consultation effort in BiH. However, by the end of 2009, she and other Helsinki Committee leaders began to question the Coalition's leadership and ability to work successfully in BiH. When discussing her goals and strategies as a leader in BiH, Letić stated that her main priority was

59 At the time, ICTJ's mechanisms (or, as they called them, pillars) were criminal tribunals, truth commissions, reparations programs, and institutional reform.

to maintain the trust of local actors, and over time, actors in BiH expressed that they did not feel that they were treated as equals in discussions about how the Coalition should conduct its work. As a result, they began to question whether the RECOM effort was a project set on a timeline for the donor agencies or a process that would actually be inclusive of the various constituencies necessary to make a truth commission possible. Her opinion reflected concerns that I heard from other advocacy organizations in Sarajevo. One BiH civil society leader working closely with a number of victims' associations explained to me that he had to work secretly with Coalition leaders because many of his colleagues opposed the effort.

These tensions contributed to a restructuring of the Coalition's leadership in BiH. In late 2009, the HLC decided to bring in the Sarajevo-based BiH Association of Journalists to help with the BiH consultations. By 2010, the Helsinki Committee for Human Rights–RS, concerned about its ability to manage the consultations and other organizational priorities, left the Coalition. Three other coordinators stepped out in the first half of 2010. Finally, in June 2010, the last of these BiH coalition leaders, the Youth Initiative for Human Rights, removed itself from the Coalition. The Association of Journalists, along with the Center for Legal and Informational Assistance in Zvornik, continued leading the BiH consultations for the rest of the year.

Nationalist media in BiH readily politicized this organizational dynamic, which created additional problems for the Coalition's work in the country. One local paper quoted Letić's boss, Branko Todorović, who was the director of the Helsinki Committee for Human Rights–RS, as making inflammatory comments about the Coalition's leadership:

> It was supposed to form a regional commission for investigating war crimes, following the example of those that existed in several countries of Latin America, but due to the extravagance and wanton conduct of Nataša Kandić, the Coalition has already lost five prominent non-governmental organizations and activists from Bosnia and Herzegovina that accused it of spending its multimillion dollar budget on their own luxuries in expensive hotels, and have the ambition for that money to win their own nomination for the Nobel Peace Prize.[60]

While the media sensationalized the issue as a dispute over financial expenditures, representatives from both the HLC and the Helsinki Committee noted that the issue between the organizations was not about money. The financing was transparent and clearly explained. Rather, the finances reflected concerns about who was dictating the agenda. With many people's livelihood dependent on foreign investment in civil society initiatives, the influx of millions of dollars to one organization fomented both competition and suspicion. As a recipient of international funds, the

[60] Press Online Serbia, "Nataša Kandić plaća milione za Nobelovu nagradu za mir!" Mar. 22, 2010, translated by author, www.pressonline.rs/sr/vesti/vesti_dana/story/107347/Nata%C5%A1a+Kandi%C4%87+pla%C4%87a+milione+za+Nobelovu+nagradu+za+mir!.html (accessed April 2, 2010).

Serbia-based HLC had to focus on holding a certain number of consultations, managing a costly media campaign, and meeting the other targets from their funding proposal. While there were several paid positions outside the HLC, including the consultation coordinatorship in BiH, most of the Coalition's work was done on a voluntary basis. This posed a problem for organizations that wanted to participate in the Coalition's activities but had to raise funds independently for staff salaries.

As the campaign dragged on, these organizational dynamics in BiH made it challenging to mobilize support for the upcoming large-scale campaign to collect one million signatures for a petition to create RECOM. In 2011, a Coalition staffer explained how difficult it was for him to pitch the Coalition to organizations they hoped would sign on to join the Coalition. He said that he "did not know the situation very well in BiH" and thought that NGOs were composed of "really nice people who would fight for something good." He continued to say that he "knew that also there were many fake projects, fake people, fake NGOs." He said that most NGOs did not answer when he called and asked them to join RECOM. He concluded, "After talking with people in NGO world, I realized there are too many organizations fighting for projects, surviving and don't care for an idea. It is about projects and money" (interview with Coalition for RECOM staffer 2011).

This negative perception of NGOs in BiH reflects not only this staffer's acute frustration, but also the structural challenges facing BiH civil society. This NGO funding scheme in BiH, whereby organizations are dependent on nationalist leaders for funds, means that it is difficult for some organizations to support an initiative such as RECOM. As the recruitment efforts faltered in BiH, some of the coalition's leadership came to question BiH civil society as much as BiH civil society questioned the Coalition. One coalition leader referred to nongovernmental organizations in BiH as "smurfs" who care little for any cause, and are only concerned about money (interview with BiH Coalition leader 2014). Looking at these organizational dynamics, an international consultant on RECOM's strategy sharply criticized the initiative for not simply being unmanageable, but not being managed well:

> RECOM is itself exclusive to the Balkans and does not involve the international community... One typical Scandinavian donor throws serious money at a deeply dysfunctional, highly conflicted, totally unorganized, as well as disorganized, group of people and basically transforms it into a feeding frenzy for project funds. What matters is money was spent. Boxes were ticked. Not too much embarrassment was caused, and what embarrassment was caused did not blow back onto anybody that matters at the political level in the funding world. That's what's going on. (Interview with RECOM consultant 2010)

While he focused on the internal organizational dynamics, his insights further show how perceptions of the malleability of a truth commission enabled this debacle. Simply put, donors thought that this campaign would be easier than it was. By promoting a truth commission under the banner of transitional justice, the Coalition was able to raise funds from foreign donors who were hoping to contribute to an intervention that would redress the war's brutal violence without the political challenges of prosecutions. However, the effort contributed not only to skepticism, but also to resistance to a regional truth commission in BiH.

THE SIGNATURE CAMPAIGN: THE LIMITS OF MALLEABILITY

By 2011, the Coalition had support from heads of state in the region, including leaders in Montenegro, Croatia, and Kosovo. However, it continued to struggle to get popular support in BiH, the key country. The signature campaign was the Coalition's most important opportunity to show government leaders that Bosnians wanted this commission. The Coalition engaged in street actions in much the same way that any popular movement might, but they simply did not have the support they needed. The leadership hoped youth would be willing to volunteer to collect signatures, but it was even hard to recruit volunteers without offering nominal compensation. Although the Coalition promoted RECOM as something that would be useful to Bosnians, they could not overcome concerns that this was yet another initiative that would be useless at best and divisive at worst.

In the beginning of the signature campaign in spring 2011, a popular T.V. program in the Federation aired a show that one interviewee described as "a massacre" of Nataša Kandić and her leadership of the Coalition (interview with Bosnian civil society leader 2011). In May 2011, paid volunteers with signature quotas described being harassed on the streets of Sarajevo for being "in the devil's army" and trying "to equalize the crimes committed by Serbia." On the days of my observations, many of these volunteers were simply ignored as they tried to engage in dialogue with pedestrians.

On May 26, the day that Ratko Mladić, the Bosnian Serb general responsible for ordering the massacre at Srebrenica, was arrested, Nataša Kandić was in Sarajevo to help with the signature campaign. Media outlets from around the world called Kandić that day, asking for her input on the Mladić arrest. She tried to bring up RECOM but, much like her challenge to get pedestrians to stop and sign the petition, the media was fixated on Mladić's arrest and future trial in The Hague. On the news, images of the Srebrenica massacre were on repeat, with Mladić calling the Bosnian Muslims "Turks" and promising revenge. On the street, it was clear that a truth commission was a hard sell when Bosniaks were thinking about punishing Mladić for the deaths of thousands of Muslim boys and men. Kandić appeared frustrated with the young adults who were collecting signatures. She encouraged them to be more proactive in engaging people walking by. The youth congregated in the background, obviously frustrated with the task.

The HLC extended the campaign for two weeks, hoping to meet its goal of one million signatures. Despite this effort, the campaign resulted in just 122,473 signatures in BiH and 542,660 in the whole region.[61] After 127 consultations, with the participation of over 6000 individuals interested in a new initiative to investigate, document, and publicize facts about the war, millions of euros spent, and three years of intense and sustained campaigning to create RECOM, the Coalition could not get the signatures. At the end of the signature campaign, the director of the Helsinki Committee for Human Rights–Republika Srpska concluded, "the entire RECOM project is envisioned completely wrong, too ambitious and is completely unrealistic."[62] In May 2011, while volunteers were strolling the streets, a well-respected civil society leader shared his perspective on the campaign with me: "RECOM is dead."

AN ONGOING CAMPAIGN, WITH ONGOING CHALLENGES

Still motivated to make RECOM a reality, Nataša Kandić eventually left the HLC to devote herself full time to promoting a regional commission. One of the initiative's newer financial backers, The Rockefeller Brothers Fund, notes in its website summary of RECOM that the organization will continuing collecting signatures until the draft statute is signed.[63]

The Coalition's leadership continued to draw on the idea of transitional justice to explain and legitimate their efforts, founding the Association of Transitional Justice, Accountability and Remembrance in BiH in 2012 and holding an "International Forum for Transitional Justice" in 2013. The Association tried to implement a number of innovative approaches to promote RECOM, continuing with public debates and sponsoring "I Run for RECOM" events throughout the region. This organization also branched out to work with the Center for Democracy and Transitional Justice in Banja Luka, the capital of RS, with a National Endowment of Democracy-funded project to collect all of the information available on detention facilities and concentration camps. However, just as RECOM has struggled to bridge divides, this project also suffered from distrust. At first, Bosniak victims' associations that had information on detention facilities rebuffed their initiative, wary of how this NGO would use their information.

After the failed signature campaign, the Coalition's leadership focused largely on gaining the support of policy makers. Leaders from Montenegro, Slovenia, Kosovo, and Croatia expressed support for the establishment of RECOM, as did the U.S.

[61] Youth Initiative for Human Rights, Newsletter, August 2011, on file with author; The Coalition, "RECOM Process: Results and Prospective," July 8, 2011, www.hlc-rdc.org/?p=13123&lang=de (accessed Feb. 4, 2017). The Coalition survey concluded that only 20% of the population in BiH had even heard of the initiative. The Coalition, "Survey of Public Opinion About RECOM," July 21, 2011, on file with author.

[62] Liljana Kovačević, "Is RECOM Collapsing?" *SETimes*, July 3, 2011, www.eurasiareview.com/03072011-is-recom-collapsing/ (accessed Nov. 30, 2011).

[63] Rockefeller Brothers Fund Grantees, Humanitarian Law Center: Documentation and Memory, www.rbf.org/grantees/humanitarian-law-center-documentation-and-memory (accessed July 18, 2016).

ambassador to BiH and the EU High Representative to BiH, but the leaders of BiH remained reluctant. In 2013, Kandić organized a meeting with envoys from Croatia, Macedonia, Montenegro, Kosovo, Serbia, and BiH to work on the government's concerns about the RECOM statute. They negotiated the length of time that the Commission could continue working (they made the deadline six months instead of indefinite) and addressed more controversial issues such as whether the commission would "morally judge" those guilty of perpetration. The Coalition characterized these meetings as "ushering in a new phase" of the RECOM Process, moving from the "civil to political level."[64]

However, tinkering with the mandate may not help these actors overcome their fundamental disagreements over the role of a truth commission in the Balkans. In particular, different parties were focused on how this commission would relate to judicial processes. In June 2014, the Coordinating Council of the Coalition in BiH met with the Bosniak president, anticipating yet another ambivalent response. According to a participant in the meeting, one of the biggest dilemmas for BiH leaders had to do with Article 14(e), the objective of researching "the political and social circumstances that decisively contributed to the outbreak of the war." Determining the circumstances that led to the war sounds like an apolitical goal, but asking what "contributed to the outbreak of war" remains one of the most politically divisive questions in BiH, as nationalistic leaders still mobilize support by emphasizing their victimhood. In a November 2014 meeting in Belgrade, Coalition leaders stated that the commission may either focus on the causes or first focus on "establishing facts." Benefitting from the malleability of a truth commission, they continued to oscillate in defining their primary goals and strategies.

Finally, even though the Coalition leaders promoted the truth commission as an intervention that would represent the interests of all national groups, as one Bosnian Serb member of the Coalition noted in 2014, "the pre-condition for transitional justice is the existence of an organized, legal state. BiH does not meet this criterion, since it barely functions as a state in its present form."[65]

By framing their agenda using the idea of transitional justice and promoting a truth commission, leaders of the Coalition were able to gain initial support for their effort, but they have struggled for over a decade to realize their goals. When I visited Sarajevo for fieldwork in 2014, just as in 2011, I still heard the refrain that "RECOM is dead" when asking civil society leaders about the initiative. The Coalition offered voice to the many participants in its forums and consultations, but it could not make political opportunities where there were none. This initiative may be doomed to be yet another disappointing attempt to create a truth commission in BiH, even though

64 RECOM, "Serbian President Appoints Judge Siniša Važić His Personal Envoy to RECOM," Press Release, www.recom.link/serbian-president-appoints-judge-sinisa-vazic-his-personal-envoy-to-recom/ (accessed Dec. 3, 2016).

65 See The Coalition, "Press Release," www.theCoalition.org/press/Public-debate-on-Transitional-Justice-hosted-in-Banja-Luka.en.html (accessed July 20, 2016).

the Coalition continues to mobilize support both within the region and abroad. By 2015, the Serbian government publicly backed the creation of RECOM, but getting the support of the diverse constituencies in BiH will remain challenging.

OTHER ATTEMPTS TO INSTRUMENTALIZE TRANSITIONAL JUSTICE

While it might be easy to attribute this failed effort to the organizational dynamics within the Coalition, other examples of efforts to instrumentalize transitional justice have been similarly ambitious and similarly challenging. The idea's malleability has facilitated its circulation into BiH, but the idea ultimately became a placeholder for actors to articulate their hopes and desires about how to overcome divisions in the region. Mobilizing around transitional justice continues to be appealing, particularly because it connects domestic organizations with transnational elites that can provide them with resources. At the same time, using the idea does little to help quell the distrust and divisions over questions of justice for the war's violence.

Notably, building on its longstanding interest in transitional justice, the United Nations Development Program was working with the Bosnian government to implement new interventions that would address growing social and political divisions. In 2007, the UNDP's Sarajevo office hired an American lawyer, John Furnari, to lead a new program called "Facing the Past: Access to Justice and Building Confidence for the Future." The goal was to develop a National Transitional Justice Strategy that the BiH government would implement.

Furnari was not familiar with transitional justice when he took the job. He became interested in international law after working as a law clerk in Guam, and had previously worked on police and judicial reform in the region. He immediately enlisted the support of the ICTJ to help develop his goals and strategies. He chose to define his project according to the ICTJ's 2007 description of the "pillars" of transitional justice: judicial mechanisms, truth-seeking mechanisms, reparation, and institutional reform. By 2009, the ICTJ had added more pillars, including memorials and gender justice, but Furnari had already committed to the definition of transitional justice as four pillars. The UNDP received instruction from transnational transitional justice professionals, specifically the ICTJ, as they were not sure what this idea offered the country. After the presentations, some were still confused. One participant explained that "the lecturers would just fly in for a day and they would leave," noting that this is the "downside" of working with big organizations. This participant noted liking the presentation but said that "maybe it was a bit too abstract for some of the participants. I mean, it's not ICTJ's [fault] – that's what they come with" (interview with UNDP staffer 2009). Similarly, another participant suggested that the presenters were "woefully academic" and "seemed frightened." He was bothered that they focused on transitional justice in general rather than on Bosnia, saying that there seemed a "lack of interest in coming to do this" when he saw inviting them as an "opportunity on a silver platter" (interview with UNDP staffer 2009).

These perspectives give additional insight into how the proponents of transitional justice keep it malleable by talking about the idea in general and giving examples of interventions in other places when asked how the idea might benefit a particular place. Interestingly, when I asked Furnari about his understanding of transitional justice, he immediately mentioned RECOM and other proposals for truth commissions. I followed up on this coupling of truth commissions and transitional justice, which I had heard from other interviewees in BiH, by asking why he immediately jumped to discussing truth commissions when I mentioned transitional justice. He answered that, based on his consultations, "many victims want their story to be told," and that they want "some semblance of symbolic level of reparation, whether it's a letter, for heaven's sake, from a tripartite presidency that says we recognize your loss" (interview with John Furnari 2009). Like RECOM proponents, rather than seeing a truth commission as a tool for documenting atrocities or any number of goals, Furnari saw it as a tool for victims to gain recognition from the state. At the same time, the UNDP's position was that BiH needed its own commission. Their strategy was to work with civil society organizations and the government to generate interest in creating a truth commission, reparations programs, and institutional reforms that would help end the nationalist divisions.

The UNDP also served as an important intermediary in spreading the idea of transitional justice into BiH by offering small grants to domestic organizations engaged in work on accountability and victims. Just like the UNDP staff, very few civil society leaders who received grants from the UNDP could explain their understanding of transitional justice. Leaders of two organizations, one that worked on democracy education programs for youth and another that provided psychosocial services to survivors, noted in our interviews that they did not identify their work as transitional justice and did not really know what the idea meant. However, they wrote proposals that related their work to their understandings of transitional justice, which they did not find challenging because the idea encompasses so many goals and strategies, in order to receive project funds.

These small grants may have done more to help bridge social and political divisions than did the UNDP's work with BiH policy makers. Under Furnari's leadership, the UNDP created a handbook on transitional justice in the Balkans and called on government to consider a truth commission, financial compensation to survivors, and institutional reforms. A UNDP staffer reflected on personal experience with this project as a clear indicator of how difficult it is to get anything done in the United Nations, as well as in BiH, because of the United Nations' approach to "delivering deliverables and products" when it is difficult to get "government partner" to work with them (interview with UNDP staffer 2009). These concerns highlight the dilemmas associated with promoting interventions that require the two entities in BiH to work together and how debates about transitional justice can simply become another opportunity to air disputes.

After Furnari's departure at the end of his two-year contract, the UNDP hired a local Bosniak journalist to lead a working group of civil society and governmental leaders in implementing the strategy. Furnari viewed his hire as the "kiss of death," as leaders of the Serb-dominated RS would not listen to a Bosniak. The head of the working group was Letić, the deputy director of the Helsinki Committee for Human Rights–Republika Srpska, who was well respected by the various parties. The working group included ten government ministers and five civil society members, three of whom represented victims' associations. The UNDP's team included both the Bosniak journalist and two Serbs who had been involved in the Coalition for RECOM. As one UNDP staff member explained, they hoped the working group might lead to new policies rather than just another "paper that is being written somewhere in some of the state institutions" (interview with UNDP staffer 2010).

Letić was hopeful about the working group's potential when we discussed the initiative in spring 2010. However, by the time I returned to BiH in 2011, this working group had splintered, with RS leaders saying that they would not participate in a collaborative effort with policy makers in the Federation. One of the UNDP staffers did not anticipate success in effecting any policy changes with this new endeavor, and wondered aloud in our interview whether he would have a job by the end of the year.

Interestingly, the United Nations persisted in its efforts, particularly on the issue of truth seeking. In 2011, it contracted former ICTJ staff, who were referred to as "international truth-seeking experts," to write a report on the need for truth-seeking initiatives to "move from a state of conflict to peace, from denial to reconciliation."[66] The UNDP continued its efforts to promote transitional justice, and specifically a truth commission, as useful for the country despite the ongoing recalcitrance from the government. Though the project's leaders hoped the idea of transitional justice would be easy to support, BiH political leaders continue to stymie efforts to bridge divisions in the country.

STILL TRANSLATING TRANSITIONAL JUSTICE BEYOND THE COURTS

For now, it seems as though foreign elites continue to draw on the idea of transitional justice to promote new initiatives, while domestic actors remain skeptical. The European Commission-sponsored Balkan Transitional Justice Initiative, for example, is a journalistic outlet proffering the same idealistic discourse as the Coalition for RECOM. It boasts that regional transitional justice is "the founding stone of any successful democracy, respect for the rule of law, human rights and sustainable peace in the region."[67] Despite ongoing and commendable work by a variety of organizations, these goals remain elusive.

Like the Coalition for RECOM and the UNDP, the International Commission on Missing Persons (ICMP) drew on transitional justice to articulate the need to

66 Simpson, Hodžić, and Bickford (2012).

67 Balkan Transitional Justice Initiative, "About Us," www.balkaninsight.com/en/balkan-transitional-justice/about-the-project (accessed July 20, 2016).

move beyond court-based strategies for social and political change. For them, the malleability of transitional justice was useful to help bridge their previous work with the ICTY and their desire to make their work relevant to the many victims of the war. The ICMP is neither a civil society nor an intergovernmental organization. Rather, it originated in a political agreement between the countries involved in the Dayton Peace Accords. The chief operating officer, Adam Boys, explained that their goal is to support "the rule of law" by "establishing some truths – for example, the number of killed and missing, the names of those people" for the courts (interview with Adam Boys 2010). Despite its scientific integrity, various media outlets and political leaders criticized the ICMP for working with the prosecutor at the ICTY. Some claimed that staff contaminated their data to prove that Serb defendants are genocidaires and inflated the number of Bosniak victims.[68] Such claims created new challenges at the ICTY, where defense lawyers for Karadžić, the famed commander of the Bosnian Serb army, challenged the validity of the ICMP's work.[69]

When the ICMP leaders realized that they needed a new approach to ensure that the "truths" produced by the organization were actually changing narratives about the violence, they looked for a new framing strategy. As part of a new program on "Mutual Understanding and Transitional Justice," ICMP staff engaged in discussions with local civil society leaders on how to memorialize victims and how to lobby the government for benefits. Moreover, the organization developed an online inquiry center for family members to track the status of a case and provide information about family members who might be able to provide DNA.

For this organization, transitional justice served as a useful frame for communicating how these different efforts fit with their earlier strategies to identify victims and work with the ICTY. One staff member, who had previously worked with the HLC and the Coalition for RECOM, explained that these new strategies are necessary to "commemorate" 20,000 who have been identified, and also to commemorate those who have not yet been identified. He explained his understanding of transitional justice as "efforts are designed to improve social relationships between the nationalist groups" with the goal to "prevent a recurrence of violence" (interview with ICMP staffer 2011). His understanding of transitional justice shows, again, how actors viewed the idea as useful for wide-ranging goals and strategies, all of which were aspirational and framed as complements to the work of the ICTY.

As transitional justice continued to circulate in BiH, other actors working to redress violence in BiH continued to express concern about the idea. The cover page of a newsletter published for Sarajevo's Peace Week in June 2014, for example,

68 See, e.g., *Prosecutor v. Vujadin Popović*, IT-05-88-T, International Criminal Tribunal for the former Yugoslavia (ICTY), 10 June 2010. Retrieved from www.unhcr.org/refworld/docid/4c1f69fe2.html (accessed July 20, 2016).

69 International Criminal Tribunal for Former Yugoslavia, *Prosecutor v. Karadžić, Order on Selection of Cases for DNA Analysis*, IT-95-5/18-T (accessed Mar. 19, 2010).

mentioned transitional justice in an article on the question of whether one should talk about the past or forget it.[70] In describing the goals of their project on memory, the newsletter put the idea of transitional justice in quotation marks. This writer was ambivalent about using the idea, though he realized that others use *transitional justice* to discuss initiatives that he referred to with the term memory. By 2014, during my last trip for fieldwork in BiH, one of the board members of the Association of Transitional Justice, Accountability and Remembrance in Bosnia and Herzegovina asserted that "transitional justice is for foreigners," but that one cannot talk about work related to accountability and remembrance without using it (interview with Bosnian civil society leader 2014). The idea continues to circulate, but some still see it as a foreign implant that is not useful for their work.

DISRUPTIVE INSTRUMENTALIZATION

This chapter points to how the malleability of transitional justice and, in particular, truth commissions made the idea and intervention appealing to a wide range of actors with a variety of goals. Looking specifically at the Coalition for RECOM, elite actors thought that a truth commission could be created between seven countries and one disputed territory and could satisfy the hopes and desires of individuals recently at war. A regional truth commission was easy to suggest, difficult to promote, and nearly impossible to create.

Translating transitional justice into political action in the BiH through this campaign was innovative and groundbreaking, but unmanageable. In part, the Coalition's dilemmas were due to the fraught organizational dynamics and political opportunities in the country, but, more broadly, they reflect the dilemmas of mobilizing around a malleable intervention onto which individuals can place their complementary, competing, or contradictory hopes and desires. This disruptive instrumentalization points to how the malleability of transitional justice and truth commissions can be both an asset and a liability, particularly in countries where there are such deep divisions. Actors may hear what they want to hear about what a truth commission will do for them. Those hoping a truth commission will reinforce judicial decisions may support one, just as those hoping a truth commission will challenge judicial decisions will support one. Survivors with different narratives about the violence may see a commission as useful to be sure their story is told in a public forum, just as political leaders who want to show that their country is socially, politically, and economically sound may see a truth commission as useful for this endeavor. Thus, actors may readily agree to create one.

[70] The event was organized by the Catholic Relief Services and was almost canceled when participating organizations expressed concerns about the fact that USAID funded it. The United States is not particularly popular in BiH, as there are many concerns about its actions in the Middle East and perceived anti-Muslim sentiment.

However, actors with competing or contradictory goals will want a truth commission to do too many things. This case reveals that promoting the procedural aspects of a truth commission may initially help overcome this challenge. Yet, if everyone affected by a truth commission has a say in how one is designed, it will be impossible to actually create a satisfactory one. Individuals in the Balkans, as in many other settings where there has been mass violence, will inevitably be disappointed because they will have not only different, but directly contradictory, hopes and desires for what a truth commission can and should accomplish. Actors may believe that a regional truth commission could bring about the social and political change that they are seeking. However, its malleability means a truth commission is more likely to reflect the social and political dynamics than to change it.

Though it is unclear if there will be a truth commission in the region, the instrumentalization of transitional justice, particularly through the Coalition for RECOM's work, did have other impacts on Bosnian society. While the previous chapter reveals the creation of elites at the transnational level, this case reveals a trickle-down effect in which the movement's professionalization can create elites within regions and nations. The Coalition would not have received the material and nonmaterial support that it did if it had not been helped along by the ICTJ, as well as other transnational scholars, policy makers, and advocates who were interested in creating a truth commission under the banner of transitional justice. The Coalition's leaders were already prominent in civil society, but by appropriating and promoting transitional justice, they gained both domestic and international recognition for this effort. Prominent actors in BiH who rejected the commission also gained public recognition for their position. Finally, other domestic organizations that appropriated transitional justice found themselves with new access to funding and support, and they will likely continue to draw on transitional justice until another idea becomes more useful for them.

Moreover, as transnational professionals provided training and political actors drew on transitional justice to describe their work, they helped spread the idealistic discourse about what a truth commission could offer, namely reconciliation. Organizations such as the UNDP and the ICMP also drew explicitly on the idea to explain new strategies to supplement the influential but divisive work of the ICTY. These efforts to promote transitional justice in BiH may not have focused explicitly on courts, but they reaffirmed the belief that criminal prosecutions are an important, if not necessary, strategy for redressing mass violence. In particular, the Coalition for RECOM's leaders decided to endorse the tribunal's highly contested findings of genocide. The ICMP, too, used transitional justice in efforts to make sure that their work on judicial accountability would bridge divides. Despite growing concerns about the ICTY's divisiveness in the region, these initiatives reinforced the importance of using tribunals to ensure accountability, improve survivor well-being, and prevent future violence.

The next chapter, on Colombia, reveals similar dynamics in terms of how the malleability of transitional justice made it a useful tool for political actors in Colombia. Just as in the Balkans, however, the malleability of transitional justice meant that actors with contradictory goals could agree that the idea and its associated interventions, particularly truth commissions, would be useful to help bridge social and political divisions in the country. However, given the strikingly different organizational dynamics and political opportunities in Colombia, the instrumentalization of transitional justice in Colombia was different. While translating the idea into political action reflected and even exacerbated existing divisions in the country, its instrumentalization also helped facilitate a peace accord with two different sets of armed actors.

4

Transformation

The Politics of Peace in Colombia

In 2016, the Colombian government signed a peace accord with the oldest guerrilla group in the western hemisphere, the Revolutionary Armed Forces of Colombia, or FARC. Opponents to the accord, led by Senator Alvaro Uribe, called the accord – particularly the way it drew on transitional justice – a "framework for impunity." Ironically, this was not the first time that Uribe spoke about transitional justice. In 2005, then President Uribe succeeded in pushing Law 975 through the legislature by referring to it as a transitional justice process. This law, also known as the Justice and Peace Law, created an alternative judicial process for demobilizing paramilitaries as well as the National Commission on Reparation and Reconciliation (NCRR), which scholars referred to a "sort of truth commission" (Laplante and Theidon 2006).

When I first went to Colombia in 2010 to study understandings of transitional justice, staff at several advocacy organizations initially refused to participate in my study, saying "we don't believe in transitional justice" (Rowen forthcoming).[71] These actors saw the idea as foreign, and part of Uribe's plan to ensure impunity for the paramilitary. However, in the course of a decade, transitional justice shifted from being seen in some circles a useless academic enterprise and part of Uribe's plan to absolve the paramilitary of liability for their crimes to being enshrined in Colombia's constitution, part and parcel of the government's day-to-day functions, and a key factor in the government peace accords with the FARC. To a large extent, this transformation happened because of how political actors drew on the idea of transitional justice. They passed laws such as the 2011 Victims Law, which provided reparations to a fraction of the millions of the conflict's victims, and called itself a transitional justice law.[72] In 2012, the government passed the Legal Framework

[71] Parts of this chapter appear in my forthcoming article on Colombia in *Law and Social Inquiry* (Rowen forthcoming).

[72] In the course of the conflict, over 7,000,000 individuals have been displaced, over 200,000 killed, and many more have been raped or tortured, lost their livelihood, and suffered other abuses.

for Peace, which was the constitutional amendment that permitted the government to create "transitional justice instruments" and mandated the creation of a truth commission, in a peace accord with the FARC.

With this law as the framework for the negotiations, the Colombian government, under the leadership of Juan Manuel Santos, and the FARC came to the historic agreement in August 2016. The accord came after four years of negotiations, nearly half of which was devoted to the question of transitional justice, which, by then, referred to the dilemmas posed by ensuring victims' rights to truth, justice, and reparation while incentivizing armed actors to demobilize. However, just as quickly as the optimism for peace arose, it quickly dissipated when a referendum approving the peace accord failed to receive a majority of votes. Colombians voted against the Octoer 2, 2016 accord for many reasons, prominent among which was the rejection of transitional justice for the guerrilla.

Looking at the evolving understandings of transitional justice in Colombia and the role of transitional justice in the peace accords, I characterize the instrumentalization of transitional justice in Colombia as transformative. This is not to suggest that the conditions that led to the violence changed, that the violence stopped, or that it will stop, given that the underlying structures that contributed to the violence have not changed. However, understandings of transitional justice changed over this period, and translating transitional justice into political action shifted the parameters and possibilities of peace accords with armed actors. The instrumentalization of transitional justice opened a space for victims to make claims against the government, for the guerrillas to agree to the terms of a peace deal, for the government to market that peace deal to a skeptical public, and for opponents of the peace accords to condemn the Santos administration.

Building on the previous chapters, this case further shows the malleability of transitional justice and truth commissions by showing how the idea was instrumentalized in a country where there was no clear political transition. In fact, both the idea and intervention were promoted as tools to end violence, not simply to redress it. In addition, the case reveals that this same malleability is both an asset and a liability for actors that promote such commissions. In Colombia, actors with contradictory agendas were able to agree to create a truth commission, yet are unlikely to be able to reconcile their different goals for a truth commission.

To make this argument, this chapter begins with a description of the conflict, followed by an examination of how transitional justice entered Colombian politics when the Uribe administration pushed through the Justice and Peace Law of 2005. It points out the contested understandings of transitional justice. Early on, skeptical advocates resisted the policy makers and transitional justice professionals who tried to convince them of the utility of this new idea, despite the fact that the armed conflict was ongoing. Understandings of the idea shifted through new legislation that drew on transitional justice, particularly the 2011 Victims Law and the Legal Framework for Peace.

Throughout this process, transitional justice served as a placeholder for political actors with different perspectives on the peace process to make claims against one another. In addition, actors with contradictory agendas came to agree that a truth commission was necessary, but they had different opinions on what a truth commission should do. This chapter also points out how, as occurred in the Balkans, the idea's instrumentalization helped create new elites, fostered an idealistic discourse, and reaffirmed the belief that criminal prosecutions are an important, if not necessary, strategy for redressing mass violence. Many actors in Colombia viewed, and continue to view, transitional justice as a lesser form of justice if it does not require prosecutions for both domestic and international crimes.

Finally, although questions about incarceration and a truth commission came to dominate media and political analyses of the peace process, Colombia's social and political divisions are deep-rooted. The malleability of a truth commission and the hopes and desires that various actors have for one imply that creating one may ultimately reproduce those divisions.

BACKGROUND ON AN INTRACTABLE CONFLICT

In Colombia, the idea of transitional justice does not refer to a past conflict but, rather, to an ongoing conflict between guerilla groups, paramilitary groups, the military, and conflict entrepreneurs such as drug traffickers and corporations that profit from Colombia's many natural resources. The length of the conflict, its complexity, and Colombia's democratic history all shape how actors think about the conflict and, thus, the meaning of transitional justice in the country.

The country has suffered from violence since its declaration of independence from Spain in 1811, and this legacy shapes the current conflict. Throughout the nineteenth century, the country was engulfed in civil wars that entrenched divides between the conservative and liberal factions in society. The most violent period in the country's history was between 1948 and 1957, after the liberal leader Gaitan was assassinated. The ensuing war between the conservatives and liberals left 300,000 people dead. After 1957, the National Front unified the two political parties and left little room for the growing communist movement. Communists moved to the countryside and claimed control of a territory known as Marquetalia. After a government crackdown in 1964, the FARC emerged to defend the communists and began expropriating land for its revolution. Wealthy landowners sought to defend themselves and, with the support of the political leaders in various locales, paramilitary groups emerged. The conflict took a new turn with the drug war of the 1970s and 1980s. Earlier ideological commitments to communism merged with interest in controlling the drug routes. By the end of the 1990s, the United States began funding the Colombian military to eradicate the drug trade, and the influx of arms heightened the violence in the countryside.

By the 1980s, the violence reached the cities, and calls for government reform reached fever pitch, as even urban elites did not feel safe in the country. Armed groups engaged in peace negotiations with the government, and amnesties and legal benefits for demobilized actors were common. When the FARC demobilized in the 1980s, it joined with the Colombian Communist Party to form the United Patriotic Front, winning elections in the countryside and in the cities. Paramilitary groups, armed forces of the state, and narco-traffickers responded by targeting the political party's leadership. Over 3000 party members were killed in what is known as *el Baile Rojo*, or the Red Dance. The FARC went back to fighting, and its distrust of the government grew.

The year 1985 marked a turning point in the conflict, as the guerrillas targeted the country's capital. The M-19 guerrillas, initially a group of urban communists, besieged the Palace of Justice in downtown Bogotá with the goal of putting President Betancur and his defense minister on trial for violating the peace accords they had signed a year and a half earlier. The ensuing battle with the military left over 100 people dead, including eleven Supreme Court justices. When the M-19 guerrilla group finally demobilized at the end of the 1980s, its members demanded electoral reform. The former guerillas immediately became active in the government and helped create new opportunities for constitutional reform. After leaders of the drug trade organized the assassination of the liberal leader Galan in August 1989, local protests finally pressured the government to hold a referendum for a Constitutional Assembly. Reformers hoped a new constitution would lead to peace in the country.

In 1991, Colombia emerged with one of the most progressive constitutions in the world, guaranteeing a healthy environment, public morality, and other novel rights. It also established an independent Constitutional Court that could hear challenges to legislation related to war and peace. Article 22 guarantees that "peace is a right and duty whose compliance is mandatory," and Article 29 guarantees that "in penal cases, a permissive or favorable law, even when ex post facto, will be applied in preference to restrictive or unfavorable alternatives." These new provisions provided the executive branch with greater latitude in negotiating peace accords, while also requiring that the government adequately sanction perpetrators. The government had not previously been deterred from providing amnesties to demobilizing actors. Laws 77 from 1989, 104 from 1993, and 418 from 1997 and Decrees 206 from 1990, 213 from 1991, and 1943 from 1991 all included some form of alternative criminal sentence or no criminal sentence for illegal actors. These laws were almost exclusively focused on the rights of armed actors, not the rights of victims. Finally, the government began passing laws to aid victims. Law 387 from 1997 provided indemnification for forced displacement and was a political milestone in recognizing that millions of individuals have suffered from the conflict.

Due to the country's history of democratic political institutions, Colombia's educated classes share an understanding of justice that Lemaitre Ripoll (2009) refers to as legal fetishism, which also shapes how they understand transitional justice. With the new Constitution, political decisions regarding peace had to withstand the scrutiny of the Constitutional Court. In addition, Colombia is party to the American

Convention on Human Rights and has granted jurisdiction to the Interamerican Court for Human Rights (IACHR). By 2015, the IACHR had ruled on the Colombian conflict fourteen times, requiring that the government investigate and punish human rights violations, provide information about individuals who were killed or disappeared, and adequately compensate victims. This court, like the Constitutional Court, was particularly concerned about the "false positives" scandal of 2008, in which the Colombian military was found to have killed civilians and dressed them as guerrillas. Moreover, in 1999, Colombia became a party to the Rome Statute, the treaty that created the International Criminal Court (ICC). The ICC has jurisdiction over the international crimes of crimes against humanity, war crimes, and genocide.[73] On March 2, 2005, the ICC Prosecutor alerted the Colombian government that it was investigating Colombia's responses to international crimes, making Colombia the first country outside of Africa that the ICC flagged for investigation.

Given its domestic, regional, and international legal obligations, as well as its interest in getting domestic and international support for its peace negotiations, the government began looking for new ways to explain and legitimate its demobilization efforts.

INTRODUCING TRANSITIONAL JUSTICE: TRUTH, JUSTICE, AND REPARATION

Soon after Alvaro Uribe was elected in 2002, his administration began a concerted effort to demobilize the paramilitary apparatus in the country. By then, the country's disparate paramilitary groups had joined under the umbrella organization of the AUC (United Self-Defense of Colombia) and decided to put down their arms. Like armed actors before them, the paramilitary wanted legal benefits such as protection from prosecution and financial support for reintegrating into civilian life. However, with the changing legal landscape, the government was no longer able to provide blanket amnesties and was under domestic and international pressure to investigate acts of violence and compensate victims.

Uribe's *mano duro*, or heavy hand, against the guerrillas curried favor with those who viewed the guerrillas as terrorists, and it was clear that he did not want to punish the paramilitaries as harshly as the guerrillas. Uribe's father, a wealthy landowner, was killed by the FARC in a kidnapping attempt. He would not acknowledge the existence of an armed conflict or its millions of victims, preferring instead to frame the guerrilla violence as terrorism and efforts to combat the violence as counterterrorism. As mayor of Medellín, Uribe had openly supported Convivir, which many consider to be a paramilitary group, to help protect Medellín residents from ongoing guerrilla threats. Convivir was later restricted from gathering intelligence and using military grade weapons, which effectively made it illegal.

[73] In 2017, the ICC may also have jurisdiction over the crime of aggression, but, due to the fact that Colombia's conflict is internal, this crime does not apply.

In the 2003 demobilization process, known as the Ralito Pact, former paramilitary members agreed to put down their arms, offer information about themselves and colleagues, and allow themselves to be monitored by the International Organization for Migration in order to assess their ongoing reintegration. However, after the Ralito Pact, the government had to develop a plan for dealing with paramilitary crimes. At first, leaders drew on the idea of restorative justice to explain their plan to sanction demobilizing actors. In proposed legislation on the demobilization of paramilitary groups, known as the *Ley de Alternatividad Penal*, the law's drafters mentioned the need for reconciliation, reparation, and forgiveness.

During these negotiations, the idea of transitional justice was just beginning to circulate in the country. As early as 2003, Ivan Orozco, a political scientist at Los Andes University, published articles on how the idea of transitional justice might inform the Colombian peace processes.[74] Pablo de Greiff, whose father was a prominent jurist in Colombia, enlisted his colleagues at the ICTJ to help consult with the government on its *Ley de Alternatividad Penal*. Both Lisa Magarrel and Mark Freeman, transitional justice professionals from the ICTJ, provided extensive comments on the law, pointing out factual and legal inaccuracies in the government's arguments for amnesty. In a report for the Colombian research group Fundación Social, the consultants suggested that the government integrate transitional justice into its proposed law:

> It is necessary to construct a politics of peace that includes elements of transitional justice. In other words, it is about creating a comprehensive idea of justice that is responsive to the urgent need for peace but that does not lose sight of the inalienable principles of truth, justice, and reparation.[75]

This document reveals how, from the beginning of its circulation in Colombia, actors explained transitional justice in Colombia as an idea that could help end violence, not simply help countries where violence had ceased. Moreover, they equated it with claims to truth, justice, and reparation – principles that the Constitutional Court and the Interamerican Court held must be considered in peace settlements. According to Magarrel and Freeman, truth refers to the individual right to know what happened to a loved one, as well as the goal of memory, or creating a "history of oppression" that would help avoid future violence. Justice refers mainly to judicial accountability in which a court provides a sanction that is effective and proportional. Reparation refers to financial compensation to the millions of victims who lost their property and livelihoods, as well as other forms of indemnity and psychological support.

74 Sanchez, L.M., 2015. *Justicia: An Ordinary Language Analysis*. Unpublished manuscript, on file with author.

75 Fundación Social, *Documento de Recomendaciones Sobre el Proyecto de ley Estatutaria No. 85 de 2003-Senado*, translated by author, e-archivo.uc3m.es/bitstream/handle/10016/19155/FCI-2004-6-botero.pdf?sequence=1.

The *Ley de Alternatividad Penal* did not pass Congress, and was heavily criticized for its leniency toward paramilitary offenders. Domestic and international observers were upset that the law might allow amnesties for clear violations of domestic and international law and did not require that perpetrators disclose information about their crimes. In response to this defeat, the Uribe administration became more interested in how the idea of transitional justice might serve its interests (Uprimny and Saffon 2008). For Uribe, the malleability of the idea seemed useful to show how his demobilization policy would serve his interests and those of his constituents.

PRESENTING THE JUSTICE AND PEACE LAW AS TRANSITIONAL JUSTICE

In 2005, the Uribe Administration succeeded in passing Law 975, also known as the Justice and Peace Law, a policy that many now refer to as the "first transitional justice law" in the country. The Justice and Peace Law created an alternative judicial process with a different set of punishments for paramilitaries than the criminal justice system's rules allow. In the judicial process, applicants for benefits, primarily former paramilitary members, were required to provide free confessions (*versiones libres*) to all crimes committed, and to indicate all illegally gained property and goods. These goods were to be delivered to the Reparation Fund for victims of violence. In a second session, a prosecutor would interrogate the applicant, and victims or their representatives could ask questions and present additional evidence. Those found guilty would receive a prison sentence of five to eight years, far less than if they were convicted through the regular court process.

In 2010, a policy maker involved in designing the Justice and Peace Law explained to me that "transitional justice is the best instrument to go from war to peace in our case, or dictatorship to democracy in the Chilean case." He explained his belief that "transitional justice makes political interpretation very flexible, which is what is needed for these changes" (interview with Colombian policy maker 2010). More specifically, this policy maker hoped that judges would not be bound by the criminal code when dealing with armed actors who were willing to demobilize. His concern was that "Colombian judges don't even know what transitional justice is, state officials don't either." He expressed worry that the government was "limping" along in its demobilization efforts, and that this ignorance "is a major pedagogical failure because some people are stuck to legality" (ibid.).

Legality, in this context, refers to the legal requirement that all individuals accused of certain acts of violence must be held accountable and punished according to existing statutes. From his perspective, appropriating and promoting transitional justice was a way to explain and legitimize the administration's interest in discouraging a strict application of the criminal code to paramilitary groups. He believed that judges should not sentence paramilitaries as harshly as they would individuals who are not affiliated with paramilitary groups.

These reflections on transitional justice provide insights into how the idea's malleability, particularly its ambiguity on the issue of judicial accountability, made it very useful for policy makers interested in pursuing peace accords that would withstand legal, as well as political, challenges. For domestic advocates skeptical of this policy, in contrast, demanding truth, justice, and reparation became a way to show their concern that this law, and the idea of transitional justice, was simply a cover for Uribe's plan to demobilize the paramilitary without adequately punishing them for their crimes (Diaz 2008).

DEFINING TRANSITIONAL JUSTICE IN THE COURTS

Soon after the Justice and Peace Law passed, advocacy groups, led by Gustavo Gallon at the Colombian Commission of Jurists (CCJ), petitioned the Constitutional Court to assert Colombia's obligations to ensure due process for victims. The ruling in *Gustavo Gallón Giraldo y Otros v. Colombia* was interpretive, meaning it clarified which of the provisions were constitutional and which were not. In doing so, it provided a foundation for laws addressing the future peace negotiations with the FARC. In decision C-370 of 2006, the Court asserted that the Justice and Peace Law struck an acceptable balance between the right to peace, enshrined in the Constitution, and the rights of victims to judicial accountability, confessions from perpetrators, and reparations. The Court ruled that the legislation was, in general terms, constitutional, but it also ruled that several of its provisions are unconstitutional.

In particular, on the question of the right to truth, the judges found that if the demobilized actors lied or committed new crimes, they could risk losing their reduced sentences. The Court decreed that, as a prerequisite for judicial benefits, confessions must be complete and truthful for the accused to receive a reduced sentence. Moreover, the accused must declare, jointly or severally, all their legally or illegally acquired assets. The judges also found that the classification of victims must be broader than that originally established in the law. The Court held that paramilitary members could not be treated as if they had committed political crimes, which would have given them legal cover, because they were not acting against the state. Moreover, the ruling stated that their crime, aggravated conspiracy, amounts to a crime against humanity and they could not be pardoned. Finally, the Court found that prosecutors did not have discretion to suspend or avoid prosecution, a legal doctrine known as the principle of opportunity.

All of these findings created dilemmas that the government wanted to address in its peace negotiations with the FARC, and it drew on the idea of transitional justice to do so. Partly, they knew that the Court might look favorably upon this framing. In its decision on the Justice and Peace Law, the Court drew on the idea of transitional instruments, a precursor to its later rulings on transitional justice, to explain how it was balancing rights to truth, justice, and reparation with rights to peace:

> The pursuit of peace is a complex legal entity, as a collective right, an essential purpose of the Colombian state and a constitutional value. Therefore, the State has the authority to provide reasonable transitional instruments, justified and proportionate, even limiting other constitutional guarantees, in order to achieve peace.[76]

The Constitutional Court further explained these transitional instruments as part of a new "theoretical frame":

> About the rights of victims and based on the same theoretical frame, the Court rules that these rights are complex and could not be reduced in an indemnity for the damage caused. Instead, it includes the right to know the truth about the facts of the crime, the right to justice, i.e. that the criminals will be prosecuted, judged and punished; and the right to damage compensation (moral and economical), and the guarantee of nonrepetition of criminal acts.[77]

The "theoretical frame" that the Court references was transitional justice, though it did not use the phrase. As described in the Attorney General's report on the implementation of the Justice and Peace Law, transitional justice became shorthand for a wide range of goals: "the realization of victims' rights to the truth, justice and reparation, the strengthening of state policies on demobilization, demilitarization and reintegration, the fight against impunity, truth, attention and holistic reparation to the victims of the armed conflict."[78] Whereas, in the Balkans, nongovernmental actors tried to get the government interested in transitional justice, in Colombia, various branches of the government saw its utility and tried to translate it in order to help the country end its decades-long armed conflict.

PROMOTING TRANSITIONAL JUSTICE

By drawing on transitional justice, the Uribe administration opened the country to an influx of international attention for its new strategy to end the ongoing violence. As a staff member at the research-oriented organization De Justicia suggested, Colombia was "*de moda*," or fashionable, for foreign donors and other actors interested in supporting organizations working on peace and justice issues. During my fieldwork in 2010, I attended weekly public events on the Justice and Peace Law and encountered a wide variety of advocacy organizations focused on how Colombia could make peace while ensuring rights to truth, justice, and reparation. This same researcher suggested that "if you stay here for a year, you are going to attend twenty-five international seminars on [transitional justice]. It's incredible." He went on to describe the many

76 Constitutional Court, Sentence C-370, english.corteconstitucional.gov.co/sentences/C-370-2006.pdf (accessed May 21, 2015).

77 Ibid.

78 Government of Colombia, Procuraduria Nacional, Observatorio de Justicia Transitional, Transitional Justice in Colombia: A Process in Construction, www.procuraduria.gov.co/portal/media/file/Justicia%20Transicional%202005%20-%202010%281%29.pdf (accessed July 14, 2015).

transitional justice professionals that came to the country: "Name one international expert and I can tell, ninety percent of them have been in Colombia in the past three years. Jon Elster was here; we actually brought him for a conference in Los Andes. Scott Lakey, Pablo [de Grieff] of course comes very often. Ruti Teitel came too."

Much like UNDP staff in Sarajevo, he was also concerned about how much useful information these leaders brought. "I would say, except for Pablo [de Grieff], I don't think many of them know the particularities of Colombia. It is more like the United Nations idea of best practices and lessons learned, like, this worked here, don't do this, in terms of mechanisms." At the same time, he noted that the "conceptual idea of transitional justice" was shaping Colombian policy due to the ways in which policy makers drew on it to explain and legitimize the Justice and Peace Law (interview with De Justicia staffer 2010). Despite his misgivings about abstract presentations, from his perspective transitional justice offered a "comprehensive" approach to truth, justice, and reparations and was helpful in his organization's work discussing the trade-offs that the government would have to make as it pursued peace agreements.

De Justicia was not the only organization interested in promoting the idea of transitional justice to help Colombians think about how to make peace with armed actors while ensuring victims' rights. Most Colombian advocates, and even policy makers, immediately mentioned the ICTJ's staff when discussing their understandings of transitional justice. The ICTJ's Bogotá office opened shortly after the enactment of Law 975 and quickly became the largest and best resourced of the organization's regional offices. For years, the office was located in a beautiful converted house in an upscale suburb of Bogotá, far from the bustle of downtown. Individuals who worked with the ICTJ came to play important roles in Colombian politics, bringing the idea of transitional justice with them. Catalina Diaz worked in the ICTJ's New York office, helped found the Bogotá office, and later played an instrumental role in the peace process with the FARC after taking a job in the Santos administration. One of the Bogotá office's early directors, Javier Ciurlizza, left the organization to run the Latin America Program at the International Crisis Group (ICG). After Ciurlizza's arrival, ICG also began drawing on the idea of transitional justice in explaining how to help resolve the conflict (interview with ICG staffer 2015).

Scholars were also quick to appropriate transitional justice, integrating the idea into academic programs related to the conflict. As noted, as early as 2003, scholars were writing about transitional justice's utility in Colombia's peace negotiations (Orozco 2003). In 2010, three Colombian professors of law and political science mentioned that their students were increasingly interested in the conflict and peace negotiations and that they were incorporating the idea of transitional justice into their courses. With new courses and ongoing seminars on transitional justice at elite universities in the capital, such as Los Andes, Rosario, and Nacional, a new generation of lawyers and other interested youth learned about transitional justice, and a new generation of scholars published articles, books, and reports on how the idea could help inform Colombia's peace processes. Moreover, given that there are regular exchanges between professors at these elite universities and government officials (many of them went to these same universities), these academics also had an influence on policy making.

By instrumentalizing transitional justice, all of these actors came to play an important role in transforming understandings of transitional justice in the country and paving the way for future peace accords. However, to be effective, they had to appease actors with contradictory perspectives on how to adequately ensure truth, justice, and reparation.

A MALLEABLE IDEA IN A CHALLENGING SETTING

As these transnational and domestic actors translated transitional justice into political action, they faced skepticism from domestic organizations that were wary of this new foreign idea and, more importantly, of how the government was utilizing it to explain and legitimize the Justice and Peace Law. The director of a victims' association, for instance, coupled her understanding of transitional justice with a critique of the ICTJ, stating, "there are organizations here like the ICTJ that are trying their hardest to say that there is a process of transition here in Colombia. We don't agree." Her concern was that transitional justice is a euphemism for impunity: "If transition is amnesty or impunity, there is no point in it." She used the word "truth and justice" to explain how to make peace, but saw transitional justice as a phrase that the government used to tell people to "forget about" their loss even "when they have to see the person who murdered their family member in the mayoralty" or elsewhere. She said that "it is very difficult" to accept the idea of transitional justice given this reality (interview with Colombian victims' association director 2010).

Actors such as this interviewee contested transitional justice, and the individuals and organizations promoting it, by asserting their rights to truth, justice, and reparation (Diaz 2008). The ICTJ's challenges, in particular, highlight how the malleability of transitional justice created dilemmas for the actors who initially promoted it. During our interviews, three staff members at the ICTJ-Colombia office mentioned that some domestic advocates refused to engage with them simply because of their organization's name. Staff struggled to clarify that they were not working on behalf of the government and that transitional justice was not a euphemism for impunity. In 2010, Michael Reed Hurtado, a lawyer trained in the United States, directed ICTJ-Colombia. Drawing from his background in human rights advocacy against the state, Hurtado was critical of the Justice and Peace Law. He worried that the government was using the idea of transitional justice to legitimize policies that did not adequately ensure victims' rights. Hurtado even participated in the 2010 IACHR case against the government for the murder of Manuel Cepeda, an assassinated leader of the Union Patriótica. In his writing and public speaking, Hurtado was emphatic that the government needed to recognize the existence of an armed conflict and its own role in fomenting violence.

Given his work to expose the government's involvement in violence, Hurtado found himself in a professional bind as a supposed proponent of transitional justice. While domestic advocates were concerned that the ICTJ was trying to justify the Justice and Peace Law, policy makers involved in the Interamerican Court case criticized Hurtado and, by association, the ICTJ for working against the government. Hurtado also encountered challenges from the ICTJ's leadership in New York, which did not want him to be such a vocal advocate against the government's policies. The ICTJ's leadership preferred to work with governments, not against them. However, critics of Uribe's policies could not ignore how the president promoted transitional justice and yet denied the existence of an armed conflict and, by extension, its millions of victims. Hurtado eventually left the organization and continued his research and advocacy at Yale University. The next director was much less critical of the government, and worked closely with the New York headquarters to help the peace accords with the FARC.

Apart from their concerns about how the Uribe administration was using the idea of transitional justice, advocates were also concerned about the utility of this seemingly foreign idea. In one example among many, the director of an organization that provides educational services and resources to indigenous communities near Santa Marta explained to me that transitional justice "experts" lack understanding of local practices:

> I hoped to get from them something I didn't already know, but something that I could also apply to my experience here. But when I go somewhere and there's the expert that thinks that we are just empty vessels to be filled without taking into account what we already have in our heads, just because they have many diplomas . . . what I end up thinking is what a waste of money on presentations and arrows and flashy things. (Interview with victims' association director 2010)

This Colombian advocate spent decades working with victims in the north of Colombia. She suggested that transitional justice is simply a term used by scholars rather than something useful for individuals working with survivors. Similarly, another advocate succinctly summarized his belief that transnational actors promoting transitional justice are "well-intentioned" but "in another world":

> I think that they are well-intentioned academics, studious people who have a prodigious mind, they have a good memory but they aren't working in reality, this is the impression I have. The problem of the academics and these types is that they think they know everything and all can be resolved in a library or computer. And the reality is different, I am sorry to say. I am sorry to say because we always generate a debate and confrontation with these types of people because we are here in the reality accompanying the victims and we know the tragedy and we are helping where we can and we are making organizational processes. These academics are in another world. (Interview with director of Colombian advocacy organization 2010)

As in the Balkans, this skepticism has as much to do with the organizational dynamics and political opportunities in the country as it does with concerns about the intermediaries that were promoting transitional justice. In 2010, when Uribe was President, distrust between the government and advocacy organizations, particularly those with left-leaning agendas, was extreme. Drawing on a malleable legal and political idea, for Uribe's critics, was simply a way to avoid concrete remedies. The director of an organization that engaged in lawsuits against the government expressed his disdain for transitional justice by saying, "there are either human rights or there are no human rights; that is to say, they kill or they don't kill, they disappear or they don't disappear." His concern with transitional justice was that it was too malleable, though he did not use this terminology. Rather, he explained that "in terms of human rights, the consequences are concrete. Either there is complete historical truth independent of the legality, either there is justice or there is impunity, either there is complete reparation or a remedy of this type, or there is prevention and guarantees of no repetition. [Either this] or the conflict continues and then there is a more serious violation" (interview with director of Colombian advocacy organization 2010).

For this lawyer, transitional justice is simply a lesser form of justice, without clear standards that will guarantee victims' rights. Another lawyer, Gustavo Gallon, from *Gustavo Gallon Giraldo y Otros v. Colombia*, became famous as an outspoken advocate of legal standards that precluded amnesties for human rights violations. His organization, the CCJ, took up two floors in a large downtown building, which revealed how well funded (partly by the Ford Foundation) the organization was throughout the 2000s. The organization drew the enmity of the government for its success in lawsuits against the Colombian government, both in the Constitutional Court and in the IACHR.

According to a Colombian government official, concerns about transitional justice, particularly the call for prosecutions, had to do with "a level of polarization where the government is the enemy in the victims' eyes." He continued to describe the "zoology" of NGOs, with "every color, every brand." His concern was that the human rights organizations fight for victims' rights, but their goal is lawsuits in front of international bodies that will demand reparations. He suggested that "they get paid in dollars; these are privileged lawyers that collect 30% in dollars for their own pocket." He criticized the "humanitarian" side of these people (interview with Colombian government official 2010).

This official also explained that transitional justice was a useful idea because it enabled the government to point out the need for alternative sanctions, and criticized organizations that denied the need for such a policy.

Looking at these different perspectives on the idea and how different actors drew on it, one sees that transitional justice served as a placeholder for these different actors to articulate their beliefs about law as a tool for social and political change. They also drew on it to express their hopes and desires for the future, and to make claims against one another. A future truth commission, too, served as a placeholder for different groups to debate their understandings of truth, justice and reparation, and became a symbol of what a transition and justice might entail.

THE "SORT OF" TRUTH COMMISSION

After the Justice and Peace Law, understandings of transitional justice in Colombia were also closely coupled with understandings of truth commissions. The director of a victims' association, for example, answered a question about her understandings of transitional justice by referring to the NCRR as part of the "fad" for transitional justice that emerged from "copying what happened in other countries" (interview with victims' association director 2010).

From this advocate's perspective, transitional justice, exemplified by the NCRR, was yet another tool for pacifying victims' claims to truth, justice, and reparations. At the same time, the NCRR represented what a future truth commission might offer.

According to Article 52 of the Justice and Peace Law, the NCRR would be responsible for (1) guaranteeing victims participation in the judicial process; (2) ensuring follow-up and verification of reintegration and reparations; (3) submitting a report on victims' reparation progress; (4) recommending criteria for victim compensation; (5) promoting national reconciliation; and (6) overseeing regional offices. Scholars referred to the NCRR as a "sort of" truth commission because of the Commission's Historical Memory Group, which worked separately from the unit in charge of reparations (Laplante and Theidon 2006). The Historical Memory Group was created to fulfill the Commission's mandate to produce a "public report on the reasons for the illegal armed actors' creation and evolution" from 1964 onward.[79]

The NCRR appeared to be an innovative new strategy in the government's efforts to ensure truth, justice, and reparation. As opposed to other investigative bodies, the Commission operated independent of government interference, at least in the beginning. The Commission was mandated to operate for a period of eight years, overseen by Uribe's Vice President Francisco Santos and Eduardo Pizarro, a former M-19 guerilla member. However, Santos did not interfere in the Commission's work, and Pizarro went to work implementing the Commission's mandate. In its twelve offices throughout the country, the Commission took statements of victims and provided financial compensation. Five commissioners were civil society leaders, including Patricia Buritica, a well-respected labor rights activist, and Jaime Jaramillo, a lawyer and peace activist who maintained his support for a peace accord with the FARC even when his oldest son was killed by one of its members. Two commissioners were representatives from victims' associations, including one long-time victims' rights advocate who coordinated a national network of victims' associations.

The commissioners received training on transitional justice and saw it as malleable enough to apply to the Colombia case. One commissioner explained to me the common understanding of transitional justice as "accepting a process in which

[79] Historical Memory Group, www.centrodememoriahistorica.gov.co (accessed June 12, 2012).

we can accomplish truth, justice and reparation in the midst of the conflict." She continued to explain that transitional justice is "an alternative justice, that offers on one hand some benefits for the offenders so they start feeling obligated to [tell] the truth, to submit themselves to justice and to the redressing of their victims. But on the other hand, a justice that also allows during this period, during this process, for victims to have their corresponding rights to truth, justice, and reparation" (interview with NCRR commissioner 2010).

She, like others who approved of the idea, understood transitional justice as broad enough to fit the Colombian context. For this commissioner, the idea was not merely a set of interventions after a conflict ends, but an idea that can help end a conflict. For skeptics, however, the idea was too self-serving for the Uribe administration. These actors pointed out that the NCRR compensation scheme affirmed their perspective because victims of the guerrillas received the most money, victims of paramilitaries received less, and victims of the state (such as children of the Union Patriótica members) received none. The director of one of the NCRR's offices shared these concerns and described to me how he saw the Commission as part of Uribe's plan to absolve the state of its responsibility not only for contributing to the violence, but also to help the victims. He explained that he decided to use his position to encourage victims to organize and make further demands on the government (interview with NCRR staffer 2010).

He was not the only staffer worried about the Uribe administration's interests. By the end of 2011, Eduardo Pizarro had resigned from the NCRR, concerned that Uribe's new vice president and NCRR co-director was trying to take more control of the process than he was comfortable with.[80] The worry was that the administration's interest was not in victims but, rather, in ways to hasten the alternative judicial process created by the Justice and Peace Law. Around the time when Pizarro decided to leave, the executive declared that it would create an independent truth commission in order to clear up the courts clogged by petitions of the 17,000 former paramilitary members.[81] That truth commission never materialized, but it was clear that support for a commission was coming from below and from above, and for different reasons.

THE APPEAL OF VOICE

While the reparations proved problematic and the alternative sanctions for the paramilitary were roundly criticized, the Justice and Peace Law's focus on truth

[80] Radio Interview with Gonzalo Agudelo, former member of NCRR in el Meta, wradio.com.co, www.wradio.com.co/oir.aspx?id=1532041 (accessed August 26, 2011). Ironically, various commissioners felt more comfortable working under the Uribe administration, where they had more independence, than under the Santos administration, where they became part of the Vice-President's office.

[81] El Tiempo, "Salidas al Limbo Jurídico de Los Desmovilizadoes en Colombia," November 27, 2011, www.eltiempo.com/justicia/salidas-al-limbo-juridico-de-los-desmovilizados-en-colombia-_8464203-4 (accessed May 14, 2015).

came to symbolize the possibility of what a peace accord with guerrillas might bring about. In particular, the NCRR's Historical Memory Group shaped understandings of what a future truth commission might do for the country.

Advocacy organizations were initially skeptical of the Group, worried that it would be another voice of the government, meaning that it would produce a narrative of the violence that absolved the government of its responsibility in the conflict. However, their fears were quelled when Gonzalo Sanchez was appointed as director. Sanchez was a well-respected historian of the conflict and did not shy away from pointing out the government's and the paramilitaries' role in the violence. The Group was primarily academic in nature, "almost like an NGO in the state," according to one of its members. The Group conducted its work from the second floor of the NCRR's main building in Bogotá and conducted focus groups and trainings throughout the country.

Providing victims with the opportunity to speak was a central part of their agenda. When discussing their work with me, Group members not only emphasized the importance of creating an accurate historical record, but were emphatic that historical memory "carries out the role of making the voices of the victims be the main focus, which isn't the only aim, but it's one of the goals that are set from the beginning" (interview with Historical Memory Group member 2010).

Members of the Historical Memory Group did not see themselves as a truth commission, thinking that a truth commission would focus on a more comprehensive account of the violence. Moreover, they saw a truth commission as a body that would provide public hearings, which they did not think was possible in the middle of a conflict. In fact, during my fieldwork in 2010, all but two of my interviewees said that creating a truth commission was not possible because it was not safe for survivors to share their experiences. At the same time, they assumed that there would be a commission if the violence ended and they should prepare for one.

Advocacy groups, as well as government agencies, began developing their goals and strategies with a future truth commission in mind. One actor working for *Verdad Abierta*, or Open Truth, a website dedicated to publishing information on the violence, with a focus on violence perpetrated by state actors, explained how the project's originators envisioned it as similar to a truth commission. The International Center for Transitional Justice published a volume titled *Remembering in Conflict: Non-official Memory Initiatives in Colombia*. This latter volume notes that authors were not trying to supplant the state's obligations to create judicial and quasi-judicial bodies such as truth commissions but rather to provide preliminary information for future bodies and to instruct the government on democratic practice (Carrillo 2009).

Mayoralties also became involved in efforts to create a truth commission. In 2009, the mayor's office in Medellín published several edited volumes with survivors' narratives, and the mayor called for a truth commission that would focus solely on that city's violence. The mayor of Bogotá created its own Center for Memory and Reconciliation, a museum and research center that began researching and publishing edited volumes with essays on what a truth commission in Colombia could offer the country. These edited volumes contained contributions from domestic and foreign scholars and provided information about truth commissions in other countries and the importance of not only clarifying the causes and consequences of the violence, but also ensuring that there was an opportunity for survivors to share their stories.

Advocacy organizations were also preparing for a future truth commission, viewing this intervention as useful for their overall goals. As part of their advocacy campaign for victims of state violence, the Movimiento de Victimas de Crimines del Estado (MOVICE) brought together a variety of advocates from Colombia and elsewhere in Latin America to create a proposal for a future truth commission. The representative explained that NCRR was part of the government's plan to ensure impunity and that "there are no conditions for a commission." She continued by explaining that "what is important for organizations is to continue to document the cases and prepare ourselves for a future truth commission." Preparing for a future truth commission was a way to ensure that they would have a say in the one they knew would be created at the end of the conflict: "[A] person that has worked for the NCRR [and] belongs to the impunity process' side cannot be part of the Truth Commission. We consider it is important that victim organizations take part in deciding who those people would be" (interview with MOVICE representative 2010).

For this representative, both the process of creating a truth commission and a commission itself should provide an opportunity for victims to be part of policy making. Only then would she trust that there was a transition, or justice, in the country. This advocate coupled transitional justice and truth commissions, and saw advocating one as advocating the other. Despite not seeing a truth commission as politically viable in the middle of a conflict, they saw this intervention as malleable enough to meet their various goals and strategies. They could agree that a truth commission was important, but they did not yet have to decide what such a commission would focus on because their calls were merely hypothetical and used to show that the government was not meeting their demands.

TRANSFORMING TRANSITIONAL JUSTICE THROUGH THE VICTIMS LAW

During my observations in the BiH from 2009 through 2015, understandings of transitional justice remained stagnant as the political impasse continued. In Colombia, in contrast, the social and political changes were striking, as was the evolving instrumentalization of transitional justice. During Uribe's administration, there seemed little chance that the government would actually negotiate peace with guerrilla groups, little chance of an actual transition from violence to peace, and little chance of a truth commission in which survivors would feel safe participating.

Despite the lack of political opportunities to ensure victims' rights, for four years two liberal senators, Guillermo Rivera and Juan Fernando Christo, sought to pass legislation that would give victims some form of financial compensation. In 2011, these policy makers succeeded in passing Law 1448, known as the Victims Law. Drafters of Law 1448 invoked the term "transitional justice" in its preamble and emphasized that this law would help lead to reconciliation. The bill's prologue explains that the Victims Law was part of Colombia's "transitional justice policy," with the overall goal of the law being to show the government's interest in "integral reparation" for victims of the armed conflict, the "strengthening of the judicial and administrative apparatus," and generating the conditions to promote peace.

The law created three units, one on land restitution, one on compensation and reparation for victims, and one that changed the previously quasi-independent Historical Memory Group into a state agency called the Historical Memory Center. The Victims Law provided for restoration to victims of land that they owned but had been forced to leave, rights to compensation and damages, social services and support systems, legal protection in court proceedings, and protective security forces. It also allowed an exemption from military service for five years, the establishment of a national holiday in memory of those who lost their lives in the decades-long conflict, and the establishment of another memorial for victims' experiences. Finally, businesses implicated in the conflict could not sell court-determined displaced land without a judge's approval, and businesses could also be held financially responsible for their roles in perpetuating the conflict.

According to one of the law's drafters, calling this a transitional justice policy was strategic. The idea of transitional justice was important to indicate that this law was "exceptional," meaning that the indemnification would only last ten years and that it was not a permanent policy of payment for victims. In addition, it was aspirational, as these senators wanted to show that the conflict would end. These policy makers were well aware that the conflict was ongoing and, at the time they were drafting the bill, they did not see an end in sight. The idea of transition in transitional justice was a way to say that they were looking forward to the day when there would be peace in the country.

The Victims Law was certainly aspirational, and its passage reveals how the government used the idea to make certain trade-offs. The short-term nature of the indemnification and the definition of who counted as a victim and who counted as a perpetrator suggest that policy makers used this law, and the idea of transitional justice, to support a particular narrative of the violence. For example, early discussions about the bill included arguments that the bill should include those who were victims starting in April 1948, when Gaitan was killed. However, the government was responsible for much of the violence that occurred after Gaitan's assassination. The Senate decided that the law would only cover those who were victimized after 1985, the year that the M-19 guerilla group besieged the Palace of Justice. By setting 1985 as the starting date, the government avoided recognizing the millions of individuals affected by the violence in previous years, particularly the victims of the violence against the United Patriotic Front.

Deciding who received benefits, and how much, was central to the narrative of violence that the government wanted to promote. In addition to the preceding example, victims of narco-trafficking could not receive benefits under the Victims Law. One of the law's drafters explained that allowing narco-trafficking victims to claim benefits would elevate the narco-traffickers to a political status that was unacceptable. More specifically, recognizing victims of narco-traffickers could pave the way for these perpetrators to negotiate some form of judicial protection. From his perspective, despite the overlapping relationships between all of these armed actors, narco-trafficking must be treated as a common crime, and not one that deserves the "exceptional" legal measures that the guerrillas and paramilitary deserve.

With the Victims Law, the government was clearly trying to respond to complaints about the Justice and Peace Law. At the same time, the law fit within the government's interest in defining the conflict a certain way, and policy makers saw transitional justice as useful for that interest.

TRANSFORMING TRANSITIONAL JUSTICE THROUGH THE LEGAL FRAMEWORK FOR PEACE

The understanding of transitional justice behind the Victims Law – as temporary and as aspirational – provides key insights into the transformative role that the idea played in the peace negotiations with the FARC. Such an accord appeared impossible under Uribe, who was barred from running for a third term. He encouraged his former defense minister, Juan Manuel Santos, to run for the 2012 presidential race and thought that Santos would continue his *mano duro* approach. After being elected, Santos immediately pursued a different approach to the conflict and began secret discussions with FARC negotiators. He quickly earned the enmity of Uribe, who continued to espouse conservative policies from his new position in the Senate. Over time, the battle between proponents and opponents of a peace accord became a battle over the meaning of transitional justice for the FARC.

In June 2012, the Colombian Congress passed the Legal Framework for Peace, a bill designed to preempt legal challenges to an eventual peace accord with guerrilla groups. The law goes beyond prior enactments that merely refer to transitional justice and defines the phrase as a set of "instruments" that will be "exceptional" and facilitate the end of the conflict while guaranteeing, "to the best level possible, rights to truth, justice and reparation."[82] As with the Victims Law, the "exceptionality" of the transitional justice instruments was key to the government's argument for the constitutionality of this bill.

A government staffer who helped design the Legal Framework for Peace explained how policy makers designed the law after reading about the idea of transitional justice in other countries. Interestingly, when asked why they drew on the idea, this staffer quickly clarified that that the idea did not fit in Colombia the way that it did in Chile, Argentina, and other countries where there had been political transitions. However,

[82] El Congreso de Colombia, Legislative Act No. 1, July 31, 2012, Articulo Transitorio 66.

transitional justice was a useful idea because it allowed the legislature, aware that the Constitutional Court might find the law unconstitutional, to emphasize that the mechanisms they were proposing were "exceptional." Knowing that the government was going to have to prosecute some actors, but could not prosecute all of them, they saw transitional justice as a useful frame to emphasize that there would be "justice" even if there were not going to be prosecutions of every individual for every crime.

The Legal Framework for Peace's description of transitional justice instruments is deliberately vague, and reveals how the idea's malleability was an asset for the government's negotiators. The Framework states that the government can create "judicial or extra-judicial bodies" to ensure that investigations and sanctions are enforced. The law has a number of stipulations about what perpetrators would have to do in order to receive alternative sentencing, including putting down their arms, releasing kidnapped and underage fighters, acknowledging responsibility, contributing to the "clarification of truth," and providing holistic reparation for victims. Importantly, the government wanted to clarify the principle of opportunity, a doctrine that leaves the government discretion in the prosecution of perpetrators. Under the Legal Framework for Peace, the Attorney General would be able to decide on extra-judicial sanctions, alternative punishment, or simply not pursuing cases against individuals. As explained earlier, this "principle of opportunity" is what hampered the Justice and Peace Law's constitutionality, because the Court did not want to allow prosecutors discretion in whom they prosecute. Policy makers hoped that their explanation of the principle of opportunity as part of transitional justice would help the bill withstand another constitutional challenge.

In addition, with the Legal Framework for Peace, a truth commission became a constitutional mandate, as the bill states that a truth commission must be created upon the signing of a peace accord. This mandate reflects the fact that policy makers viewed a truth commission as a politically viable alternative to a judicial process and a crucial transitional justice instrument. One of the law's drafters, who later worked for the Office of the High Commissioner on the peace negotiations with the FARC, explained how the law's drafters "did not want to commit to the idea that there was going to be a truth commission because you do not necessarily create a truth commission by a constitutional amendment." She suggested that there were other ways, such as in decrees and agreements, but that they knew they were going to have to write a law that mentioned alternatives to courts if they wanted the law to pass: "we just never thought it should be said in the constitution, but it was basically how the coalition was built for the amendment to pass" (interview with Colombian government staffer 2015).

As this staffer tells it, proposing a truth commission helped bring together various political constituencies that were concerned about what kind of alternative judicial mechanism they would create for the guerrillas. Those pressing for prosecutions were more receptive to a truth commission, which they saw as an alternative to courts, whereas those who wanted prosecutions viewed a truth commission as a precursor. Either way, it was easy to support a truth commission.

INSTITUTIONALIZING TRANSITIONAL JUSTICE

The Santos administration was so committed to promoting the idea of transitional justice that it renamed various ministries with the label. In 2014, the Attorney General's office changed the name of the unit pursuing cases under Law 975 from the Justice and Peace Division to the Transitional Justice Division. In May 2015, the signs in the office still read as Division of Justice and Peace, a throwback to the 2005 demobilization policy and an indication of how understandings of transitional justice evolved from the Justice and Peace Law. Similarly, the Ministry of Justice and Human Rights established the Transitional Justice Unit in 2011, working under the Deputy Ministry of Political Crimes and Restorative Justice. The head of the Unit was Catalina Diaz, who, by that point, had worked for five years with ICTJ's office in New York and in Colombia and was a well-respected civil society leader on issues related to the peace processes.

The Transitional Justice Unit's definition of transitional justice further reveals how the malleability of the idea enabled enterprising political actors and transitional justice professionals to make broad claims about how the idea and its associated interventions could help forge a peace accord. Emphasizing that the idea refers to justice in political transition, the Unit specifies that, in the context of an armed conflict, the idea refers to ways to end the conflict through political negotiation (in contrast to a military defeat, which was Uribe's goal) while ensuring justice. In its description of the "mechanisms or tools" of transitional justice, the Ministries website lists truth commission above tribunals, reparation, and guarantees of nonrepetition, matching the popular slogan "truth, justice, reparation, and guarantees of no repetition."[83]

The Ministry drew explicitly on the idealistic discourse of transitional justice, suggesting that the third goal of transitional justice, after recognition of victims and their rights and fostering civic trust, is reconciliation. Well aware of transitional justice skeptics within the country, they also pointed out what they believe transitional justice is not – a soft form of justice to ensure impunity. Like the Coalition for RECOM, this Ministry engaged in what they call "knowledge production" on transitional justice, including "regional forums" throughout the country on the concepts of transitional justice. One of the trainers explained to me that many of the participants (there had been nearly 3000 by summer 2016) viewed transitional justice as a euphemism for impunity, this time for the FARC and not the paramilitaries. The Transitional Justice Unit, along with proponents of transitional justice hoped to convince Colombians around the country that the idea and its associated interventions would help ensure peace in the country, not impunity.

[83] Ministry of Justice, "Transitional Justice," www.justiciatransicional.gov.co/articulo/que-es-justicia-transicional (accessed August 23, 2016).

CHALLENGING TRANSITIONAL JUSTICE IN COURT

The idea may have helped the Santos administration pass the Legal Framework for Peace, but transitional justice's malleability also made it easy for different actors to draw on it to make claims against one another. Notably, after championing an alternative penal process for paramilitaries, Uribe became the most prominent opponent of the bill, calling it a "framework for impunity for terrorism."[84] His comments foreshadow the ways in which transitional justice became not only a placeholder for actors to articulate contradictory beliefs about the peace process, but also a potential political landmine in a country that had experienced nearly sixty years of armed conflict.

Ironically, Uribe and Gustavo Gallon, a major critic of the former president, found themselves in agreement on the question of alternative sanctions for the FARC. As he did with the Justice and Peace Law, Gallon challenged the Legal Framework for Peace in court, arguing that the bill violated constitutional rights that perpetrators should be prosecuted, judged, and sanctioned. Gallon insisted that international crimes should not be the only crimes worthy of judicial proceedings. In Decision C-579 of August 28, 2013, the Court rejected the claim and emphasized that it was guaranteeing peace and democracy by upholding this law. Borrowing the government's argument, the Court described how transitional justice mechanisms are exceptional and temporary, which makes them constitutional.[85] With the Constitutional Court's affirmation of the Legal Framework for Peace, transitional justice became a "constitutional category," the first time that a Constitution actually included a provision for alternative judicial sanctions (Sanchez and Ibañez 2014). In its decision, the Court reaffirmed international criminal law by stating that judicial accountability is necessary for "serious violations," which would be determined by looking at the "gravity of the crime." This language also echoes the ICC and reflects the influence of the ICC's ongoing pressure on the peace negotiations. In just one example of the ICC's ongoing pressure, in summer 2013, ICC Prosecutor Fatou Bensouda reiterated that if Colombia were to negotiate a peace deal that included amnesty for serious human rights violations, the international court would be compelled to act on its own to prosecute ex-guerrillas or members of the security forces. The same would likely occur, she stated, if Colombia were to adopt an arrangement that included trials but no punishments, such as suspended sentences in exchange for full confessions. Bensouda warned that "The decision to suspend a prison sentence would suggest that the proposed judicial process has the purpose of removing the accused from his criminal responsibility."[86]

84 Branden Barret, "Legal Framework for Peace Moves Closer to Passing," *Colombia Reports*, May 31, 2012, colombiareports.com/legal-framework-for-peace-moves-closer-to-passing/ (accessed May 16, 2015).

85 Colombia Constitutional Court, Decision No. C-579, August 28, 2013.

86 See Washington Office on Latin America, www.wola.org/commentary/colombia_peace_process_update_november_15_2013.

Recognizing that these courts were interpreting transitional justice as an idea that prioritized prosecution for certain crimes even if it did not guarantee prosecution for all crimes, some earlier skeptics came to see the malleability of transitional justice as advantageous. Reflecting on the case in our 2015 interview, Gallon suggested that, in upholding the law, the Court rejected his petition but agreed with its substance about the need to prosecute perpetrators of certain crimes. He remained one of the most outspoken critics of alternative sanctions, but explained how he came to accept that transitional justice was now central to domestic politics. From his perspective, Colombian society misunderstood transitional justice as a euphemism for impunity, and he saw his role as educating others that the idea required prosecution, particularly for international crimes (interview with Gustavo Gallon 2015). This famous advocate's understandings of transitional justice evolved, and the Santos administration hoped other skeptics of transitional justice might accept the idea as well.

FACILITATING A PEACE NEGOTIATION

After the Constitutional Court upheld the Legal Framework for Peace, Santos' administration had the legal protection it wanted to pursue peace negotiations with the FARC. Along with advocacy organizations promoting transitional justice, the government hoped that it could convince Colombian and international observers that transitional justice was not a euphemism for impunity but, rather, a way to balance the trade-offs inherent in pursuing a peace negotiation with the oldest guerrilla group in the world. As much as transitional justice's malleability was an asset in bringing the FARC to the negotiating table, the idea's ambiguity on the question of prosecution became a liability as the negotiations dragged on.

Secret talks between the government and FARC began in Havana, Cuba soon after Santos took office. Even before the talks were public, the Santos administration was gleaning insights from academics on the idea of transitional justice and how it might help facilitate peace. Ivan Orozco from Los Andes University became a consultant with the government in its negotiations, as did others from elite universities. The government also drew on the expertise of transnational professionals, including current and former ICTJ staff. Mark Freeman, who played a key role in organizing RECOM and had commented on Colombia's earlier demobilization policies, also consulted with the Santos administration. By that point, Freeman had left the ICTJ and founded a new organization called the Institute for Integrated Transitions, and he worked with the Colombian government throughout the accords. American scholars such as Doug Cassel, one of the early academics writing about tribunals and truth commissions, also helped negotiate the process.[87]

[87] At the end of the negotiations, before Colombians rejected the deal, the Colombian government awarded Cassel the Order of Merit, the highest honor the government can offer a foreigner.

The talks formally began in November 2012, when the two sides formulated a "General Agreement for the Termination of the Conflict and the Construction of a Stable and Lasting Peace" with six points that the parties would have to agree upon before a final peace accord could be signed: agrarian reform, political participation, drug trafficking, demobilization, victims' rights, and a public referendum, which they called a plebiscite, so that Colombians could vote on whether the accord would go into effect.

While it took only six months for both sides to agree on policies regarding agrarian reform and illicit drugs, the issue of victims' rights took nearly eighteen months. The main questions at the negotiation table were whether the FARC would face incarceration for the crimes they committed and how a truth commission might interact with a judicial process. To facilitate the negotiation, the governmental body in charge of the negotiations, the High Commissioner for Peace, created its own Transitional Justice Unit.

Both parties were under domestic and international pressure to clarify what transitional justice for the FARC would entail, and the government found itself struggling to explain its position on amnesty. The issue came down to which crimes could be amnestied, which crimes could receive reduced punishments, and which crimes had to be punished according to existing domestic and international law. In early 2015, Kofi Annan visited Havana and reiterated that FARC members responsible for international crimes could not avoid punishment. The FARC responded to these demands for incarceration by stating that they would not put down their arms in order to go to prison, and that they did not believe in transitional justice. Rather, they supported social justice.[88]

In this battle over transitional justice for the FARC, the guerrillas emphasized the responsibility of multiple actors and noted that the state is the most responsible for violations of human rights, and cannot be the source of justice. In addition, they stated that they did not believe that they were responsible for crimes against humanity or crimes of war because they were a legitimate army in rebellion. Moreover, they claimed that they have been engaged in political crimes and would not accept incarceration as the only sanction. The FARC wanted their crimes of kidnapping and extortion to be seen as part of the crime of sedition, which they believed should be amnestied as a political crime. Finally, they asserted their need to create their own framework for justice for all parties involved in the conflict.[89] For them, the government's understanding of transitional justice was just another unilateral government imposition that they would have to negotiate.

[88] "Kofi Annan Se Equivoca, No Vamos a Pagar Ni Un Dia de Carcel," *Semana.Com*, March 2, 2015, http://www.semana.com/nacion/articulo/farc-dicen-que-no-pagaran-carcel-en-respuesta-declaraciones-de-kofi-annan/419700-3 (accessed March 2, 2015).

[89] Carlos Medina Gallegos, "Justicia Para la Paz: Una Reflexion Desde Los Imaginarios de los FARC-ELP," Centro de Pensamiento y Siguimiento del Proceso de Paz, Universidad Nacional de Colombia, May 10, 2015, on file with the author.

In May 2015, there were near-daily public events and newspaper articles on the question of transitional justice in the peace accords. On May 13, 2015, at a public forum at Rosario University on "Transitional Justice and the Role of the International Criminal Court," Colombia's Attorney General and Ombudsman squared off on the issue of incarceration. The Attorney General insisted that armed actors must have alternative sanctions and followed up on his public statements with bold actions. Two days after his appearance at this meeting, he dropped 167 charges against a notorious FARC leader. Following the Attorney General's presentation, the Ombudsman, a well-known and outspoken ally of Uribe, said that it would be unacceptable to propose an agreement that did not include incarceration. The deputy prosecutor of the ICC, James Stewart, was also at the meeting and took a more measured tone. He seemed almost apologetic, suggesting that the ICC would not try to disrupt a successful peace accord by pursuing prosecutions. In addition to emphasizing the ICC's standards on international crimes, he expressed the concern that the Colombian people might not accept a peace agreement that did not ensure judicial accountability for international crimes. The President of the ICTJ, David Tolbert, also spoke, and reiterated that transitional justice is not a euphemism for impunity and that it entails respect for international criminal law.

All of these different perspectives fell under the banner of transitional justice, but theoretical views on punishment were not helping the government's negotiators. By the summer of 2015, the peace talks were stalled on the question of victims' rights. In May, the FARC broke their unilateral ceasefire, which began in December 2014, and killed twenty-three soldiers. Support for the ongoing peace negotiations plummeted, and Santos' approval ratings dipped down into the teens.

AGREEING TO TRANSITIONAL JUSTICE, IN THEORY

In June 2015, the FARC and the government finally agreed to create a truth commission in the event of a peace accord, which they had been negotiating for months. The FARC insisted that they would not agree to a truth commission unless it was extra-judicial. The government obliged, but they still could not agree on the issue of sanctions. That same month, the FARC's leaders declared, "Justice is a dead mule on the road to peace."[90] Their position was clear. If the government insisted on sanctions that required imprisonment, the FARC members would never put down their arms.

The government found itself in a challenging position. The negotiators were desperate to get an agreement, but they also knew that the majority of Colombians would not approve of a deal that did not punish perpetrators with jail. Public opinion surveys (usually conducted in Colombia's five biggest cities, thus excluding

[90] Alfredo Molano Jimenez, "Justicia es Una Mula Muerta en el Camino de Paz: Ivan Marquez," *El Espectador*, May 30, 2015, www.elespectador.com/noticias/politica/el-tema-de-justicia-una-mula-muerta-el-camino-de-paz-iv-articulo-563635.

the sizeable rural population most affected by the violence) consistently showed that the majority of urban Colombians believed that the FARC should face jail time and should not be eligible to participate in politics after they put down their arms. As the negotiations dragged on, the polarization around punishment for the FARC stifled public debate about the peace process. Several Colombian scholars mentioned that critiquing the idea of transitional justice, and even critiquing a future truth commission, could be interpreted as critiquing the peace negotiations. At the end of summer 2015, a new survey revealed that only 29% of Colombians supported the peace process.[91] Proponents of the peace negotiations found themselves defending a president who was floundering amid critiques that he was ensuring impunity for the FARC and that the FARC were merely using this negotiation to take a break from their guerrilla war.

On September 2015, the FARC and the government finally came to an agreement on the question of victims' rights, which news media referred to as an agreement on transitional justice.[92] The agreement stated that the FARC would put down their arms and submit themselves to a special tribunal called a Superior Tribunal of Peace that would evaluate charges of international crimes, including war crimes and crimes against humanity. The government offered amnesty for the crime of sedition, as the FARC negotiators maintained that they would not demobilize without this promise, but the details of this deal would be left to the Congress.[93] Narco-trafficking would also be included in the list of crimes that could be considered political.

While amnesty was one concern, one of the most controversial parts of the deal was the "effective restriction of liberty" of five to eight years, which is the punishment mandated by the agreement provided that the FARC tells the "truth" and takes "responsibility" for crimes that would not be amnestied. The question, of course, was what an "effective restriction of liberty" meant? Again, this dilemma continued to be framed as a question of transitional justice. One journalist clarified the problem, noting that actors in Colombia are still unsure of what transitional justice means: "If the restriction of movement consists only of not being able to leave the country

91 *Telesur*, "Poll Reveals Increase in Support for Peace Process in Colombia," October 5, 2015, www.telesurtv.net/english/news/Poll-Reveals-Increase-in-Support-for-Peace-Process-in-Colombia-20151005-0010.html.

92 For example, the news source Telesur pointed out, "the topic of transitional justice was seen as one of the more contentious topics during the talks and the signing on an agreement on the topic was so significant that both the FARC and the government felt confident enough to commit to having a final deal by March 23, 2016." *Telesur*, October 9, 2015, www.telesurtv.net/english/news/FARC-and-Government-to-Settle-Dispute-Over-Transitional-Justice-20151009-0050.html; Sibylla Brodzinsky, "FARC peace talks: Colombia Nears Historic Deal After Agreement on Justice and Reparations," *The Guardian*, September 23, 2015. Even Democracy Now, a progressive US news outlet, reported on the peace accords as an agreement on transitional justice. *Democracy Now*, Headlines, June 23, 2016, www.democracynow.org/2016/6/23/headlines/colombian_government_and_farc_to_sign_historic_ceasefire.

93 *NoticiasCarocol.com/AFP*, "Si no hay una ley de amnistia no habra acuerdo final," August 5, 2016, noticias.caracoltv.com/colombia/si-no-hay-una-ley-de-amnistia-no-habra-acuerdo-final-farc (accessed June 23, 2016).

or a department, or if the labor restriction consists of going to Congress or the town council, it will be very hard for people to trust in transitional justice. If it is more strict, it could give the system more legitimacy."[94]

Even with an agreement in place, actors from the political left and right still argued over transitional justice in order to articulate their understandings of how to use law to bridge social and political divides. The director of Human Rights Watch for Latin America referred to the deal as a "piñata of impunity,"[95] much like Uribe's position. After the FARC and the government signed the agreement on victims' rights in December 2015, Uribe asserted, "More than the presumption of innocence and other universal guarantees . . . in the Havana accord with FARC, the government has newly equated the armed forces of our democracy with a terrorist organization and wants to apply the same transitional justice."[96] Though Uribe championed transitional justice for the paramilitaries, he worried that this idea would be applied in different ways to different armed actors. For him and his supporters, much like the human rights organizations dedicated to prosecutions, transitional justice was too malleable, and punishment for the FARC had to include incarceration.

A FUTURE TRUTH COMMISSION

While much of the media attention on the peace accords fixated on the public debates over incarceration, few questioned the truth commission that the government and FARC agreed to in June 2015. That year, all of my interviewees said that a truth commission was inevitable, and that this was a good thing.[97] Quickly, money came pouring in from abroad to finance this future commission. President Obama pledged to support *Paz Colombia*, or Peace Colombia, a reference to the notorious Plan Colombia that provided millions of dollars of military support to eradicate the drug trade. In September 2015, just after the FARC and the Colombian government publically announced the agreement on victims' rights but when they had not yet signed the agreement, let alone the final accord, USAID published a call for proposals for a $50 to $55 million "Reconciliation Activity." The call for applications emphasized that USAID had developed a "theory of change" for countries wrestling with mass violence. The first part of their theory was that a nationwide truth-telling

94 Juanita Leon, "Las diez cosas que se necesitan para que la justicia transiciona no sea un fiasco," *La Silla Vacia*, lasillavacia.com/historia/las-diez-cosas-que-se-necesitan-para-que-la-justicia-transicional-no-sea-un-fiasco-52629 (accessed August 18, 2016).

95 See Human Rights Watch, *Analysis of the Colombia FARC Agreement*, www.hrw.org/news/2015/12/21/human-rights-watch-analysis-colombia-farc-agreement (accessed December 23, 2015).

96 *El Tiempo*, "Uribe insiste en que Gobierno iguala a militares con guerrilleros," December 22, 2015, translated by author, www.eltiempo.com/politica/congreso/opinion-de-uribe-sobre-justicia-transicional-de-militares/16464979 (accessed December 23, 2015).

97 During my fieldwork in 2010, only one interviewee, a former NCRR staff member, was skeptical of a future truth commission in Colombia, largely because he thought that victims prioritized money and that a truth commission would be a wasteful academic enterprise. In 2015, no one expressed concern about a future truth commission; they just had different ideas about what one should do.

process is necessary for reconciliation, and the grant objective is "to measure the degree of progress toward a national truth commission."[98] In September 2015, ACDI/VOCA, a Washington, DC-based NGO that has been working since 1963 to promote broad-based economic growth, advertised for a "senior truth commission building expert" for Colombia in anticipation of receiving the grant.

This jump to financing a truth commission as part of a reconciliation project reveals just how appealing truth commissions are, and the idealistic discourse used to explain and legitimize them. However, if past experience holds, it will be very difficult to create a commission that does not entrench social and political divisions in the country. As the political analyst Cesar Torres aptly noted in April 2015, armed actors, including the state, fear the truth more than they fear incarceration.[99]

When contemplating the challenges of a future truth commission in Colombia, one need not look further than the commission that the FARC and the government had already created. In 2014, as they were negotiating the question of victims' rights, the government and FARC representatives agreed to create a Historical Commission on the Conflict and Its Victims (HCCV), a precursor to the truth commission that they agreed upon in June 2015. The Commission was to "produce a report on the origins and multiple causes of the conflict, the principal factors and conditions that contributed to its persistence, and the most notorious effects and impacts on the population."[100] The Commission finished its work in February 2015, producing yet another lengthy document that reveals divergent opinions about the conflict's causes and consequences.

A simple reading of the HCCV highlights the fact that there is still no general understanding of how and why the violence occurred, or how to explain it. Whereas the Victims Law put the start date of reparations at 1985, this Commission began the analysis of the conflict in 1958, the year that the communists retreated to the countryside. For the FARC, and for the victims, the start date is crucial. The government was responsible for most of the violence that occurred before the communists took up arms. In addition, despite starting with the same date, the HCCV report focuses on very different aspects of the violence. The Commission was composed of twelve researchers and two well-known writers, chosen by both the FARC and the government. Several of the historians focused on the FARC. Another offered an explanation of Colombia's development as a nation-state, while another pointed out the fallacy of thinking that one can identify a beginning and an end of the country's ongoing conflicts. As the previous chapter's analysis of debates over RECOM reveals, disputes about the causes and consequences of violence can create political maelstroms.

98 USAID, "Reconciliation Activity," www.usaid.gov/sites/default/files/documents/1862/NOFO%20Reconciliation%20Activity.pdf (accessed November 7, 2015).

99 Cesar Torres, "Transición, Verdad, Justicia, Cárcel, Reparation," *El Tiempo*, April 28, 2015.

100 Comisión Histórica del Conflicto y Sus Víctimas, February 2015, p. 2, www.mesadeconversaciones.com.co/sites/default/files/Informe%20Comisi_n%20Hist_rica%20del%20Conflicto%20y%20sus%20V_ctimas.%20La%20Habana%2C%20Febrero%20de%202015.pdf (accessed July 14, 2016).

THE APPEAL OF VOICE, AGAIN

Throughout my discussions of a future truth commission in Colombia, it was clear that actors had different perspectives on what the commission should focus on, including whether to address the role of the United States in it, narco-traffickers, and other conflict entrepreneurs. However, what all could agree upon was that a future truth commission must enable survivors to participate and get public recognition for what they suffered. The experience of the Historical Memory Group, which focused both on providing a historical account of the violence and on providing victims with the chance to share their stories, highlights how appealing the emphasis on voice may be, but how providing voice about a conflict as complex as Colombia's can also reproduce and entrench divisions in a country.

When the Victims Law changed the status of the Historical Memory Group to a governmental agency called the National Center for Historical Memory, the organization lost its prior independence and became the voice of the government. The Center took charge of all archives related to the conflict, including state actors, human rights organizations, and victims' associations. These groups all have competing narratives about the causes and consequences of the violence, and the Center had to make decisions about how to prioritize these different perspectives in its work. The Center's director, Gonzalo Sanchez, described his reluctance to include the voices of all of the actors who were party to the conflict. Mainly the concern was "being receptors of testimonies of the perpetrators [in order] to solve their judicial situation" when the Center had worked so hard to "establish a relationship of trust with the victims" (interview with Gonzalo Sanchez 2015).

In other words, representing all the sides of the conflict presented an inherent contradiction. As the purveyor of the nation's "truth," the Center found itself at the center of a legal dilemma, not just a political one. Sanchez joked about the irony that, before it became a government agency, he and other members of the Historical Memory Group might go to jail for defamation if they published names of perpetrators that the courts absolved of responsibility. He expressed relief that, at least under the Victims Law, the newly formed Center would be protected from such a legal hazard. At the same time, he wondered how to reconcile the different "voices" in the conflict without furthering divisions:

> The disappeared, the disappeared victims want their [own] truth commission. The [victims of] kidnapping want their own truth commission, the guerrilla in a way also wanted a commission of their own to be created . . . In the near future, there will be a truth commission. (Interview with Gonzalo Sanchez 2015)

Negotiating over a truth commission may have helped smooth the peace negotiations, but the agreement to create one may also belie a shallow, self-serving commitment to the truth. Throughout the negotiations, the FARC maintained that a future truth commission must address questions about businesses, narco-traffickers, and the United States' role in perpetuating the violence through its efforts to eradicate cocaine. These are politically sensitive questions that the FARC wanted to bring to the fore in order to emphasize that their crimes were always political in nature. The government, of course, wanted to avoid these larger questions and focus directly on the FARC's actions rather than the broader political system.

Talking to other actors involved in documentation efforts revealed how many different actors want a truth commission to tell their story. In particular, victims are not a unified group and, with over seven million displaced individuals and nearly every Colombian affected in some way or other by the violence, a truth commission obviously will not be able to provide voice to every individual, let alone group, who wants a story to be part of the official record.

National studies about how Colombians view a future truth commission similarly reveal shared hopes and concerns about the inevitability of a truth commission in Colombia. The Ministry of Justice and Human Rights' study of over 500 victims reveals that a majority support a truth commission and view it as vital to disclose the complicated history of the violence. At the same time, the authors cite a "minority" who expressed concern that a truth commission would simply duplicate the work of existing investigations, that the country does not have enough money for it, that there is no guarantee that victims will be able to participate, and that there should be no talk of a truth commission until the violence has actually stopped.[101] Another comprehensive survey of the Colombian public, conducted by University of Los Andes political scientists, similarly reveals that truth-seeking efforts may have little impact on Colombian society. The majority of the population were unaware of the work done by the Historical Memory Center. Moreover, less than half the population said that making memory (*hacer memoria*) is necessary to recognize and respect victims, while a quarter said that making memory would not help society advance.[102]

While it may be relatively easy to get buy-in for a truth commission, particularly from foreign donors, actually designing and implementing a truth commission may be as politically contentious as the battle over alternative sanctions for armed actors and reparation for victims, if not more so. With so many actors responsible for the violence, the truth commission will have to make politically sensitive choices about what to focus on, and how to appease the many parties who want the truth commission to tell their stories.

TRANSFORMATIVE INSTRUMENTALIZATION AND THE FUTURE OF TRANSITIONAL JUSTICE IN COLOMBIA

This case, perhaps more than the others, reveals how the malleability of transitional justice proved to be both an asset and a liability for actors who mobilized around it. Over the course of a decade, scholars, policy makers, and advocates drew on the idea to transform the political opportunities for peace, and succeeded – up to a point. After

[101] Ministerio de Justicia, *La Justicia Transitional Vista desde Las Regiones*, 2015, on file with author, pp. 80–81.

[102] Center for Historical Memory, *Encuesta Nactional: Que Piensan Los Colombianos Despues de Siete Anos de Justicia y Paz*, September 2012, on file with author, p. 92.

the government and the FARC signed the agreement on victims' rights in December 2015, Uribe argued for Colombians to reject the accord, as "civil disobedience" and as a sign of their commitment to peace. In the aftermath of the failed plebiscite on October 2, 2016, one of Colombia's senators most involved in the peace accord suggested that "getting rid of transitional justice," as he believed Uribe was proposing, "was getting rid of the peace accord."[103] This comment reflects the fact that different actors could agree to support transitional justice while not necessarily agreeing on the most contentious issues in the peace processes. In other words, all could agree that transitional justice was necessary, but they could not agree on what the idea means for Colombia.

Although one might point to this dynamics as evidence of disruptive instrumentalization, transitional justice played an important role in transforming the nature of the political debate about demobilization and victims' rights. Furthermore, as debates over prosecutions stymied the peace accords, a truth commission emerged both as a pragmatic compromise and as a symbol of a peaceful future. A truth commission was an aspiration to peace in the country. Actors saw this intervention as one that could meet their specific needs, whether to bring opposing politicians together to agree to alternative sanctions, or to ensure that victims of violence would have a chance to participate in designing and implementing the policies that affect them.

In part, this transformative instrumentalization of transitional justice reflects the distinct organizational dynamics in Colombia, as the active NGO sector was able to maintain sustained pressure on the government to respond to claims for truth, justice, and reparations. These advocates understood that the malleability of transitional justice enabled the Uribe administration to draw on it to explain and legitimate the Justice and Peace Law, and that they could similarly draw on it to make their claims. In addition, advocates were familiar with truth commissions and aware that they had to wait for the right political opportunities, and continued to slowly mobilize around one in preparation for that time to come.

In addition, the transformative instrumentalization of transitional justice in Colombia reflects the changing political opportunities for truth, justice, and reparation in the country. Given their desire to create a peace accord with the FARC that was politically and legally viable, policy makers drew on transitional justice to explain why both following and deviating from established laws would be necessary. As domestic, regional, and international courts sided with victims' claims to truth, justice, and reparation, the government had to ensure that a new peace accord with the FARC fulfilled these claims, at least nominally. Moreover, when the administration shifted between Uribe and Santos, understandings of transitional justice transformed further. Critics of transitional justice as a euphemism for impunity maintained their concern, but a transition from armed conflict to peace was finally

[103] CNN *Espanol*, "Are Uribe's Proposals Viable in Order to Achieve a Peace Accord with the FARC?" October 10, 2016, http://cnnespanol.cnn.com/2016/10/10/son-viables-las-propuestas-de-uribe-para-lograr-un-acuerdo-de-paz-con-las-farc/ (accessed October 16, 2016).

possible. The new transitional justice dilemma was how the Santos administration would ensure victims' rights while incentivizing the FARC to demobilize.

Despite the idea's utility in the negotiations with the FARC, it is too soon for transitional justice proponents to claim victory in Colombia. The same qualities that made the idea useful, particularly the idea's ambiguity with regard to judicial accountability and the idealistic hopes for what a truth commission might offer, will no doubt create political strife when the interventions are actually created. As noted, the plebiscite, which Santos promised Colombians so that he might show popular support for the accords and thereby make the reintegration of the FARC smoother, was narrowly rejected on October 2, 2016. Many of those supporting the no vote emphasized that they wanted the FARC to be adequately punished for their crimes, and they believed that the accord's transitional justice plan had insufficient penalties and too many benefits.[104] This surprising outcome (most polls showed the yes vote ahead) temporarily put the entire peace process into disarray, and revealed just how politicized transitional justice became through the peace negotiations.

In response to the plebiscite, Uribe listed a new set of conditions for himself and his political followers to support the crimes. These demands include ensuring that the FARC do not have automatic seats in Congress, that their "effective restriction of liberty" be clarified, that the crime of narco-trafficking not be included in the amnesty, and that the "transitional justice" mechanism be part of the existing court system and not special tribunals. Colombia's Congress narrowly approved a revised peace accord on November 30 and are continuing to implement their transitional justice plan. However, Uribe and his followers protested the vote, claiming that Congress' action went against the popular will.

Given Uribe's popularity, it is possible that the agreement, which Uribe and his supporters criticized as a tool for impunity, will contribute to a resurgence of the ultra-right in the country. Santos' popularity plummeted and never recovered as he pursued this peace negotiation. While his political stance may seem illogical in a country that has suffered from such a longstanding conflict, Uribe had the political influence to upend the entire peace process by working with other leaders to convince Colombian voters that this peace accord symbolized not simply a vote on justice but, rather, the future of the country's national identity.

There are ongoing protests by Uribe's supporters. Notably, at the April 1, 2017 country-wide marches that were supposedly against corruption, opponents of the peace accord spoke out with great fear and anger. At the march in Barranquilla, which took place in an upscale suburban park, organizers reiterated their belief that Santos ignored the will of the people by forging ahead with the peace accord after the No vote. They expressed their trepidation that, if the peace accord went through, the country would become like Venezuela, their taxes would go up, and their family

104 See Boris Miranda, "Las Razones por Las Que el 'No' Se Impuso en el Plebiscito en Colombia," *BBC El Mundo*, October 3, 2016, www.bbc.com/mundo/noticias-america-latina-37537629 (accessed Dec. 4, 2016).

values would be undermined by the accord's references to gender. Indeed, many of the participants who stayed to listen to the speeches wore shirts saying "protecting the family; I'm with Christ" and with images of a blue, a pink, and two white figures representing a father, a mother, and two children.

These different actors were able to politicize transitional justice so effectively because they could use the idea to articulate their agendas while not specifying where they actually stood on the most difficult political questions: what would be a "just" punishment for decades of massacres and terror, can there actually be a unified narrative of "truth" for the violence, and how can the government help "repair" the damage done by over sixty years of armed conflict? The longstanding divisions in the country will no doubt come to the fore if and when a truth commission makes decisions about which parts of the conflict it will address and which parts it will leave out. With so many Colombians affected by the violence, a national truth commission will have to prioritize which voices to include.

Moving beyond the peace accord, the transformative instrumentalization of transitional justice in Colombia had other important social and political effects. As in the Balkans, the instrumentalization of transitional justice in Colombia created new sets of elites that were able to shape understandings of transitional justice in the country and abroad. It fostered an idealistic discourse about what a truth commission might offer, and, simultaneously, reaffirmed the belief that prosecutions are an important, if not necessary, strategy to redress the violence. The plebiscite rejecting the peace accords brought this point home in a frightening way.

Furthermore, despite peace accords with the paramilitary and the guerrillas, violence will continue to destabilize Colombia. The FARC are vulnerable to vigilante justice, just as they were when they demobilized in the 1980s. The instability in the countryside is no longer caused by violence between paramilitaries and guerrillas, but by illegal armed gangs fighting for control of the drug routes and by foreign companies engaged in resource extraction and displacing residents. Colombia is second to Brazil as the most economically unequal country in Latin America. Without structural reforms that will help create more economic equality and provide sustainable solutions for its millions of impoverished citizens, many of whom have been directly impacted by the ongoing armed conflict, a tribunal, a truth commission, or a reparations payment plan will have little effect on survivor well-being and preventing future violence.

Transitional justice professionals may have come to offer training in Colombia over the past decade, but now Colombian actors from the government, from NGOs, and from leading universities regularly present abroad on Colombia's experience. Through their work, the transformative instrumentalization of transitional justice in Colombia is helping transform understandings of transitional justice more broadly. However, as the October 2, 2016 plebiscite revealed and the following analysis of transitional justice in the United States similarly points out, the malleability of transitional justice has its limits. Many actors still see the idea as a way to explain and legitimize interventions that provide less justice, and reject the idea.

5

Decoupled

Transitional Justice in the War on Terror

On February 9, 2009, less than one month after President Obama took office, the chairman of the Senate Judiciary Committee, Patrick Leahy, announced that the United States should create a Truth and Reconciliation Commission similar to the South African Truth and Reconciliation Commission. He stated that "Rather than vengeance, we need a fair-minded pursuit of what actually happened" with regard to the treatment and possible torture of terrorism suspects in U.S. custody. Leahy outlined his proposal during a speech at Georgetown University, saying, "Sometimes the best way to move forward is getting to the truth, finding out what happened, so we can make sure it does not happen again."[105] Leahy noted that a TRC was not foreign to the United States, as there had already been a TRC in 2004 that focused on racial violence in Greensboro, North Carolina.

Leahy was not alone in advocating a commission to investigate, document, and publicize the violence caused by detention policies. Beginning in 2008, scholars who were critical of the Bush administration began calling for a truth commission to investigate allegations of torture at U.S. military bases, and a group of prominent advocacy organizations, including the International Center for Transitional Justice, joined in a coalition to create a "commission on accountability." In 2009, it was unclear where these efforts would lead. After all, a truth commission seemed impossible to create in Colombia in 2010, whereas by 2015, a commission was inevitable. However, in the United States, not only was a truth commission not created, but also efforts to promote one never took off. Some actors resisted efforts to create any type of investigative commission, while others were interested in a commission but against the label of "truth commission."

[105] Philip Rucker, "Leahy Outlines Panel to Investigate Bush Era," *Washington Post*, February 10, 2009, www.washingtonpost.com/wp-dyn/content/article/2009/02/09/AR2009020903221.html (accessed March 1, 2010).

Given this resistance, I refer to the instrumentalization of transitional justice in the United States as decoupled. A variety of actors were interested in a truth commission, at least by the standard definition of "truth commission," but not in labeling it as such. Their instrumentalization shows both the success of the movement in popularizing truth commissions and the limits of the idea and intervention's malleability. Other scholars similarly noted at the time that there was growing interest in how transitional justice might apply to the United States, but there is little written on how various political actors utilized the idea (see Sarat 2012, p. 6). While a truth commission resonated, to some extent, with actors in the BiH, and more so in Colombia, few actors in the United States wanted to frame their efforts as promoting a truth commission, with many viewing it as an intervention that was not adaptable to the U.S. context.

To make this argument, this chapter describes how the issue of state-sponsored torture in U.S. detention centers became a national and international scandal. It goes on to explain how campaigns by different sets of actors – scholars, policy makers, and advocates – sought to address the violence. The analysis points to the variety of actors who decided to mobilize around a commission to investigate the causes and consequences of the violence, hoping that the transition between the Bush and Obama administrations would provide an opening for critiquing detention policies. Their efforts ultimately failed, as the campaigns went nowhere. Whereas actors in other countries were able to use the ambiguity of the concept of a truth commission, particularly with regard to judicial accountability, to their advantage, that same ambiguity was a liability in the United States, as individuals who were unfamiliar with truth commissions were worried that promoting one was promoting amnesty, or that calling for a truth commission would make an implicit comparison between the United States and places where truth commissions had been created for much more extreme violence.

This case provides yet another example to show that it may be easy to get initial interest and support for a truth commission, but that support can be hard to sustain because political actors have different opinions about what truth commissions are and what they do. Moreover, even though actors around the world continue to mobilize around truth commissions and draw on transitional justice to explain and legitimate their strategies, the resistance to transitional justice in the United States highlights how contested understandings of transitional justice are. For many U.S. advocates, the idea was not only foreign, but something for people and places where "real justice," i.e., criminal justice, is not possible.

THE NATURE OF THE VIOLENCE: DETENTION POLICIES IN THE WAR ON TERROR

Just one year after 9/11, 598 individuals were detained in U.S. custody at Guantánamo Bay, while at least 119 were held in secret CIA prisons around the world. These detainees were being held without charges, and were called enemy combatants rather than civilians or militants in order to remain outside the purview of the Hague and Geneva Conventions.[106] Reinterpreting domestic and international law in the name of national security, the Bush administration went to work developing its own framework for detainee treatment. In January 2002, Major General Michael Dunlavey sought the approval of nineteen techniques, separated into three categories that were outside traditional guidelines for military interrogation, to enable so-called enhanced interrogations. Category 1 included techniques such as yelling and deception. Category 2 included putting detainees in stress positions, depriving them of light and sound, hooding, removal of clothing, and forced shaving of facial hair. Category 3 included waterboarding and convincing the detainee that he or his family was at risk of death or pain.

Given that the United States is a party to the Convention against Torture and has its own domestic implementing legislation, the Torture Victims Protection Act, the executive branch decided to define torture as a very narrow set of practices so that the executive would have maximum flexibility to engage in so-called enhanced interrogations without fear of prosecution. John Yoo, a lawyer working for the Office of Legal Counsel (OLC) and a member of the War Council, worked with Assistant Attorney General Jay Bybee, the head of the OLC, on briefs now referred to as the Torture Memos. As part of his efforts to limit congressional and judicial restrictions on the executive, Yoo articulated a theory of presidential power that argued that the Bush administration could approve these techniques in the name of national security. Moreover, drawing on legal cases in which emergency medical services were provided to individuals with severe pain and suffering, Yoo concluded that torture required the intention to cause organ failure or death. His interpretation contrasted with more common understanding of torture as cruel, inhuman, or degrading treatment and provided legal cover for the enhanced interrogations.

The Torture Memos were formally withdrawn by the OLC soon after they were written, due to their poor interpretation of relevant law, but their effects were already felt. With the ability to subject prisoners to increasingly harsh techniques, including stress positions, twenty-four-hour interrogations, harsh noises (such as babies crying and loud western music), extreme temperatures, and extended periods of solitary

[106] Protections for POWs are provided for in the Geneva Convention Relative to the Treatment of Prisoners of War (Geneva Convention No. III), Aug. 12, 1949, 6 U.S.T. 3316, 75 U.N.T.S. 135. The term "enemy combatant" comes from *Ex Parte Quirin*, a U.S. Supreme Court case decided during World War II, in which the Court said that the government could detain enemy soldiers as illegal combatants because they slipped into the Unites States without any insignia identifying them as enemy soldiers. *Ex Parte* Quirin, 317 U.S. 1, 13 (1942). This seems contrary to the current situation, in which government agents sent individuals to U.S. soil, calling them enemy combatants. In February 2002, the Council wrote that the war in Afghanistan was subject to the Geneva Conventions; thus the Taliban could receive protections as prisoners of war. However, these rights would be withdrawn if Taliban members did not follow the laws of war themselves. In addition, they determined that Al Qaeda was not affiliated with a state and, therefore, its members could not qualify as protected combatants.

confinement, interrogators working at Guantánamo, as well as at the CIA black sites, were causing harm to individuals and to the United States' image and legitimacy in conducting the War on Terror. While anti-torture advocates focused on waterboarding to demonstrate a clear violation of international and domestic law, the infliction of psychological distress was also a key part of the military's strategy for dehumanizing detainees and ostensibly getting information about terrorism. The CIA, in particular, worked closely with psychologists who had trained U.S. soldiers in how to resist psychological torture, and turned those techniques on detainees. Later reports showed that one of the CIA's so-called high-value detainees, Abu Zubaydah, was placed in a wooden box, left to defecate on himself, and held in isolation for forty-seven days.

Soon, information about detainee abuse began to circulate, leading to concerns that the CIA, the FBI, and even the U.S. military might be complicit in torture. In December 2002, Secretary of State Rumsfeld approved of harsher interrogation techniques. Alberto Mora, the General Counsel of the United States Navy, learned about abuses at Guantánamo that month. He believed that that these harsh interrogation techniques were not just morally troubling, but created a legal quagmire. He alerted his colleagues about his concerns, but lawyers loyal to the Bush administration continued to emphasize that the interrogation techniques were legal (see Mayer 2008). As early as 2002, reports revealed that as many as a third, meaning 200 of the then 600 detainees, were at the Guantánamo detention facility by mistake, but there was no clear procedure to secure their release (Fletcher et al. 2008, p. 2).

In spring 2004, the Abu Ghraib scandal broke, confirming speculations that U.S. military personnel were torturing detainees. The Geneva Conventions covered detainees at Abu Ghraib, and the images revealed that the enhanced interrogation practices that were given legal cover at Guantánamo had migrated. Interrogators had asked prison guards to help them by breaking detainees down and making them more compliant, and several soldiers had photographed their exploits. The images showed frightened prisoners cowering from dogs, a hooded prisoner with electric wires attached to his fingers and penis, and sexually humiliating poses with naked detainees. The Bush administration responded quickly to the scandal and claimed that the military guards were to blame. Government reports on the abuse focused on the fact that the guards did not have proper training to deal with the overcrowded conditions, but they did not condemn the legal framework that gave rise to the abuse.

That same year, the Torture Memos were leaked. As public awareness of detainee treatment grew, so did public protest and demands that someone be held accountable for the violence against detainees. However, it was unclear who could or should be held accountable. When Attorney General Ashcroft blocked Yoo from directing the OLC, Yoo returned to his position as a tenured professor at Berkeley School of Law. By that point, Jay Bybee had become a federal judge. In Berkeley, protesters against Bush's detention policies showed up in the back of lecture halls and even at the 2009 law school graduation. They dressed in orange jumpsuits to symbolize the connection between the memos and the torture at Abu Ghraib, and carried signs saying, "John Yoo is a war criminal." However, given Yoo's tenure, these protesters had little long-term impact on his professional life.

Lawyers were also working to address the allegations of torture, pursuing both remedies for survivors and legislative change. In 2006, lawyers were restricted from entering Guantánamo, and many of those who did were criticized as supporters of terrorists (Meyerstein 2007). Eventually, lawyers working at organizations such as Reprieve and the Center for Constitutional Rights, which came to represent over 150 Guantánamo clients, found ways to work on behalf of clients they were not able to meet.

These lawyers translated the political quagmire of Guantánamo into a legal one. In *Rasul v. Bush*, the Supreme Court found that U.S. courts have jurisdiction over Guantánamo despite the government's argument that the base is not in the United States. In *Hamdi v. Rumsfeld*, the Court determined that prisoners could not be held indefinitely, and that a neutral third party must determine the status of detainees. The administration responded with the Military Commissions Act, creating Combatant Status Review Panels. In 2006, the Supreme Court intervened again. In *Hamdan v. Rumsfeld*, the Court held that the government's procedures for determining combatant status were unlawful under the Uniform Code of Military Justice (UCMJ) and that, as part of the UCMJ, the procedures also violated the Geneva Conventions. Finally, in the 2008 decision *Boumedienne v. Bush*, the Court held that U.S. courts should be able to review detention decisions.

At first, mobilizing law through the courts seemed to be having an impact on U.S. policies. By 2006, the Bush administration decided to change its policy on torture, aware that its detention policies had become an international and domestic scandal. However, even the new policy authorized potentially illegal practices. The OLC's new memo suggested that techniques such as waterboarding are permissible as long as any pain was not for an extended duration, and that officials could not be held liable for torture if they were following previous orders in tension with existing law.

Around this time, information about Guantánamo detainees came into the spotlight, and advocates began demanding that the United States close the base and provide information on what happened to detainees there and elsewhere. A 2007 *New York Times* article revealed that the CIA had taped the harsh interrogations of Abu Zubaydah and another detainee, but had destroyed the tapes and was recalcitrant in providing information to the 9/11 Commission created to investigate the causes and consequences of the attack on the World Trade Center.[107]

While the violence was only aimed at suspected terrorists, concerned observers noted that the violence in detention centers reflected the broader problems with the

[107] Mark Mazetti, "9/11 Study Panel Finds the CIA Witheld Tapes," *New York Times*, Dec. 22, 2007, www.nytimes.com/2007/12/22/washington/22intel.html (accessed March 24, 2009).

War on Terror. Media began reporting on the earlier, secret, internal discussions at the Pentagon over the utility as well as the legality of the interrogation techniques, with some officials worried that the tactics might constitute war crimes.[108] Investigative journalists and scholars published information about the detainees, confirming advocates' suspicions that the United States was violating domestic and international law with its interrogation techniques.[109] Detainees reported beatings, sleep deprivation, prolonged solitary confinement, what Fletcher et al. (2008) explain as a "cumulative" effect that advocates contended fell well within these legal scholars' understanding of cruel, unusual, and degrading treatment. Furthermore, it was unclear whether the detainees should have been detained in the first place. By 2008, 520 of the 779 individuals who were detained at Guantánamo had been released, and only 23 had been charged with war crimes.

The topic of torture dominated the 2008 presidential elections, as candidates were forced to reflect on U.S. foreign policy during the Bush administration. After 9/11, public opinion polls showed that Bush had an approval rating of 83%, which had plummeted to 24% by the time of the election.[110] By then, 62%of the population stated that there should be criminal investigations into policies that permitted torture.[111] Jane Mayer's 2008 book on U.S. policies in the War on Terror, which outlined how the Bush administration paved the way for torture, became a national bestseller, and public opinion polls showed significant public interest in curbing detainee abuse (Mayer 2008). Moreover, the issue of torture was not a point of contention between the two main candidates. Presidential candidates Barack Obama and John McCain were both against the torture policies. McCain, part of Bush's Republican party but also a survivor of torture, introduced an amendment to the 2005 Defense Appropriations Bill that would have prohibited inhumane treatment of prisoners, even at Guantánamo.[112] With the support of the country's youth, Democratic candidate Obama defeated McCain in the 2008 election. He campaigned under the banner of "change," and many observers hoped his presidency would actually usher in a

[108] See Bill Dedman, "Gitmo Interrogations Spark Battle over Tactics," *MSNBC*, Oct. 23, 2006, www.msnbc.msn.com/id/15361458/#.TyH5knqrG8o (accessed March 24, 2009).

[109] *New York Times*, "The Guantánamo Bay Docket," projects.nytimes.com/Guantánamo (accessed March 24, 2009); *Washington Post*, "Names of the Detained in Guantánamo Bay," projects.washingtonpost.com/Guantánamo/ (accessed March 24, 2009); Andy Worthington, "The Definitive Prisoner List," *Huffington Post*, March 5, 2009, www.huffingtonpost.com/andy-worthington/Guantánamo-the-definitive_b_172134.hTSMl (accessed March 24, 2009).

[110] Pew Research Center, Bush and Public Opinion, December 18, 2008, www.people-press.org/2008/12/18/bush-and-public-opinion/ (accessed March 24, 2009).

[111] See John Cohen and Jennifer Agiesta, "Public Supports Closing Guantánamo," *Washington Post*, Jan. 22, 2009, at A6; *USA Today*, "Poll: Most Want Inquiry into Anti-terror Tactics," February 12, 2009, www.usatoday.com/news/washington/2009-02-11-investigation-poll_N.hTSM (accessed March 24, 2009).

[112] Bush did sign the bill into law, but Addington drafted a signing statement to clarify that the President reserved his rights "as the unitary executive and as commander in chief." In essence, he could still authorize inhumane treatment if he deemed it necessary.

political transition with regard to foreign policy. More specifically, critics of the War on Terror's effects on civil liberties hoped that Obama would renounce Bush's policies on detainee treatment.

During his campaign, Obama was emphatic that the United States must reestablish itself as a leader of human rights law and repair its tarnished image from the War on Terror. After the election, Obama declared that the first thing he would do as president would be to shut down the Guantánamo Bay detention facility. He sharply questioned the legality of the detention policies and made an emphatic statement that the United States would not torture.[113] In one of his first acts as President, Obama signed four executive orders related to detention policies. The orders banned the CIA's use of secret prisons and enhanced interrogations. His order also included a protocol to review the 245 remaining prisoners at Guantánamo one by one and determine who was releasable and who would need to be transferred to another facility. The orders were clearly aimed at denouncing torture. As Army Major General Paul Eaton commented during the signing, the use of torture was "for the lazy, the stupid and the pseudo-tough"; Eaton called it a "recruiting tool for terrorists."[114]

Despite these promises to change U.S. policy, domestic actors concerned about torture wanted more than just a promise to close the detention center at Guantánamo Bay. Some wanted to punish the architects of the policy, others wanted to release the detainees, and still others wanted guarantees that the executive branch would no longer have the power to unilaterally adopt policies that they believed facilitated torture. As they contemplated their options, several scholars, policy makers, and advocates decided that a truth commission might help ensure their goals. Their efforts show how the malleability of a truth commission made this intervention appealing, but how difficult it was to overcome the belief that truth commissions do not belong in the United States.

EFFORTS TO CREATE A TRUTH COMMISSION: 2008–2013

The push for a truth commission started even before Bush left office, and actors promoting one had a variety of goals in mind. Nicholas Kristof, an outspoken *New York Times* columnist who specializes in human rights issues, published an op-ed in July 2008, calling for "a national Truth Commission to lead a process of soul searching and national cleansing." He wrote that this was a first step to accountability, and pointed to the South Africa TRC, as well as former commissions in the United

113 See "Obama Signs Order to Close Guantánamo," *CBC*, January 22, 2009, www.cbc.ca/news/world/story/2009/01/22/obama-Guantánamo.hTSMl (accessed Dec. 15, 2011); *CBS*, "60 Minutes," March 22, 2009, www.cbsnews.com/stories/2009/03/18/60minutes/main4873938.shTSMl (accessed March 24, 2009).

114 Joby Warrick and Karen de Young, Obama Reverses Bush Policies on Detention and Interrogation, *Washington Post*. January 23, 2009, p. 2, www.washingtonpost.com/wp-dyn/content/article/2009/01/22/AR2009012201527_2.html?sid=ST2009012204161.

States that addressed racial issues and Japanese military internment. He, like others concerned about allegations of torture, particularly at Guantánamo, hoped the future president would create a truth commission that "would issue a report to help us absorb the lessons of our failings, the better to avoid them during the next crisis."[115]

Also in 2008, John Conyers and Patrick Leahy, two outspoken critics of the Bush administration, began proposing investigative commissions that would establish accountability for the violence. U.S. media began reporting on these calls for investigations into torture as efforts to create a truth commission.[116] For these policy makers, mobilizing around a commission became a useful strategy for dramatizing the negative consequences of the War on Terror and further politicizing an already contentious issue in U.S. politics. In January 2009, Representative John Conyers and twenty-four co-sponsors introduced a bill titled "To Establish a National Commission on Presidential War Powers and Civil Liberties."[117] The legislation proposed an independent commission – bipartisan and without government affiliation – with the goal of issuing a final report on alleged violations of civil liberties under the Bush regime.[118]

Conyers recognized how inflammatory promoting an investigative commission might be, as the Republican and Democratic parties, as well as their supporters, were deeply divided by the end of Bush's term. He stated in his press release that "investigations are not a matter of payback or political revenge – it is our responsibility to examine what has occurred and to set an appropriate baseline of conduct for future administrations."[119] In his hearing on whether to create such a commission, he and another speaker mentioned that impeachment hearings were not off the table.

Leahy took a more measured approach, proposing a Truth and Reconciliation Commission modeled after that in South Africa. Like Conyers, Leahy's proposed commission would focus on the "use of torture, warrantless wiretapping,

[115] Nicholas Kristof, "The Truth Commission," *New York Times*, July 8, 2008, www.nytimes.com/2008/07/06/opinion/06kristof.html (accessed July 18, 2016).

[116] *Voice of America*, "Some US Lawmakers Call for Truth Commission to Investigate Bush Policies," February 25, 2009, www.voanews.com/english/2009-02-25-voa58.cfm (accessed May 25, 2012).

[117] John Conyers, "To Establish a National Commission on Presidential War Powers and Civil Liberties," H.R. 104, 111th Congress, 2009-2010.

[118] Section 1 of the bill states: "There is established the National Commission on Presidential War Powers and Civil Liberties (hereinafter in this Act referred to as the 'Commission') to investigate the broad range of policies of the Administration of President George W. Bush that were undertaken under claims of unreviewable war powers, including detention by the United States Armed Forces and the intelligence community, the use by the United States Armed Forces or the intelligence community of enhanced interrogation techniques or interrogation techniques not authorized by the Uniform Code of Military Justice, 'ghosting' or other policies intended to conceal the fact that an individual has been captured or detained, extraordinary rendition, domestic warrantless electronic surveillance, and other policies that the Commission may determine to be relevant to its investigation (hereinafter in this Act referred to as 'the activities')." Id. §1.

[119] John Conyers, Press Release, "Judiciary Chairman Conyers Issues Report Documenting Bush Abuses, Calling for Further Committee Investigation, Blue-Ribbon Panel, and Criminal Probes," January 13, 2009.

extraordinary rendition, and executive override of laws."[120] Departing from the South African model, he was not interested in providing a public platform for the actual survivors of violence. Rather, he compared this effort to the Church Committee's investigations of surveillance during the Vietnam War, a government commission that revealed abuses perpetrated by the government. Leahy's goal was "reconciliation" within the deeply divided country, and the commission was predicated on immunity in exchange for testimony.[121]

Leahy's calls for a truth commission reveal just how appealing and malleable these quasi-judicial bodies are. While most scholars consider truth commissions to be ad hoc, victim-centered bodies that focus on past violence (see Hayner 2002), Leahy drew on the label to describe something very different. His truth commission would be ad hoc, but it would be focused on uncovering the process of policy making and not on the survivors. Moreover, the violence was ongoing. While detention policies had changed, Guantanamo was still open, and individuals were still being held without any formal charges.

Leahy's call for a Truth and Reconciliation Commission inspired scholars, policy makers, and advocates who were interested in what a truth commission might offer the United States. Army Major General Taguba, who wrote the internal report on Abu Ghraib, former FBI director William Sessions, former Undersecretary of State Thomas Pickering, and Juan Mendez, along with the eighteen human rights organizations, signed on to a letter in February, calling for a commission that a later *Guardian* report referred to as an effort to create a "truth commission."[122] Similarly, the National Religious Campaign against Torture, which formed after the Abu Ghraib scandal broke, released a letter on March 3, 2009 that called for a commission of inquiry, which they sent to the Senate Judiciary Hearing on Leahy's proposal. The letter was signed by twenty-five religious leaders and endorsed by 7000 people. By April, NRCAT joined a coalition organized by the Open Society Institute (OSI), the Soros-funded organization that had supported the 1992 Salzburg conference on Justice in Times of Transition, created to pressure the government to create a presidential commission of inquiry on the detention policies.

Leahy also inspired Stephen Soldz, a Boston-based psychology professor who founded the Coalition for an Ethical Psychology. Soldz thought that a truth commission would be useful for making psychologists reflect on their role in torturing detainees and for preventing medical professionals from aiding abuse in the future.

120 Patrick Leahy, "The Case for a Truth Commission." *Time*, February 19, 2009. See also *Time*, "Leahy's Plan to Probe Bush Era Wrongdoings," February 13, 2009; *Huffington Post*, "Exclusive: Leahy Talks to White House about Investigating Bush," February 10, 2009, www.huffingtonpost.com/2009/02/10/exclusive-leahy-talks-to_n_165774.hTSMl (accessed March 24, 2009); *MSNBC*, The Rachel Maddow Show, February 10, 2009, www.msnbc.msn.com/id/29137822/ (accessed March 24, 2009).

121 The interesting point about this assumption is that the South Africa Commission was not predicated on blanket amnesty. There were clear rules regarding who could receive amnesty and who could not.

122 Spencer Ackerman, "Inside the Fight to Reveal the CIA's Torture Secrets," *The Guardian*, September 9, 2016, www.theguardian.com/us-news/2016/sep/09/cia-insider-daniel-jones-senate-torture-investigation (accessed October 10, 2016).

According to Soldz, colleagues had said it was "propaganda" to have a public hearing about the issue, but Soldz, reflecting on his days as an anti-war activist, thought a truth commission would be a useful strategy to get the issue of torture back on the public agenda (interview with Stephen Soldz 2015). For him, like the other proponents described here, a truth commission's goal would be "to expose the legal rationales that justified abuse,"[123] as well as to reveal the "role of psychologists in the design, implementation, standardization and dissemination of U.S. torture and detainee abuse."[124] Through a truth commission, he sought change within the profession, saying that a commission would examine the "professions themselves and the institutional, organizational, policy, and ethical failures that allowed such widespread abetting of government torture."[125]

Like Soldz, Peter Honigsberg, a law professor, was outraged by his profession's role in state-sponsored torture. From his perspective, the United States should be compared with other countries that have engaged in mass violence. In January 2009, Honigsberg published a blog post the *Huffington Post* entitled "Establishing a Truth Commission for Guantánamo":[126]

> This truth commission will collect the stories of their detention and abuse. This truth commission will also interview habeas lawyers who represented the detainees, translators who worked in Guantánamo, and anyone else who elects to testify, such as guards or soldiers. The observations of the detainees and the others will reveal the human narrative of the detainment facility at Guantánamo Bay. Our goal is to collect, document and archive witness testimony to show the truth of what happened at Guantánamo.[127]

Honigsberg's proposal for a truth commission was different from these other proposals in that he wanted to focus on the victims, not the policies, and hoped he could host a nongovernmental truth commission at his university. The mission was personal for Honigsberg, who saw parallels between state-sponsored torture and Nazi era violence. After writing the blog post, Honigsberg was granted initial funds to develop his proposal for a truth commission, and actively sought advice on how to make such a commission a reality.

Finally, while Honigsberg was planning his initiative, he contacted Almerindo Ojeda from the University of California – Davis. Ojeda, a professor of rhetoric originally from Peru, had developed "the Guantánamo Project," which was a

[123] Steven Soldz, "Psychologists Defying Torture: The Path Ahead," *Physicians for Human Rights Newsletter*, November 2008, p. 20, www.psysr.org/archives/newsletters/PsySR_Herald_Nov_2008.pdf (accessed December 10, 2015).

[124] Rule of Law Oral History Project, Interview with Steven Soldz, p. 83, www.hoffmanreportapa.com/resources/INTERVIEWSOLDZ.pdf (accessed December 10, 2015).

[125] Ibid, p. 84.

[126] Peter Jan Honigsberg, "Establishing a Truth Commission for Guantánamo," *The Huffington Post*, Jan. 9, 2009, www.huffingtonpost.com/peter-jan-honigsberg/establishing-a-truth-comm_b_156826.hTSMl (accessed December 27, 2011).

[127] Ibid.

comprehensive website containing information on every detainee known to be held at Guantánamo, along with published statements by military and other professionals working at the detention center. Working as both a scholar and an advocate, Ojeda was also interested in creating a truth commission on state-sponsored torture, and did not shy away from comparing the United States to countries where a truth commission had been created:

> I come from Peru. I lived through the very violent end of the 20th century there in 1980s, 1990s where Maoist insurgency – the Shining Path tried to take over the country by force – a very violent group. After 2001 – 9/11, I started seeing the same kind of rationale with the same kinds of backdoor in-the-dark actions. And the point came where I said, "I can't take anymore. I have to do something," and the Guantánamo Bay Project is what I began. (Interview with Almerindo Ojeda 2010)

Ojeda did not see the United States as a country where a truth commission does not belong, in contrast with a variety of actors discussed below, and wanted to be sure that the United States did not shy away from its obligations to redress its victims. In 2009, Ojeda coordinated a meeting with fifteen military and civilian lawyers, including eight law professors. They called their Coalition "the Davis Group" and drafted a proposal for a "Commission on Detentions" that would investigate the detention policies, focusing on the legality of the policies and making recommendations so that they did not happen again.

Ojeda hoped to contribute to the TRC that Leahy proposed. However, that initiative never got off the ground, and the leaders of these other campaigns shifted their goals and strategies. Part of the problem was that Obama's policy priorities shifted as he focused on getting his healthcare bill passed. He did not want to upset Republicans by focusing on censuring the Bush administration. At the same time, examining these actors' understandings of truth commissions and transitional justice revealed that there was more to the failed campaigns than a lack of political opportunity. Various actors were interested in creating an ad hoc government commission but resisted framing their mobilization strategies as promoting a truth commission. Actors such as Honigsberg, who initially were interested in this label, later dropped it. Understanding the evolution of these campaigns reveals that the same malleability that makes transitional justice useful in some places, for some types of violence, can make it problematic in other settings.

THE PROBLEM WITH A TRUTH COMMISSION IN THE UNITED STATES

The Congressional debates over Leahy's proposed Truth and Reconciliation Commission provide initial insights into why the label "truth commission" did not resonate with U.S. actors. While media referred to Conyers' proposed commission as a truth commission, he never adopted this label. In contrast, Leahy did use the label, and the debates over his proposed commission reveal why this framing strategy helped get attention to the issue. However, this framing also turned off individuals who may have had similar goals but were concerned about the political implications of mobilizing around a truth commission.

In spring 2009, Leahy's online petition to "investigate abuses during the Bush-Cheney Administration – so they never happen again" had nearly 100,000 signatures.[128] However, immediately after Leahy made this proposal in February 2009, U.S. media reported on the dilemma of Leahy's framing of his proposed commission as a Truth and Reconciliation Commission, as well as of the need for a commission at all. John Q. Barrett, a renowned legal professor who has expertise in both constitutional and criminal law, expressed concern that "creating a whole new entity would be a huge bureaucratic exercise," an "effort to shunt off something that can be done by Congress."[129] Another academic, a political philosopher from the University of Chicago, condemned the proposal because it implicitly compared the Bush-era policies with apartheid or the Argentine juntas. For these public intellectuals, a truth commission is useful for a different type of violence in a different type of political system.

In the Judiciary Committee's March 9, 2009 hearing on Leahy's proposal, the senator addressed these concerns by explaining a truth commission as a political and pragmatic compromise. He phrased his proposal as a commission of inquiry to "get to the truth" and argued that it would be the best compromise for those calling for judicial accountability and those suggesting that it was better to move on:

> There are some who resist any effort to look back at all, while others are fixated on prosecution, even if it takes all of the next eight years, or more, and further divides this country. Over the last month, I have suggested a middle ground to get to the truth of what went on during the last several years, in a way that invites cooperation. I believe that that might best be accomplished through a nonpartisan commission of inquiry ... to understand the full extent of what our country did and why it happened.[130]

Leahy and others who testified drew on transitional justice discourse, with expressions such as *moving forward* and *reconciliation* and references to academic debates about truth vs. justice, to explain what this commission might do in the United States. Thomas Pickering, a career diplomat who once served as the Undersecretary of State for Political Affairs, stated that "we must assess the policies that led us to our current position in order to learn how to move forward."[131] He suggested that the commission should have subpoena power and noted that questions of immunity remain at the forefront of discussions about a commission. From his perspective, there should be no blanket immunity, but those who participated in the Commission should not be held liable for what they say. His explanations echo the dilemmas

[128] See "Take Action: Support a Truth and Reconciliation Commission," ga3.org/campaign/btcpetition (accessed March 24, 2009).

[129] Bobby Ghosh, "Leahy's Plan to Probe Bush Era Wrongdoings," *Time*, February 13, 2009.

[130] Patrick Leahy, Senate Judiciary Committee, March 4, 2009.

[131] Thomas Pickering, Senate Judiciary Committee, March 4, 2009.

debated in the wake of the South Africa TRC, as well as the issues proponents of truth commissions in the Balkans and in Colombia were considering, namely whether punishing the architects of policies that lead to violence is politically feasible and, if not, what other interventions might deter future violence?

At the same time, like those who criticized the proposed commission to the media, participants in the judiciary hearing did not want to compare the United States to countries where truth commissions had been created. In particular, actors who were less critical of the Bush administration would not support an intervention that seemed too easy to politicize. David Rivkin, Jr., a Federalist Society lawyer who represented Croatia against Serbia at the International Court of Justice (he also represented states opposing the Medicaid revisions in Obamacare), also testified at the hearing. He argued that the proposed commission, which he believed was modeled on Conyers' proposal, was more of a criminal investigative body than a commission of inquiry. He pointed out that Conyers had suggested extending the statute of limitations on torture and war crimes in order to "rein in the Imperial Presidency."[132] Rivkin noted that the proposed commission would deal with acts that are regulated by criminal law and would be geared toward high-level lawyers and policy advisors. Thus, he argued, the proposed investigative commission should not be created because it violates the Constitution's separation of powers.

Professor Jeremy Rabkin, who was teaching constitutional history at George Mason University, was the most thorough and explicit about why a TRC did not belong in the United States. In his written testimony, Rabkin put the words *truth commission* in quotation marks, which highlights his concern about the label. Rabkin opened his testimony by noting that he had worked at the United States Institute for Peace, an organization that helped promote truth commissions around the world. However, as he saw it, this professional experience made him reluctant to promote one in the United States. He suggested that promoting a bipartisan commission to establish a consensus truth is "really naive" and that calling it a "truth commission" would not give it "any magical power."[133] He explained this position by pointing out that even Nelson Mandela was critical of the South Africa Truth and Reconciliation Report, and there was little consensus on the utility of a truth commission in Chile. Furthermore, Rabkin was concerned that labeling the proposed commission a truth commission would misrepresent the violence. He noted that the truth commissions in South Africa and Chile were in "extraordinary" circumstances where policy makers had issued blanket amnesties and where military coups were possible. He suggested that truth commissions are alternatives to courts and have been used when prosecutions might threaten political stability. Rabkin stated that the United States is not even "remotely" in this situation and, thus, "We do not need an extraordinary alternative to the normal process of criminal justice."

[132] David Rivkin, Jr., Senate Judiciary Committee Hearing, March 4, 2009.

[133] Jeremy Rabkin, Senate Judiciary Committee Hearing, March 4, 2009.

These different opinions show how the malleability of a truth commission made it salient for actors like Leahy, who saw a commission as a political compromise between those pushing for prosecutions and those arguing to move on. However, for others, a truth commission was simply not something that belonged in the United States. These skeptics did not want to suggest that allegations of U.S. torture were as grave as violence elsewhere, and they did not want to promote a quasi-judicial body that might equate the United States to other countries where courts could not address issues of state-sponsored violence. Their understandings of truth commissions, ranging from seeing them as a euphemism for impunity to seeing them as a euphemism for criminal investigations, shows how this intervention's malleability meant that opponents could also make claims about what truth commissions are and why they are a bad strategy for redressing violence.

ADVOCATES FOR AND AGAINST A TRUTH COMMISSION

The OSI coalition members were also interested in promoting a presidential commission, for contradictory reasons. Fritz Schwarz, who had spoken at the Conyers and Leahy hearings, responded to my first question about how his organization, New York University's Brennan Center for Justice, became involved with the Commission on Accountability by explaining his past experience investigating the Nixon administration. His interest in a commission had to do with his belief that criminal prosecution "was (a) not gonna happen and (b) probably, in most instances, would be unfair" (interview with Fritz Schwartz 2010).

For Schwartz, a commission was an alternative to prosecutions while, for others, a commission would be their precursor. Jonathan Tracy, assistant director at the National Institute of Military Justice at American University, similarly highlighted his desire for prosecutions and his acceptance that a commission would be a second-best option, "more feasible than prosecutions." He worried about "the partisan bickering that obviously will take place, and people claiming that [prosecutions] will be a witch hunt." He thought that "having a commission is probably better at this point just so that there's some sort of mechanism for getting at the truth and having the truth see the light of day and then, maybe at a later date, hopefully, go through other mechanisms to have actual criminal responsibility" (interview with Jonathan Tracy 2010).

Yet another participant, Jonathan Whitehead, from the Rutherford Institute, an organization dedicated to civil liberties and human rights, highlighted how a commission's ambiguity made it easy for them to support, as they would not have to specify whether they were promoting one as an alternative or as a precursor to future prosecutions:

> As an organization, we did wrestle some with the question of, "Are we calling for a commission of inquiry only, or are we also asking for investigations for criminal

> culpability?" And we concluded that we are doing both, but that we would put the emphasis on the commission of inquiry. (Interview with Jonathan Whitehead 2010)

Though these actors debated questions about whether to pursue "some sort of mechanism for getting at the truth" versus "investigations for criminal culpability," they still avoided the label "truth commission." Their resistance to so labeling their proposed commission was not for lack of knowledge about truth commissions or transitional justice. For example, Nathaniel Raymond, who represented Physicians for Human Rights in the coalition, explained that "we have been very aware of and steeped in the transitional justice tradition: The South African TRC, the ICTY/ICTR, Sierra Leone Special Court, etc. are venues we have been involved with" (correspondence with Nathaniel Raymond 2010). Further, in addition to the organizations' own work on truth commissions, the ICTJ was part of this coalition and provided information to other members on the idea of transitional justice and the use of truth commissions in different settings. The ICTJ obviously saw utility in taking the truth commission model from abroad and applying it to the United States. This organization had consulted with the Greensboro TRC and promoted this truth commission model to other U.S. communities that were interested in creating a TRC to deal with racial violence.

However, when it came to U.S. detention policies, even this organization was less sanguine about using the label. With new funding from the OSI, the ICTJ was able to hire Carolyn Patty Blum, a legal scholar and advocate who founded the International Human Rights Clinic at Berkeley School of Law. As part of the newly developed U.S. Accountability Project, Blum and her colleagues began to publish information on why the idea of transitional justice would be useful to advocates interested in detention policies.[134] The ICTJ framed its goals and strategies in much the same way that it would for its work in other countries:

> The U.S. Accountability Project develops realistic policy options for addressing the serious and systematic violations of human rights incurred through U.S. counterterrorism operations after September 2001. It makes informed analysis and technical assistance available to advocates and policymakers on accountability issues. In undertaking this work, the project applies ICTJ's in-depth international experience and draws comparative lessons appropriate to the U.S. context.[135]

In their report, the ICTJ mentions the need for "commissions of inquiry, prosecutions, reparations and security system reform." Though they saw the utility of the idea of transitional justice, they avoided the phrase "truth commission." An ICTJ staffer working on this issue noted that, although there were some parallels between

[134] See ICTJ, Responding to U.S. Abuses in the War on Terror, ictj.org/sites/default/files/ICTJ-USA-Accountability-Abuses-2009-English.pdf (accessed Jan. 26, 2012).

[135] ICTJ, *After Torture: U.S. Responsibility and the Right to Redress*, 2010, www.ictj.org/sites/default/files/ICTJ-USA-Right-Redress-2010-English.pdf (accessed Apr. 5, 2014).

the issues facing U.S. and foreign advocates, the United States should not be compared with other countries that had established truth commissions. She suggested that "there is some question in a lot of people's minds about what is the relevance of other experiences" and that she thinks that the questions "are correct to some extent." She worried that the United States was a different context: "a lot of the situations where we see truth commissions operating is a very different context in a sense that it's usually about citizens of a state and the state's relation with those citizens rather than the kind of amorphously defined global 'War on Terror.'" Mainly, the nature of the violence, being perpetrated far away and on people with little connection to U.S. citizens, meant that it would be difficult to "motivate citizens of the country that is perpetuating abuses to care about the broader context" (interview with ICTJ staffer 2010).

For this ICTJ staffer, the question was not so much whether courts were useful, but what the goal of a commission in the United States would be. The ICTJ's understanding of a truth commission was focused on citizens and their state. When it came to state-sponsored torture in the United States, the violence was not being done to citizens. In addition, rather than encouraging survivors to talk about their experiences, the commission they were interested in was focused on U.S. policy making. Thus, this staffer was not sure the label was appropriate.

Another coalition member who was similarly familiar with truth commissions noted that he "argued not to have it be known as a truth commission." He explained his understanding that truth commissions "go back through to see not only what happened and the who, what, where, when, and why, but also to find out what happened to society as a result of that." He was clear that the proposal was not a commission to do that but, rather, "was a commission that would look at policy." He concluded that he hoped that no one would refer to the proposed commission as a truth commission (interview with U.S. human rights advocate 2010).

For this advocate, who had worked on investigations for courts and truth commissions around the world, the name of their proposed commission was more than a question of labels. Rather, it reflected larger questions that participants had about what they hoped to accomplish. They were less interested in enabling the survivors of violence to provide information, and to show the effects on the larger society. Rather, they were interested in policies that led to the violence. They did not see the label of "truth commission" as useful for that investigative goal, suggesting that malleable understandings of truth commissions have their limits.

The coalition ultimately defined its goal as creating a Commission on Accountability that would be similar to the 9/11 Commission. They avoided mentioning their interest in judicial accountability, but emphasized their hope that a Commission would strengthen rule of law in the United States:

> The commission, comparable in stature to the 9/11 Commission, should look into the facts and circumstances of such abuses, report on lessons learned, and recommend measures that would prevent any future abuses. We believe that the

> commission is necessary to reaffirm America's commitment to the Constitution, international treaty obligations, and human rights. The report issued by the commission will strengthen U.S. national security and help to re-establish America's standing in the world.[136]

Like government proposals for a truth commission, the Commission on Accountability did not materialize. However, several coalition members remained committed to their goal of creating a comprehensive account of the causes and consequences of violence. The Constitution Project, one of the coalition members, decided to organize a nongovernmental, nonpartisan "task force." In December 2010, the Constitution Project sent out a press release about its new initiative. It described the project's goals in relation to domestic and international law:

> [The] [i]ndependent, bipartisan, blue-ribbon Task Force is examining the federal government's policies and actions related to the capture, detention and prosecution of suspected terrorists in U.S. custody during the Clinton, Bush, and Obama administrations. Created late in 2010, the goal of the Task Force is to provide the American people with a broad understanding of what is known – and what may still be unknown – about the past and current treatment of suspected terrorists detained by the U.S. government. The Task Force seeks to identify and promote detention policies and practices that comply with the nation's legal obligations, foreign policy objectives, and values.

Notably, the opening paragraph in the project's report explains how this initiative was inspired by Leahy's call for a TRC, but it still did not refer to the initiative with this label or suggest the creation of a truth commission. The Task Force, like a truth commission, focused on the causes and consequences of violence, and published their final report in 2013. The report focused on the legal and political consequences of U.S. detention policies (only 15 pages of the 600-page report discuss the detainees) and provides detailed information and legal analysis that would support a future tribunal interested in trying individuals for committing torture.

REJECTING A TRUTH COMMISSION: U.S. EXCEPTIONALISM

This overview of the OSI's campaign reveals that even actors familiar with truth commissions saw the label as problematic for the United States. Several prominent civil society organizations that engage in court-based mobilization strategies considered joining the coalition to create a Commission on Accountability, but they ultimately declined. Their perspective was that the United States is simply different from other countries where truth commissions might be useful, and that these quasi-judicial bodies are simply tools for amnesty. For these actors, the malleability of a truth commission was deeply problematic.

136 See Commission on Accountability, www.commissiononaccountability.org (accessed December 9, 2011).

In a discussion of a potential truth commission with a staff attorney for the American Civil Liberties Union (ACLU), the attorney emphatically noted that truth commissions are for countries that are "in such an unstable situation" that they cannot have courts deal with the issue. He invoked the idea of transition, suggesting that "we have had numerous successful and peaceful transitions of power since our beginning, and we're in no real danger of threatening our democracy by simply applying our existing laws to all who violate them" (interview with ACLU staff attorney 2010). His perspective reveals the common belief that truth commissions are for countries where transitions are violent and where courts cannot address domestic and international crimes. While this remains a common belief, by 2010, South Korea had created a truth commission, Canada had created a truth commission, and the Greensboro TRC had completed its work in the United States; but many actors still saw truth commissions as useful primarily for countries that are unstable.

To a large extent, his legalistic perspective reflects organizational identity, as the ACLU was famous for pursuing social change through the courts, and even turned to the Interamerican Court for Human Rights to address issues of torture and indefinite detention.[137] He was concerned that promoting a quasi-judicial body such as a truth commission might undermine the ACLU's ongoing lawsuits to provide redress to specific detainees and to compel the government to disclose information about detention policies. At the same time, his statement also highlights the prevalent belief that political opportunities in the United States are distinct from political opportunities in other countries, even though U.S. courts seemed unwilling or unable to challenge executive authority on the issue of torture, the court cases were moving at a snail's pace, and the public was losing interest.

The Center for Constitutional Rights (CCR) also contemplated joining the OSI Coalition, but declined for similar reasons. The organization was the first to send lawyers to defend detainees in the military trials. Since its early days of defending civil rights activists, the Center conceived of itself as a "social movement support" team, an organization that "accepts cases and projects based on principle and the value of the struggle itself, not solely by using a calculus of victory."[138] The organization was actively litigating cases on torture both domestically and internationally, and staff saw little point in a strategy that was not aimed at judicial accountability. According to one CCR staff attorney, a commission was not needed for the United States, because there was no need for more information to be discovered. The dilemma was that it was classified. He saw truth commissions as useful for places like South Africa and Argentina, where the information "is buried in the consciousness of someone who is the only witness and doesn't want to talk about it." In addition to mentioning

[137] See *El-Masri v. Tenet*, Petition to the IAHCR, April 9, 2008, www.aclu.org/files/pdfs/safefree/elmasri_iachr_20080409.pdf (accessed Jan. 26, 2012).

[138] See Center for Constitutional Rights, "Mission and History," www.ccrjustice.org/missionhistory (accessed Feb. 22, 2012).

the "information gap," he also suggested that there was not "the same sort of national cleavage" that would require a truth commission (interview with CCR staff attorney 2010). Like participants in the Congressional hearings, his concern centered on the belief that the political context in the United States was unique, that the violence was problematic but not as pervasive as in places where there have been truth commissions, and that a truth commission would not help stop the violence.

The ACLU staff attorney echoed him, reiterating the common misconception based on the ICTJ's success in promoting the South African model. When I asked about the OSI initiative, he suggested that "that type of truth commission model relies on generally giving immunity to most to find out details about what took place and then to have a public reconciliation." Again, he mentioned that such a commission is "mainly needed" in places such as South Africa and places where there is "a fledgling democracy that wouldn't survive protracted investigations, where the very horrendous abuses that had taken place would literally threaten the democracy that was forming" (interview with ACLU staff attorney 2010). The staff attorney from the CCR also noted that truth commissions are essentially tools to exchange truth for immunity.

In addition to showing how understandings of the South African TRC affect understandings of truth commissions more generally, these lawyers' opinions reveal how the malleability of truth commissions, particularly with respect to judicial accountability, was not an asset but a liability. For them, truth commissions are useful where prosecution is not possible, and prosecution is possible in the United States. While some actors who joined the OSI coalition saw the utility of promoting a commission as a precursor to prosecutions, these actors saw a commission as an alternative and something that would undermine their efforts. They continued to sue the U.S. government, as well as private contractors involved in developing and implementing the enhanced interrogation policies, on behalf of detainees.

Another organization, the Bill of Rights Defense Council (BORDC), contemplated whether a truth commission might help change public perceptions of torture and emerged with similar concerns about whether promoting a truth commission would undermine efforts toward prosecution. The former executive director, Shahid Buttar, is a lawyer, but BORDC did not focus on legal mobilization through the courts. Rather, it worked on grassroots campaigns, encouraging local policy makers to address the issues of detention and allegations of torture. Buttar, like other advocates, had heard about truth commissions in other countries and suggested to his colleagues that they promote one. He described to me knowing very little about these quasi-judicial bodies, but was attracted to the idea of investigating, documenting, and publicizing information about abuse, because such a strategy might call public attention to the issue and lead to future prosecutions. However, he faced opposition from his colleagues, who were emphatic that prosecutions were necessary, and who thought truth commissions provide amnesties. Buttar let go of his interest in promoting a truth commission and continued to call for prosecutions.

This sense of truth commissions as second best was not unique to actors in the United States. This book shows similar perspectives in the Balkans and in Colombia. However, what made the U.S. case different was that some of these actors simply did not want to compare the United States to other countries or to say that the United States could learn from their experiences. For them, appropriating and promoting a seemingly foreign intervention was not a strategy worth entertaining.

NO POLITICAL OPPORTUNITIES FOR A COMMISSION

While part of the reason these strategies never got off the ground had to do with organizational goals and strategies, the main dilemma was that there were no political opportunities to create a commission, let alone develop other strategies that would bring public attention to the issue of torture.

Some interviewees blamed politicians for not paying sufficient attention to the issue of torture, but most suggested that the problem ran deeper than political elites. John Whitehead emphasized that the Coalition's challenges were mostly related to public apathy and the fact that torture was now accepted. He suggested that "the problem with these kinds of projects is that a large cross-section of Americans are not just in the right." He singled out "some of what you might call classic liberals" who "believe that torture is okay." This worried him, as he saw this belief as one of the reasons that the OSI project and projects like it were stalled: "It's tough to get a politician to move forward on anything if he thinks the poll's the other way" (interview with John Whitehead 2010).

While actors in BiH and Colombia similarly had to address issues of apathy, the U.S. context was distinct. In BiH and Colombia, the violence affected most of the citizenry, whether directly or through interactions with individuals who were affected. By 2009, the economic crisis overshadowed interest in Guantánamo Bay and the War on Terror, and the media had moved on from the issue. Nathaniel Raymond, from Physicians for Human Rights, explained his perspective on how challenging it was to get public attention to the issue:

> American people don't care about torture anymore. It is six years since Abu Ghraib. People on the ground in the military were twelve when Abu Ghraib happened. They have captains who weren't out of high school. The military establishment, general public, have been hearing about this a long time, it would have happened if it were going to happen. (Interview with Nathaniel Raymond 2010)

Raymond went on to say that his organization decided to study human experimentation at Guantánamo in order to explain to the American public that what was going on could be compared to Nazism. This was a last-ditch attempt to get the "human rights community" to "wake up and smell the coffee . . . it was a political nightmare that they needed to put in legal jeopardy." He expressed his frustration, suggesting that "at this point there [is] nothing we can throw up that they have to react to. We are running out of time and money. Funders won't fund on this after this year unless it changes" (interview with Nathaniel Raymond 2010).

Physicians for Human Rights eventually released a report that suggested detainees were used for medical experiments.[139] His organization continued to work on the issue of torture, but they no longer saw promoting a national commission as a viable strategy. For them, the time to get public attention to the issue passed along with Obama's interest in the issue.

DECIDING AGAINST A TRUTH COMMISSION: SCHOLAR–ADVOCATES

Finally, the scholars I interviewed about their campaigns – who really functioned more as scholar–advocates – were more committed to the label of a truth commission than policy makers or staff at advocacy organizations. At first, they believed that they could adapt truth commission models from abroad to fit the U.S. context. However, they too eventually shied away from this label, worried that it was not useful for their mobilization campaigns.

Soldz, who had promoted a truth commission for psychologists, recounted that he was not very familiar with truth commissions when he proposed one. Like others interviewed for this study, Soldz wanted to do something to prevent torture, knew about the South Africa TRC, and figured that a commission would be a useful intervention to help get prosecutions in the future. However, as he learned more about these quasi-judicial bodies, he realized that the U.S. context was different from the political contexts where truth commissions had been created. In our interview, he referenced Africa, which is where he thought most truth commissions had been created. He described learning more about these quasi-judicial bodies and came to see commissions as better for reconciliation and worse for truth. His interest was in exposing information about medical professionals, and he stopped seeing the creation of a truth commission as the most effective way to ensure that goal. He hoped that at some point, if political power changed in Congress, he would be able to get public hearings on the role of health professionals in torture. However, with no political opportunities on the horizon, he decided to offer support to existing investigative efforts, such as the Constitution Project's Task Force, rather than continue to pursue an independent commission.

Similarly, Honigsberg, who had considered creating a nongovernmental commission at his university, learned more about the OSI initiative and talked with fellow

139 Physicians for Human Rights, Evidence Indicates that the Bush Administration Conducted Experiments and Research on Detainees to Design Torture Techniques and Create Legal Cover: Illegal Activity Would Violate Nuremberg Code and Could Open Door to Prosecution, Press Release, June 7, 2010, physiciansforhumanrights.org/press/press-releases/news-2010-06-07.hTSMl (accessed Dec. 21, 2011). Although various bloggers mentioned the report, there was little response from the mainstream media or the government. See, e.g., Our Campaigns, "Evidence Indicates that the Bush Administration Conducted Experiments and Research on Detainees to Design Torture Techniques and Create Legal Cover," www.ourcampaigns.com/NewsDetail.hTSMl?NewsID=67876 (accessed Dec. 22, 2011).

actors about transitional justice and truth commissions. Reflecting on these other initiatives, he ultimately decided that he would not call his proposed commission a truth commission or pursue a public recounting of violence at Guantánamo. Rather, he would redirect his efforts toward providing voice for survivors through a different medium. His new effort was titled "Witness to Guantánamo," and he promoted it as an oral history project to gather videos of detainees willing to describe their experiences in detention centers. Interestingly, on the site, he framed the ultimate goal as accountability, and saw providing voice as a way to get there: "W2G's [Witness to Guantánamo's] filmed narratives have helped transition former detainees from being faceless, nameless victims of abusive interrogation policies to individual human beings with personal stories of survival." He noted that recognition of survivors might "educate the public and mobilize pressure to hold U.S. government officials and private actors accountable."[140]

Even after Honigsberg redirected his efforts away from promoting a truth commission, the new initiative proved challenging. The project manager for the initiative described it "stop and go" as they tried to gain funds and access to former detainees. Ultimately, the organization did receive some support from the University of San Francisco and several family charities, as well as the OSI. Moreover, Honigsberg's interest in providing an opportunity to speak did not always align with the survivors' interests. Staff noted that they tried to find various ways to explain to the detainees the value of recording their stories, as some survivors were less interested in offering their stories for educational purposes. By 2015, the Witness to Guantánamo Project succeeded in collecting interviews with almost fifty former detainees and dozens of individuals who worked in the facility, an important contribution to information about the detention facilities, but far less than the original hope of securing the testimony of all detainees.

Finally, Ojeda also redirected his efforts back to his website, which, like Honigsberg's new project, focused on providing a virtual platform for survivors to tell their stories. Ojeda's goal had been to support Leahy in his proposal, but with Leahy following Obama's lead, their call for a commission became yet another stunted mobilization campaign.

DECOUPLED TRANSITIONAL JUSTICE INITIATIVES

Efforts to shut down Guantánamo and redress torture victims continued long after these mobilization campaigns ended. However, mobilizing around a truth commission in the United States, or even pursuing legal action against those who helped design the torture policies, did not have the effect that proponents hoped it might. The 2016 election of Donald Trump, who pledged to bring back waterboarding and promised "far worse" for suspected terrorists, was a far cry from the 2008 campaign

[140] See Witness to Guantánamo, "About the Project," witnesstoGuantánamo.com/about/about-the-project.

where McCain and Obama publicly repudiated Bush's detention policies. Trump's entire platform was predicated on U.S. exceptionalism, including exceptionalism with respect to issues of international law. Although Trump later modified his stance on bringing back "enhanced interrogation techniques," his rhetoric during the campaign suggests the futility of efforts to publicize information about the violence caused by Bush's detention policies.

The Senate, for its part, did launch an investigation, which disclosed detailed information about the CIA's role in torture. Staff for Senator Dianne Feinstein, a California Democrat, worked tirelessly gathering information on the CIA's program despite the lack of support from the White House. On August 1, 2014, President Obama notoriously quipped, "We tortured some folks," but did not want to investigate further.[141] The Senate and the CIA's relationship soured during the investigation, as the CIA went so far as to hack Senate computers to find out if and how one of their documents made it into Senate's investigation. Eventually, a heavily redacted report on the detention program was released to the public. Even this report, which clearly showed that the CIA engaged in torture, did not spark much public interest. In a cynical departure from his campaign promises, Obama worked to minimize its political impact.

Lawsuits against military contractors are proceeding at a snail's pace in U.S. courts, but hold some promise for detainees hoping at least to get information about U.S. policies, which has often been withheld on the basis of national security claims. In October 2016, the *New York Times* reported on long-term consequences of torture in CIA detention, trying again to bring attention to the long-term impacts of U.S. policies[142]. However, as the 2016 election revealed, none of these disparate efforts have resulted in renewed or sustained attention to condemning state-sponsored violence by the United States, or helping to redress victims. Public opinion surveys show that a majority of Americans express the belief that torture is justifiable, and that opposition to torturing suspected terrorists is decreasing.[143]

As Acharya (2004) notes, foreign ideas spread most effectively when transnational actors are able to make ideas culturally resonant in particular locales. Without resonance, foreign ideas appear exactly that: foreign. Despite the fact that transnational transitional justice organizations such as the ICTJ and USIP are located in the United States and truth commissions are being created in countries that are not undergoing regime change, including the United States, actors interested in

[141] Ackerman, note supra.

[142] Matt Apuzzo, Sheri Fink and Jame Risen, "How Long Term Torture Left a Legacy of Damaged Minds," *New York Times*, October 9, 2016, https://www.nytimes.com/2016/10/09/world/cia-torture-guantanamo-bay.html (accessed October 10, 2016).

[143] Americans are more likely to think torture is justified than are any other nations. "Global Opinion on Use of Torture," Pew Research Center, www.pewresearch.org/fact-tank/2016/02/09/global-opinion-use-of-torture/ (accessed Dec. 3, 2016). See also, At the same time, data suggest that approval of torture is highly partisan; see "No, Americans Aren't Fine with Torture, They Strongly Reject It," *Washington Post*, Dec. 22, 2014, www.washingtonpost.com/posteverything/wp/2014/12/11/no-americans-arent-fine-with-torture-they-strongly-reject-it/ (accessed December 3, 2016).

redressing torture at U.S. detention centers were resistant to promoting a truth commission in the United States, seeing either the strategy or the label as problematic.

In resisting the label of "truth commission," actors mobilizing around U.S. detention policies were implicitly rejecting the idea of transitional justice, which they saw as something useful for other countries. At the same time, regardless of what they wanted to call it, this chapter further reveals how, for many, truth commissions have become a default way to *do something* to redress mass violence, particularly state-sponsored violence. Actors who saw them as precursors or as alternatives to courts could agree to create one. Similarly, actors who wanted to focus on the policies behind the violence, or the survivors of the violence, thought a truth commission would be useful. The malleability of truth commissions made them appealing to these scholars, policy makers, and advocates, but that same quality made them seem an ineffective approach to others more interested in either prosecutions or a more limited investigation.

Although resistance to a truth commission in the United States may suggest that this case provides little insight into the instrumentalization of transitional justice, the idea's absence is also telling. As Finnemore and Sikkink (1998, p. 268) point out, choosing a particular frame can define issues by naming, interpreting and dramatizing them. Some saw the label of truth commission as a frame that would help to define state-sponsored torture as a crime against domestic and international law, while others saw it as a frame to dramatize the impact of violence on victims and the overall image of the United States in the world. Those who drew on the idea viewed the United States' policies on torture as comparable to those of other regimes that had engaged in torture, and they wanted to make that point. However, others saw the frame as a misrepresentation of both the violence and what should be done to redress it. For them, a truth commission was foreign, useful in places where there was a different type of violence and a different judicial system.

In other words, rejecting the label of a truth commission was also a way to name, interpret, and dramatize violence. Some advocates who rejected the label of a truth commission wanted to name the violence at U.S. detention centers as a crime in need of a judicial remedy, others rejected it because they did not think the allegations of torture were severe enough to warrant a truth commission, and others saw a truth commission as a much more ambitious endeavor than what they were proposing. Regardless of why they rejected the label, their rejection reveals how they understood the nature of the violence and their preferred remedy. In addition, their skeptical perspectives on a truth commission in the United States further reveal the malleability of these quasi-judicial interventions and how that malleability is both an asset and a liability in campaigns to redress mass violence.

At the same time, though to a lesser extent than in the Balkans and in Colombia, mobilizing around a truth commission helped create new sets of elites, here in the form of different coalitions and scholar–advocates inspired by Leahy's call. Actors who chose the label of a truth commission also promoted it with the idealistic discourse that characterizes the transitional justice movement, hoping that there could be reconciliation within the politically divided country. In addition, many of these actors decided to promote a truth commission in order to achieve their long-term goal of prosecutions for the violence.

Furthermore, as occurred in the Balkans and in Colombia, transitional justice became a placeholder for actors to articulate their different beliefs about law as a tool for social and political change and to make claims against one another. Even if they did not call their proposed commission a truth commission, mobilizing around a commission enabled these actors to condemn the earlier administration's policies in the War on Terror and explain their hopes and desires for social and political change in the country. Ironically, although Leahy promoted a truth commission as a political compromise and a way to ensure reconciliation, the proponents of a truth commission were all heavily critical of the Bush administration. Looking at the process of mobilization suggests that actually creating a truth commission might have reproduced, or entrenched, social and political divisions that grew throughout the Bush era. The election of Donald Trump confirms this concern, as the country's divisions on issues of national security have returned to the foreground, and there is little hope that the administration will revisit questions of unlawful detention policies.

In these ways, the decoupled instrumentalization in the United States provides additional insight into why truth commissions are being promoted around the world, as well as how the transitional justice movement is evolving. The malleability of transitional justice has helped the idea spread to countries where there is no political transition, but it is still seen as a lesser form of justice. Actors who promote transitional justice see it as useful in some countries but not others, and for some conflicts but not others. Finally, as the concluding chapter elaborates, their rejection of truth commissions suggests that transitional justice may be yet another Western export, like rule of law, development, or even human rights, that actors in powerful countries can say they do not need for themselves but need to promote elsewhere.

6

The Power of Legal Ideas

This conclusion draws together the main arguments from this book in order to further elaborate on this book's original puzzle, which is why actors in such politically disparate settings were promoting truth commissions? In answering this question, this book points to the larger phenomenon of transitional justice, arguing that transitional justice is an idea around which a movement has emerged, professionalized, and promoted truth commissions as one of its signature interventions. In studying understandings of transitional justice and truth commissions, the empirical analysis shows that actors mobilize around truth commissions for a variety of reasons. The malleability of both the idea and the intervention help explain why actors around the world choose to appropriate and promote them. At the same time, this malleability is also a liability, as actors with contradictory goals can decide that a truth commission is useful, and will, at some point, have to reconcile those differences.

Revisiting these arguments, the following discussion further explains the relationship between truth commissions, transitional justice, and legal politics. First, it elaborates on the concept of a truth commission as a quasi-judicial medium (Rowen 2012), which helps clarify how the intervention's malleability is both an asset and a liability. Following this, it discusses how the malleability of transitional justice made it easy for a movement to emerge and professionalize around the idea, as well as how this professionalization has contributed to the creation of new elites and an idealistic discourse about what truth commissions offer. Next, it discusses how the professionalization of the movement has, ironically, contributed to the anti-impunity turn in human rights advocacy (Engle, Miller, and Davis 2016). In each of these cases, actors interested in transitional justice had to explain their goals and strategies in relation to judicial processes, thus reaffirming prosecutions as an important, if not necessary, strategy to redress mass violence.

While mobilization around truth commissions illustrates the emergence and professionalization of the transitional justice movement, the movement is an illustration of how actors mobilize law to achieve political, social, moral, and even economic ends (Massoud 2013). In addition to elaborating on the malleability of both transitional justice and truth commissions, this conclusion also discusses how the idea serves as a placeholder for actors to articulate their different beliefs about law as a tool for social and political change, as well as to make claims against one another. More broadly, examining how transitional justice is translated into political action reveals that actors continue to mobilize the law as a "salvation" for societies that have experienced mass violence (Massoud 2013, p. 221). However, what this book asserts, as do similar critiques of legal mobilization around human rights, transitional justice, rule of law, development, and other aspirational ideas, is that legal mobilization tends to reproduce social and political divisions in society rather than changing them.

Building from these insights, the conclusions reiterate the importance of ongoing research on who is promoting transitional justice, how, and why. Although the transitional justice movement has succeeded in popularizing the idea and its associated interventions, this book has shown that there is skepticism, ambivalence, and even active resistance to the movement. As such, its future is uncertain.

THE TRUTH COMMISSION AS A QUASI-JUDICIAL MEDIUM

The fact that scholars, policy makers, and advocates in these disparate settings have mobilized around a truth commission reveals just how appealing truth commissions are. Further, that individuals in such different places thought they could adapt the same intervention to meet their particular goals reveals just how malleable they think the intervention is. In each case, understandings of truth commissions varied, with actors seeing them as an alternative or a complement to judicial accountability, as a mechanism to get an accurate historical record, as a tool to provide individuals with the chance to tell their stories in a way that affirms their dignity, or as a combination of the above. Regardless of their long-term goals, they thought a truth commission would get them there.

Given that many proponents of truth commissions prioritized public hearings, one way to think of truth commissions is as voice commissions, bodies that will ensure that individuals have the chance to tell their stories and receive public recognition for their suffering. Thinking of truth commissions as voice commissions helps reveal why, after the South Africa TRC's model of "revealing is healing," these commissions piqued the interest of scholars, policy makers, advocates, and donors looking for innovative strategies to redress mass violence. Thinking of them as voice commissions also explains the efficacy of the ICTJ's initial efforts to spread the South African experience. Many survivors want public recognition for what they have suffered, and advocates serving survivors saw a truth commission as useful for that goal. As Martha Minow, a leading scholar on the South Africa TRC, suggested, "The chance to tell one's story and be heard without interruption or skepticism is crucial to so many people, and nowhere more vital than for survivors of trauma"

(Minow 1998, p. 324). RECOM's move toward prioritizing this voice function of a truth commission underscores this point. Colombian actors, too, emphasized the importance of giving survivors a chance to participate in the creation of a truth commission, as well as its implementation. While the emphasis in U.S. efforts was on policy makers, some actors also saw the South African model as a useful one, and the truth commission proponents hoped public hearings might bring public attention to the issue. Their approach resonates with research that suggests that the more "public" a truth commission is, the more likely it is to lead to higher levels of democracy (Taylor and Dukalskis 2012). From this perspective, truth commissions should prioritize an inclusive process in which it holds public hearings, releases a public report, and names perpetrators.

However, if truth commissions have become voice commissions, then there is an additional problem with their ongoing appeal. Actors who promote the voice function of truth commissions may be ignoring important research on the double-edged sword of procedural justice. These studies emphasize that focusing on voice, or giving individuals the chance to feel heard, can lead individuals to accept outcomes, fair or unfair, simply because they believe they have a say in them (MacCoun 2005). Moreover, as the BiH and Colombia cases suggest, allowing people to speak may be less threatening to power holders than trying to explain the causes and consequences of violence. However, survivors of mass atrocities are particularly susceptible to exploitation and manipulation of interventions that prioritize voice. Studies reveal that survivors of international crimes want the chance to be heard, but they want to discuss community harms, not simply personal harms (Koenig and Smith Cody forthcoming). Moreover, while victims in domestic trials may be satisfied with a procedure if they feel respected by court personnel, survivors of international crimes want recognition, not only from the court, but also from the larger community. For them, recognition is not only about words of respect, but also about material support. In other words, survivors may want voice, but they will likely be disappointed if, like the South African TRC, a truth commission does not lead to some sort of financial compensation and/or changes in government policies.

While it may be easy to point to the South African TRC as a standard, and certainly the professionalization of the movement helps make it one, this book shows that understandings of truth commissions are much more varied, and actors interested in a truth commission often resist the South African model. Elsewhere, I have suggested that truth commissions can be understood as a quasi-judicial medium (Rowen 2012). The findings of this book, which focus on the malleability of the truth commission, provide further insights into the utility of this theoretical concept, which emphasizes how truth commissions channel contradictory, competing, and complementary beliefs about law as a tool for social and political change.

The utility of thinking of a truth commission as a quasi-judicial medium is that the theoretical concept provides insights into why so many different political actors are interested in them, why support for them may be shallow, and why realized truth commissions often disappoint their proponents. First, their quasi-judicial nature brings in the legitimacy of the state, which makes these bodies seem more capable of ensuring social and political change. Actors who want punishment may believe that the truth commission is a first step to judicial accountability, particularly if the truth commission focuses on the causes of the violence. Moreover, when conducted in a public forum, such as the South African TRC, the truth commission hearings resemble court proceedings, with commissioners asking questions of parties that have different perspectives on the violence.

The dilemma is that, as a *medium*, actors have contradictory goals about what these quasi-judicial bodies should do. As Naftali (2016) emphasizes, the appeal of truth commissions has coincided with a movement to promote the "right to truth," whose success derives from "its capacity to accommodate a plurality of causes." Naftali deftly explains how these varied goals may also turn into a constraint as "strategies of alignment and disalignment among truth entrepreneurs that may reinforce or undermine each other's cause" (Naftali 2016, p. 19). This book similarly reveals the contradictory goals of actors interested in promoting truth commissions. For some, they are a precursor to prosecutions. For others, they are an alternative. For many, the goal has less to do with punishment than with providing voice, as explained above, while, for others, a truth commission is actually a way to investigate, document, and publicize information that will serve communities.

Furthermore, a truth commission may prioritize the process as much as the end goals. These bodies enable actors with contradictory or competing beliefs and practices to engage in a performance that defines problems and solutions, much as mediation does (Merry 2013). The majority of contemporary truth commissions have made recommendations for prosecutions, institutional reforms, reparations, and other country-specific suggestions, but few of these recommendations ever come to fruition. These cases suggest that even promoting a truth commission can provide individuals with the opportunity to voice their grievances and articulate hopes for a better future (see Merry 2006). This makes promoting a truth commission a useful strategy for getting support for broader goals, whether or not a truth commission is actually created.

Given the malleability of truth commissions, it is easy to be skeptical of these quasi-judicial bodies. Critics may see them as purveyors of harmony ideology, the belief that the existence of conflict is necessarily a bad or dysfunctional thing and that a healthy society is one that minimizes conflict and confrontation (Nader 1991). Certainly the South African Truth and Reconciliation Commission promoted harmony. With its focus on reconciliation, this truth commission appealed to power holders who wanted to quell claim-making and did not want to disrupt the social order they were trying to create (Nader and Grande 2002; Wilson 2001). These concerns echo Steinberg, who critiques proponents of truth commissions as drawing on "a promiscuous collection of vaguely defined ideas relating to truth, healing, and reconciliation is deployed to conceal pragmatic compromise" (Steinberg 2011, p. 35).

At the same time, my findings leave room for optimism about reproducing the harmony ideology of the South African TRC. Most of my interviewees were well aware of the limitations of truth commissions, and rejected the South African model of "revealing is healing" and forgiveness over vengeance. Rather than viewing them as a panacea, these actors view truth commissions as a way to *do something* to redress mass violence. Many of these actors promoted truth commissions with a self-reflexive awareness that these commissions are very limited tools, and promoting them is politically pragmatic. Though the intervention they promoted was malleable, many of these actors had more concrete goals.

Next, thinking of a truth commission as a quasi-judicial medium gives insights into the ways that the label of a truth commission can serve as a frame that actors will use to inspire and legitimate their campaigns. In Colombia, for example, before the peace negotiation with the FARC was under way, a variety of actors promoted a truth commission in order to emphasize that such a body could only be created if the violence ceased. In the United States, actors avoided the label in order to point out their understanding of the violence and the remedy, which, for many, was prosecution. In both cases, these framing strategies reflect perceived political opportunities for actors to realize their goals, and whether or to what extent they believed a truth commission would aid them.

Finally, on a methodological note, while is it tempting to compare features of truth commissions or discrete variables about the social and political contexts where they are created in order to explain why they are created and when they are effective, this methodology cannot capture the social and political relationships that shape a truth commission's design, implementation, and ultimate efficacy. The Coalition for RECOM's difficulty in gaining popular support in BiH exemplifies the importance of understanding who is promoting a truth commission, how, and why, as do the case studies in Colombia and the United States. Sustained focus on the relationships between civil society and policy makers, the relationships between advocacy organizations, and understanding the incentives for different political actors not only to express support for a truth commission but also to use their political capital to create one, will provide much more useful insights into the conditions under which a truth commission will be realized and/or be effective.

PROFESSIONALIZING AROUND A MALLEABLE IDEA

Just as the malleability of truth commissions made it easy for actors with diverse goals and strategies to promote them, the malleability of transitional justice made the idea a "coalitional glue" that brought diverse sets of actors together, both at the transnational and at the domestic level (Evangelista 1995). At the same time, the malleability was also a liability for those who wanted to ensure accountability, improve survivor well-being, and prevent future violence. Actors with competing goals could draw on the idea to make competing claims, particularly about the value of prosecutions, and skeptics of the idea could readily point out why transitional justice and its associated interventions were either not useful or counterproductive. More simply, its malleability is the reason it was easy to instrumentalize, and why it was instrumentalized in such different ways.

Part of the idea's malleability lies in the idealistic discourse about what transitional justice interventions offer countries seeking to redress mass violence. The discourse includes vague but appealing terms such as reconciliation, truth, reparation, and even justice, and debates about how policies should ensure these different goals. Given this idealistic discourse, which is part and parcel of the idea's malleability, coupled with ambiguity about the value of prosecutions, the transitional justice movement has been able to succeed where the human rights movement has struggled in terms of blending relativist and universalist approaches to law. Transitional justice, like human rights, is an "emancipatory script" designed to bridge cultural differences while offering defined prescriptions for countries wrestling with legacies of violence (Santos 1996). With the universally appealing notion of justice and the ambiguous notion of transition, the idea continues to circulate because actors can draw on it to promote any number of widely accepted goals.

In addition, looking at this idealistic discourse provides insights into how the idea has circulated between the global North and the global South. In a process of reverse vernacularization, transnational actors borrowed beliefs and practices from Eastern Europe, Latin America, and Africa, and then decontextualized and recontextualized them as a new way to think about justice in order to suggest that they had something novel to offer countries where mass violence had occurred. With the fame of the South Africa Truth and Reconciliation Commission, actors could point to this commission to make the claim that truth commissions lead to the vague, idealistic goal of reconciliation, and could explain and legitimate the idea and intervention in reference to one another. Over time, scholars, policy makers, and advocates broadened definitions of transitional justice to include even more goals and strategies, suggesting that truth commissions and other associated interventions might contribute to more complex political challenges such as economic development and redressing the historic injustices of colonialism (Nagy 2008).

This idealistic discourse, thus, goes hand and hand with the professionalization of the movement. A distinguishing feature of a profession is the belief that an occupation has "considerable public importance" and requires certain knowledge or training (Posner 1998, p. 2). Given the difficulty, if not impossibility, of realizing idealistic goals such as truth and reconciliation, there is now a "professional mystique" around transitional justice that allows certain individuals to claim knowledge of how to ensure these goals (Posner 1998). Further, the movement is composed of actors who continue to produce knowledge that reinforces their status as experts (Eyal 2013). With a market for this kind of expertise, individuals are personally invested in making sure truth commissions and other transitional justice interventions continue to be created.

However, for critics of transitional justice, as well as its proponents, it will be important to continue to study elites such as the ICTJ and the broader political economy of the movement. Clearly, the ICTJ became a transnational powerhouse when it received an unprecedented grant from the Ford Foundation. By promoting transitional justice as an idea that could apply to any number of countries, opening regional offices, and working with local civil society and political leaders, the organization also helped create new sets of elites and new opportunities for funding in the places where it worked. Given the idea's malleability and its growing ubiquity, domestic and transnational actors drew on the idea to get resources and to legitimate their work. This suggests that organizations may just as well choose a different idea with which to frame their goals and strategies when that framing strategy becomes more useful. Furthermore, given that the availability of resources to mobilize around transitional justice can foster competition and distrust between organizations with different goals, or simply with different framing strategies, the incentives behind the spread of transitional justice require further examination.

For international relations and political sociology scholars, this analysis of transitional justice's professionalization also points to new directions for research on transnational collective action. Given the role of scholars, policy makers, advocates, and donors in shaping this movement, transitional justice transcends the categorical boundaries between transnational advocacy organizations, epistemic communities, and social movements. Although this book does not discuss the details of the multiple networks in which these professionals work, it was clear in this research that individuals were moving through positions with NGOs, domestic governments, international organizations, and universities and spreading their understandings of transitional justice with them. Like other transnational movements, transitional justice includes an elite class of cosmopolitan activists to which institutions provide resources, opportunities, and incentives (Tarrow 2001). These are the actors that scholars critique as transitional justice entrepreneurs, but they are not the only ones appropriating and promoting the idea (Madlingozi 2010). In Colombia, especially, and to a lesser extent in the United States and BiH, academics played a central role in the instrumentalization of transitional justice. Understanding the contours of this movement, particularly the role of academics in it, and similar forms of transnational collective action around new legal and political ideas can help illuminate new players that are shaping international politics in important ways.

Finally, countries that are in the midst of conflict, emerging from conflict, or even stable but dealing with violence in the past are, obviously, not blank slates. Looking at the different ways in which the idea was instrumentalized reveals that domestic actors translate new ideas according to incentives that may be harder to identify. Future research should continue to explore the professionalization of the transitional justice movement and what it tells us about why actors continue to mobilize around idea. Malleability may make it easy to appropriate and promote an idea, but it may also mean that the idea is easy to coopt, and that actors appropriate and promote transitional justice for self-serving goals. In other word, transitional justice's malleability means the idea serves as a coalitional glue, but more research is needed to explain what makes it continue to stick.

TRANSITIONAL JUSTICE IN THE ANTI-IMPUNITY (RE)TURN

Ironically, while early transitional justice proponents initially conceptualized the idea as a way to think about alternatives to punishment, the movement has also helped affirm prosecutions as an important, if not necessary, strategy for redressing mass violence. Like Subotić (2012), who refers to this affirmation as the legalization of transnational transitional justice advocacy, this book reveals how central prosecution has become to understandings of transitional justice. Engle (2015) explains a similar phenomenon, which she calls the anti-impunity turn in human rights advocacy. Engle points to Amnesty International's argument that not only is impunity a human rights violation, which courts such as the Interamerican Court of Human Rights have suggested, but also impunity leads to human rights violations (Engle 2015, p. 1077). These changes all reflect the "justice cascade," which is the increasing use of trials around the world to redress human rights violations (Lutz and Sikkink 2001). For a brief period after the South Africa TRC, international law scholars pointed to the dangers of prioritizing criminal justice above other goals related to social and political change. However, these cases reveal that transitional justice movement has contributed to the anti-impunity turn, or better return, by which I mean a renewed emphasis on prioritizing prosecutions to redress mass violence.

Looking at domestic advocacy organizations, this book suggests that this anti-impunity return is coming from above and from below, and largely for the same reasons. TRCs became part of this anti-impunity turn as the "right to truth" emerged within domestic and international law (Naftali 2015, 2016). This book has shown that various actors in the Balkans, Colombia, and the United States viewed criminal prosecution as the ideal of justice and resisted thinking that they needed a different standard of justice, which is how they understood transitional justice. Scholars interested in this anti-impunity turn, particularly those who study international law, should continue to study the role of domestic advocacy organizations, not just elite transnational organizations, in promoting prosecutions in the wake of mass violence. The turn may have as much to do with court decisions as it does with organizational goals and strategies. Courts can create new political opportunities that lead to new organizational campaigns, and organizational campaigns can lead to court decisions about rights to truth as well as punishment for mass violence.

Understanding this relationship between criminal courts and other political institutions within the transitional justice movement is particularly challenging, as international criminal courts have emerged as a new player in international and domestic politics (see, e.g., Simmons and Danner 2010). When "transitional justice" was coined in the early 1990s, it was unclear whether there was going to be a permanent court that would prosecute international crimes, and whether South Africa-style amnesties would be restricted. The Rome Statute that created the International Criminal Court (ICC) was not signed until 1999. In the following years, countries domesticated the statute by developing their own legislation that outlawed amnesties for international crimes. As the ICC began to exert pressure on governments that were contemplating peace negotiations, it was no longer politically palatable to suggest that amnesties were necessary. Actors who promoted transitional justice had to emphasize that they were not undermining prosecutions for international crimes, thus elevating prosecutions as a default strategy to redress mass violence, with truth commissions as a complement.

This emphasis on prosecutions was most clear in Colombia, where proponents of transitional justice were interested in avoiding investigation by the ICC. There, actors promoting transitional justice had to make reference to international criminal law and their limited ability to create amnesties. When the plebiscite failed in October 2016, one commentator suggested that Human Rights Watch was to blame on account of the role it played in condemning the peace accords' terms of punishment (Grandin 2016). In the Balkans, actors explained transitional justice in relation to the International Criminal Tribunal for the former Yugoslavia (ICTY), which many individuals viewed as a model of what justice could and should be (Nettelfield 2010). In the United States, mobilizing around transitional justice did not occur in the shadow of an international judicial body but, rather, a domestic one.

In each place, mobilization around transitional justice required actors to address how they would contribute to judicial accountability, not undermine it. The fact that they had to articulate their goals with judicial accountability as the reference point underscores the strength of the anti-impunity turn or, better, return, in human rights advocacy. While mobilizing around truth commissions may once have been a politically pragmatic compromise that avoided the problems of prosecutions, this is no longer the case. Truth commissions are now understood as a complement to prosecutions, if not a precursor, and mobilizing around one further contributes to the anti-impunity agenda, for better or worse.

TRANSITIONAL JUSTICE AS A PLACEHOLDER

Looking at the malleability, idealism, and legalism present in these different case studies, this book reveals that transitional justice serves not just as a coalitional glue but also as a placeholder for actors to articulate their beliefs about law as a tool for social and political change and their hopes and desires for the future, as well as to make claims against one another. Just as proponents of truth commissions can promise everything from voice to prosecution, transitional justice has become a black box into which actors can throw situations ranging from colonial violence to civil war, where the goals are everything from restorative to procedural to retributive to economic to social justice. The dilemma is that, as a placeholder, transitional justice interventions may, at best, reflect social and political divides and, at worst, reproduce and entrench them.

This predicament of reproducing divisions was most clear in BiH, where mobilizing around a truth commission became another opportunity for disappointment and the chance to express nationalist divisions. This dilemma was less clear in Colombia but, perhaps, more dangerous. At first glance, the instrumentalization of transitional justice appeared to have helped open up new possibilities for peace negotiations. On closer inspection, however, the underlying social and political dynamics that fomented the violence has not changed, and the fixation on how the peace agreement will deal with transitional justice has deflected attention from other, pressing concerns about demobilization. Moreover, the idea has become so politicized that opponents of so-called transitional justice for the FARC may undermine the peace process and polarize Colombian society further. In the United States, promoting a truth commission appeared as a thinly veiled attempt to criticize the Bush administration and a tool of partisan politics.

The decoupled instrumentalization of transitional justice in the United States provides additional insights into how transitional justice serves as a placeholder for different political interests, and how its malleability is an asset and a liability. Many U.S. actors rejected truth commissions as an intervention that simply did not fit the context, based on their understanding of what truth commissions are for. Rejecting a truth commission and, along with it, the idea of transitional justice suggests that transitional justice resonates with actors mobilizing around certain types of violence in certain places. It is now common to talk about racial and colonial legacies with the idea of transitional justice, even in the United States, and to describe interventions in Iraq, Afghanistan, and Syria with the idea (Nadery 2007; Stover et al. 2005; Balint et al. 2014). However, certain topics remain outside the movement's reach, further highlighting that many actors working to redress violence see transitional justice as a lesser form of justice, not necessarily a more comprehensive one.

Finally, understanding the process of mobilization around a truth commission can illuminate the radiating effects of this strategy for social and political change. During my observations, no truth commission was created in BiH or the United States, and it is unlikely that one will be. At the same time, these mobilization efforts had social and political effects. In BiH, the effort to create a truth commission brought millions of dollars into the regional economy, groups from around the region came together to talk about their experiences, and, for a time, there was renewed international attention to the region. The efforts to promote a truth commission in the United States brought together a variety of actors with similar goals, and their work led to investigations that are being used in court cases against officials in the Bush administration, as well as others responsible for torture at detention sites. Looking at how transitional justice serves as a placeholder reveals what the idea does for those who appropriate and promote it, even if it does not lead to their stated goals.

LAW, IDEAS, AND IDEOLOGIES

By characterizing transitional justice as an idea and focusing on how actors translate the idea into political action, it is easier to recognize the ideology that sustains the movement, as well as other movements predicated on legal mobilization to redress mass violence. Scholars use the term *ideology* to refer to many things, but here I use it to refer to systems of ideas that inform behavior, where both the idea and behavior are maintained regardless of their benefit (Nader 1991; Freeden 2006). The idea of transitional justice supports the ideology that Western liberal law, in the form of judicial and quasi-judicial interventions geared toward individual liberty, is necessary to ensure accountability, improve survivor well-being, and prevent future violence.

The danger of ideologies about Western law is that certain beliefs become so commonplace that it is hard to recognize the behaviors they inform. In writing about the "human rights idea," Henkin describes "international human rights" as an "international movement to promote and protect and assume and assert international responsibility for *national* human rights, that is, rights within national societies" (Henkin 2000, p. 8). Human rights has become far more than a theoretical tool; different actors utilize to make claims about what their governments owe them, as well as what the international community owes them. For many proponents of the idea, protecting or enforcing human rights is a universal good. For example, Teitel's *Humanity's Law* suggests that international criminal courts and doctrines such as R2P (responsibility to protect), which enables countries to violate norms of sovereignty in order to prevent individuals from human rights violations, reflect international law's shift from serving governments to serving humanity (Teitel 2011).

For skeptics of human rights, however, ideas that are predicated on Western liberal legality can easily be abused. In "Against Human Rights," Žižek (2005) condemns human rights as the "ideological foundation for the fundamentalism of the politically correct," providing a "symbolic fiction" that serves as an "alibi for militarist interventions," and as the "sacralization for the tyranny of the market." In pointing to the ideology behind R2P, Žižek suggests that there is violence embedded in human rights discourse, as this discourse facilitated the United States' military intervention into Iraq and its dire consequences.

Transitional justice, like human rights, is predicated on Western liberal law as a tool for social and political change, and can be critiqued on the same grounds of supporting an ideology that ultimately serves power holders. However, as Donnelly points out, hegemonic ideas such as human rights attract power rather than create power (Donnelly 2007, pp. 106–7). Furthermore, hegemonic ideas such as human rights or, in this case, transitional justice usually remain promotional because actually ensuring rights or justice would require material sacrifices that power holders are not willing to make. Looking at the hegemonic nature of transitional justice in different settings can reveal why promoting the idea is easy but implementing its associated interventions is more challenging.

Further, while transitional justice is less of an alibi than human rights for militarist interventions (it seems the very definition of irony to invade a country under the banner of promoting transitional justice), Andrieu (2010a) rightly points out that the idea of transitional justice, along with the creation of its associated interventions, is part of top-down social engineering designed to provide cover for the violence caused by neoliberalism. The idea may have been conceptualized in relation to earlier democratic transitions from communism and authoritarianism, where law was supposed to ensure individual liberty and equality in relation to the state. However, both domestic and international law increasingly faciliate governance according to market criteria (Brown 2006). The Colombia case most strikingly shows how efforts to promote transitional justice can become a distraction from a country's neoliberal policies that will continue to promote inequality in the country. If there is a truth commission, it will no doubt tread lightly on the most politically sensitive issues of how businesses profited from the conflict and the commission will be exalted as evidence of why the country is safe for investment (Oomen 2005).

At the same time, it is just as easy to dismiss transitional justice as a hegemonic imposition from Western elites as it is to embrace it as an emancipatory script. Embracing or dismissing the idea obviates an understanding of what the idea does for those who promote and appropriate it. As Cotterrell (1997, p. 3) notes, law, in its broadest sense, is a field of experience shaped and structured by problems of government, social control, and social order. Massoud (2013, p. 222) similarly emphasizes that law is a system of values, and that actors have an intuitive belief in the value of law. Transitional justice's circulation reflects this enduring hope that law can help bridge entrenched social and political divisions.

In sum, the transitional justice movement provides yet another example of law's inherent social and political functions. While legal ideas such as transitional justice can sustain hegemonic practices, these practices vary by setting (McCann 2006). To assess how ideas transform into ideologies and whether or to what extent they become hegemonic, this book has shown that it is crucial to take a ground up approach to look at the relationship between law, ideas, identities, and social and political action.

MOVEMENTS AROUND MALLEABLE LEGAL IDEAS

Just as this book has offered a new lens for understanding transitional justice as an idea around which a movement emerged and professionalized, future studies might compare transitional justice with similarly abstruse movements that promote law as a tool of social and political change. Prior movements around ideas such as rule of law, law and development, and even human rights share similar assumptions about law's ability to foster social and political change. As in these other movements, transitional justice proponents have argued that the idea offers an inclusive, responsive, and comprehensive approach to law that will prevent violent conflict. Over time, however, participants in these earlier movements found themselves disillusioned, and recognized that the domestic social and political context shapes the efficacy of legal interventions far more than legal interventions shape the context.

One can easily look to the law and development movement to gain insights into the potential trajectory of the transitional justice movement. Throughout the 1960s and 1970s, actors mobilizing around law and development promoted a variety of strategies, from training law students in Western-style legal education to privatizing public industries. Like transitional justice, development is a malleable idea, both universal (who wouldn't want development?) and ambiguous (what exactly is development?). By 1980, when Gardner (1980) published his famous manifesto on law and development as legal imperialism, it was clear that the legal reforms of the law and development movement, particularly in Latin America, were serving the interests of authoritarian regimes (Trubek and Galanter 1974). In response, the human rights movement tried to promote law as an idea that actors could use against the state. However, that movement, which was largely financed by Western donors, also helped to maintain a liberal legal order that prioritized the United States' geopolitical interests (Dezalay and Garth 2002; Mouralis 2013).

The movement around rule of law is also relevant to this discussion, because transitional justice emerged from programs focused on promoting the rule of law. The main difference between rule of law programs and transitional justice is that proponents of the former are explicit about their faith in Western liberal legality. Actors who promote rule of law suggest that, with the right laws, properly enforced by democratic political institutions, social and political change will occur. Rule of law programs often focus on creating an independent judiciary, which is the cornerstone of a Western legal system. However, the ongoing failures of rule of law programs in places with no history of independent judiciaries reveal that, rather than being an exogenous force in society, law is part and parcel of the social fabric. Creating independent judiciaries in countries that have never had them requires far more than new bills, training, and the other limited interventions at the movement's disposal. In addition, the apolitical phrase "rule of law" provides cover for an imperial approach to Western legal systems as the only acceptable way to organize society (Mattei and Nader 2008). While most actors in the transitional justice movement posit that the whole point of the movement is to promote an understanding of justice that is contextual, the transition and justice of transitional justice are similarly premised on the superiority of democratic governance and Western liberal legality.

Over time, it is likely that disappointments with transitional justice interventions will continue and the disillusionment that plagued these other movements will similarly affect proponents of transitional justice. Mainly, these dilemmas stem from the malleability of law more generally, not simply the ideas in which this malleability manifests. As Gomez (2013, p. 511) notes, studies on how law is instrumentalized often focus on "law either as a tool geared towards the realization of praiseworthy goals, or, conversely, as a politically manipulated weapon deployed to achieve selfish or socially undesirable objectives." Along these lines, over the past decade, it has become increasingly fashionable within the scholarly community to criticize the idea of transitional justice as an industry or discourse that promises far more than it delivers. Perhaps not surprisingly, these important critiques do not seem to have much influence on policy decisions. In Colombia, most strikingly, millions of dollars are going into efforts to create a truth commission that will inevitably disappoint its many proponents and may simply entrench political divisions, rather than reconcile them. In the Balkans, donors offered millions to a regional truth commission that sounded promising but may have been doomed from the start. In the United States, it is difficult to assess what other mobilization strategies might have been more effective than promoting a truth commission. As of this writing, Guantánamo remains open, nearly a decade after President Obama promised to close it, and Donald Trump vowed to bring back waterboarding in his presidential campaign.

From the perspective of those who see law as a tool of the powerful, these examples suggest that promoting truth commissions may be yet another disappointing movement strategy predicated on the false belief that law, specifically legal ideas and legal interventions, can help the less powerful. However, thinking of law as malleable helps avoid the pitfalls of thinking solely in terms of good or bad and enables a more nuanced analysis of how law can be a tool of society's power holders rather than the powerless (see Massoud 2013). Malleability is a double-edged sword; it cuts both ways. For scholars interested in how a new legal idea will be instrumentalized, which can provide insights into how the idea will help the powerful or the powerless, this comparative analysis suggests that they must pay attention to the social and political context, particularly organizational dynamics and political opportunities.

Finally, this analysis of the double-edged sword of malleability applies not only to seemingly progressive ideas such as human rights, but also to decidedly conservative and more narrowly focused legal ideas. Textualism, for example, is a quintessential legal idea, encompassing elements of legal doctrine and the reasoning and forms of interpretation that surround these elements (Cotterrell 1998, p. 177). Judges draw on textualism to explain their reasoning in particular cases and suggest that they are interpreting the statute without the bias that comes from interpretation that includes information beyond the written word. By claiming to be following the written law, proponents of textualism suggest that their interpretation is the correct one because it is not informed by their own ideologies or geared toward specific policy outcomes. However, it is clear that conservative jurists rely on textualism to explain and legitimate their ideological positions. The most famous example is Antonin Scalia, who argued that banning discrimination against homosexuals was the same as granting them "special rights" and that the Voting Rights Act was a "racial entitlement."

More relevant to this book, textualism played a key role in the Supreme Court's determination of whether noncitizens are entitled to the writ of *habeas corpus* in a case brought on behalf of non-citizen detainees at Guantánamo. The majority under Kennedy drew on a textualist interpretation of the statute in question to claim that noncitizens in U.S. detention are entitled to the writ, while Scalia, Thomas, and Alito dissented and used their dissent to emphasize that granting the writ "will make the war harder on us" and will certainly "cause more Americans to be killed."[143] Notably, Scalia gave his opinion about this issue in a public statement in Switzerland prior to this case, noting that "if [a detainee] was captured by my army on a battlefield, that is where he belongs. I had a son on that battlefield, and they were shooting at my son, and I'm not about to give this man who was captured in a war a full jury trial. I mean, it's crazy."[144] Though they may suggest that textualism is a value-neutral legal idea, Scalia and other conservative legal and political actors often use the idea to provide cover for value-laden opinions about social policy.

More generally, this book points to the importance of understanding malleability not only as a feature, but also as a strategy, for political actors. Keeping transitional justice malleable helped actors promoting the idea market it to diverse constituencies. At the same time, this strategy has led to the current predicament around transitional justice's future in academic, policy making, and advocacy circles.

SEARCHING FOR TRUTH IN THE TRANSITIONAL JUSTICE MOVEMENT

The circulation of transitional justice will continue, especially as actors promote and appropriate the idea and its associated interventions in new settings. Recent calls for truth commissions in countries such as Taiwan and Sri Lanka highlight just how popular truth commissions still are. However, given the ongoing critiques of transitional justice and truth commissions, of which this book is just one, in the near future it is likely that scholars, policy makers, and advocates will find a new justice-related idea or intervention that infatuates them. Already, scholars are trying to develop new ideas such as transformative justice and building on established ideas such as peacebuilding to emphasize the dilemmas associated with legalized understandings of transitional justice (Gready and Robins 2014; Laplante 2008; Sharp 2013). Reflecting on the case studies in this book reveals that developing better definitions or new ideas that extol law will not change the underlying dilemma of mobilizing the law to ensure accountability, improve survivor well-being, and prevent future violence.

Looking to the future of transitional justice, it remains unclear whether this loosely structured movement will coalesce or be replaced by a movement around another malleable legal idea. However, given the ongoing scholarly efforts to define

[143] U.S. Supreme Court, *Boumedienne et al v. Bush, President of the United States et al* 533 US (2008), no. 06-1155, p. 111.

[144] Jonathan Turley, "Our Loquacious Justices," *Los Angeles Times*, March 28 2006, http://articles.latimes.com/2006/mar/28/opinion/oe-turley28 (accessed December 4, 2016).

transitional justice, particularly in relation to international criminal law, the movement is likely headed toward formalization or fragmentation as proponents of "bottom-up" approaches clash with proponents of more standardization. Calls to "localize" transitional justice point out the utility of community-based truth telling initiatives and other alternatives to nationally or internationally driven interventions (Shaw et al. 2010). Ironically, this analysis suggests that formalizing understandings of transitional justice and truth commissions will undermine their malleability, which is what makes the idea and intervention so appealing. At the same time, that same malleability means that truth commissions may ultimately lose their purchase if actors promote or create them to undermine calls for justice, or if the actors draw on the label in more arbitrary ways to present their preferred narrative of the violence.

In the end, it is fatuous to reiterate that truth commissions, or any intervention associated with transitional justice, cannot ensure accountability, improve survivor well-being, or prevent future violence, and that they are bound to disappoint their proponents. At the same time, this book reveals how both the idea and the intervention are potent political tools. As such, they must be promoted with caution and ongoing awareness of how domestic organizational dynamics and political opportunities shape how they are understood, how they are promoted, and what their effects will be. Soon, actors interested in accountability, survivor well-being, and the prevention of future violence will likely find a new intervention to promote. Hopefully, they will be able to approach their goals and strategies with caution, and awareness that the social and political context will shape an intervention far more than an intervention will shape the social and political context.

References

Acharya, A., 2004. How Ideas Spread: Whose Norms Matter? Norm Localization and Institutional Change in Asian Regionalism. *International Organization*, 58(2), pp. 239–75.

Ancelovici, M. and Jenson, J., 2013. Standardization for Transnational Diffusion: The Case of Truth Commissions and Conditional Cash Transfers. *International Political Sociology*, 7(3), pp. 294–312.

Andrieu, K., 2010a. Civilizing Peacebuilding: Transitional Justice, Civil Society, and the Liberal Paradigm. *Security Dialogue*, 41(5), pp. 537–58.

2010b. Transitional Justice: A New Discipline in Human Rights. In *Online Encyclopedia of Mass Violence*, pp. 1–32, available at http://www.sciencespo.fr/mass-violence-war-massacre-resistance/en/document/transitional-justice-new-discipline-human-right, accessed March 6, 2017.

2016. An Unfinished Business: Transitional Justice and Democratization in Post-Soviet Russia. *International Journal of Transitional Justice*, 5(2), pp. 198–220.

Appadurai, A., 1996. *Modernity At Large: Cultural Dimensions of Globalization*, 1st ed., Minneapolis: University of Minnesota Press.

Arthur, P., 2009. How "Transitions" Reshaped Human Rights: A Conceptual History of Transitional Justice. *Human Rights Quarterly*, 31(2), pp. 321–67.

Backer, D., 2010. Watching a Bargain Unravel? A Panel Study of Victims' Attitudes about Transitional Justice in Cape Town, South Africa. *International Journal of Transitional Justice*, 4(3), pp. 443–56.

Bakiner, O., 2015. *Truth Commissions: Memory, Power, and Legitimacy*, Philadelphia: University of Pennsylvania Press.

Balint, J., Evansy, J. and McMillan, N., 2014. Rethinking Transitional Justice, Redressing Indigenous Harm: A New Conceptual Approach. *International Journal of Transitional Justice*, 8(2), pp. 194–216.

Bandy, J. and Smith, J., 2005. *Coalitions across Borders: Transnational Protest and the Neoliberal Order*, Lanham, MD: Rowman & Littlefield.

Basu, A., 2003. Globalization of the Local/Localization of the Global: Mapping Transitional Women's Movements, in Carole R. McCann and Seung-kyung Kim (eds.), *Feminist Theory Reader: Local and Global Perspectives*, New York: Routledge, pp. 68–77.

Bebbington, A., 2007. Social Movements and the Politicization of Chronic Poverty. *Development and Change*, 38(5), pp. 793–985.

Bell, C., 2009a. The "New Law" of Transitional Justice. In K. Ambos (ed.), *Building a Future on Peace and Justice: Studies on Transitional Justice, Conflict Resolution and Development: the Nuremberg Declaration on Peace and Justice*, Berlin: Springer, pp. 105–26.
2009b. Transitional Justice, Interdisciplinarity and the State of the "Field" or "Non-field." *International Journal of Transitional Justice*, 3(1), pp. 5–27.
Benford, R.D. and Snow, D.A., 2000. Framing Processes and Social Movements: An Overview and Assessment. *Annual Review of Sociology*, 26, pp. 611–39.
Bhabha, H., 1994. *The Location of Culture*, New York: Routledge.
Brahm, E., 2007. Uncovering the Truth: Examining Truth Commission Success and Impact. *International Studies Perspectives*, 8(1), pp. 16–35.
Brahm, E., Dancy, G. and Kim, H., 2010. The Turn to Truth: Trends in Truth Commission Experimentaion. *Journal of Human Rights*, 9(1), pp. 45–64.
Brockett, C.D., 1991. The Structure of Political Opportunities and Peasant Mobilization in Central America. *Comparative Politics*, 23(3), pp. 253–74.
Brown, W., 2006. American Nightmare: Neoliberalism, Neoconservatism, and De-democratization. *Political Theory*, 34(6), pp. 690–714.
Carrillo, Felix, 2009. "The Victims Remember: Notes about the Social Practice of Memory," in M. Briceño-Donn, F. Reátegui, M.C. Rivera, and C. Uprimny Salazar (eds.), *Recordar en Conflicto: Initiativas No Oficiales de Memoria en Colombia*, Bogotá, Colombia: International Center for Transitional Justice, pp. 17–42.
Carmichael, W., 2001. The Role of the Ford Foundation, in C. E. Welch (ed.), *NGOs and Human Rights: Promise and Performance*. Philadelphia: University of Pennsylavia Press, pp. 248–60.
Carruthers, B.G. and Halliday, T.C., 2006. Negotiating Globalization: Global Scripts and Intermediation in the Construction of Asian Insolvency Regimes. *Law and Social Inquiry*, 31(3), pp. 521–84.
Cassel, D.W., Jr., 1993. "International Truth Commissions and Justice," *Aspen Institute Quarterly* 5 (Summer): 69–90.
Chandler, D., 2000. *Bosnia: Faking Democracy after Dayton*, London: Pluto Press.
Chandler, D. and Heins, V., 2007. *Rethinking Ethical Foreign Policy: Pitfalls, Possibilities and Paradoxes*, New York: Routledge.
Chapman, A.R. and Ball, P., 2001. The Truth of Truth Commissions: Comparative Lessons from Haiti, South Africa, and Guatemala. *Human Rights Quarterly*, 23(1), pp. 1–43.
Chapman, A.R. and Van der Merwe, H., 2008. *Truth and Reconciliation in South Africa: Did the TRC Deliver?* Philadelphia: University of Pennsylvania Press.
Charmaz, K., 1995. *The Logic of Grounded Theory*. London: Sage Publications.
Checkel, J.T., 1999. Norms, Institutions, and National Identity in Contemporary Europe. *International Studies Quarterly*, 43(1), pp. 84–114.
Clark, J.N., 2009. Plea Bargaining at the ICTY: Guilty Pleas and Reconciliation. *European Journal of International Law*, 20(2), pp. 415–36.
Clarke, K., 2009. *Fictions of Justice: The International Criminal Court and the Challenge of Legal Pluralism in Sub-Saharan Africa*. New York: Cambridge University Press.
Clarke, K. and Goodale, M., 2009. *Mirrors of Justice: Law and Power in the Post-Cold War Era*, New York: Cambridge University Press.
Collier, D., 2011. Understanding Process Tracing. *PS: Political Science and Politics*, 44(4), pp. 823–30.
Cotterrell, R., 1997. *Law's Community: Legal Theory in Sociological Perspective*. New York: Oxford University Press.

1998. Why Must Legal Ideas Be Interpreted Sociologically? *Journal of Law and Society*, 25(2), pp. 171–92.

Daly, E., 2008. Truth Skepticism: An Inquiry into the Value of Truth in Times of Transition. *International Journal of Transitional Justice*, 2(1), pp. 23–41.

Dancy, G., Kim, H. and Wiebelhaus-Brahm, E., 2010. The Turn to Truth: Trends in Truth Commission Experimentation. *Journal of Human Rights*, 9(1), pp. 45–64.

Danner, A.M. and Martinez, J.S., 2005. Guilty Associations: Joint Criminal Enterprise, Command Responsibility, and the Development of International Criminal Law. *California Law Review*, 93(1), pp. 75–169.

Davis, G.F., 2005. *Social Movements and Organization Theory*, New York: Cambridge University Press.

De Brito, A.B., Gonzãlez Enríquez, C. and Aguilar, P., 2001. *The Politics of Memory: Transitional Justice in Democratizing Societies*, Oxford: Oxford University Press.

De Greiff, P., 2012. Theorizing Transitional Justice, in M. Williams, R. Nagy, and J. Elster (eds.), *Transitional Justice: NOMOS LI*, New York University Press, pp. 31–77.

De Greiff, P. and Duthie, R., 2009. *Transitional Justice and Development: Making Connections*, New York: Social Science Research Council.

Della Porta, D., 2007. *The Global Justice Movement: Cross-national and Transnational Perspectives*. New York: Paradigm Publishers.

Della Porta, D. and Diani, M., 2006. *Social Movements*, 2nd ed. Oxford, UK: Blackwell.

Delpla, I., 2007. In the Midst of Injustice: The ICTY from the Perspective of Some Victim Associations, in X. Bougarel, E. Helms, and G. Duijzings (eds.), *The New Bosnian Mosaic – Identities, Memories and Moral Claims in Post-war Society*. Aldershot, UK: Ashgate Publishing Company, pp. 211–34.

De Sousa Santos, B., 1999. Towards a Multi-cultural Conception of Human Rights, in M. Featherstone and S. Lash (eds.), *Spaces of Culture: City, Nation, World*, New York: Sage, pp. 214–29.

De Sousa Santos, B. and Rodríguez-Garavito, C., 2005. *Law and Globalization from Below: Towards a Cosmopolitan Legality*, New York: Cambridge University Press.

Dezalay, Y. and Garth, B., 1996. *Dealing in Virtue: International Commercial Arbitration and the Construction of a Transnational Legal Order*, Chicago: University of Chicago Press.

2002. *The Internationalization of the Palace Wars: Lawyers, Economists, and the Contest to Transform Latin American States*, Chicago: University of Chicago Press.

Diaz, C., 2008. "Challenging Impunity from Below: The Contested Ownership of Transitional Justice in Columbia," in K. McEvoy and L. McGregor (eds.), *Transitional Justice from Below: Grassroots Activism and the Struggle for Change*, Portland, OR: Oxford Hart, pp. 189–216.

DiMaggio, P. and Powell, W., 1983. The Iron Cage Revisited: Institutional Isomorphism and Collective Rationality in Organization Fields. *American Sociological Review*, 48(2), pp. 147–60.

Dimitrijevic, N., 2008. Serbia after the Criminal Past: What Went Wrong and What Should Be Done. *International Journal of Transitional Justice*, 2(1), pp. 5–22.

Donnelly, J., 2007. *International Human Rights*, Boulder, CO: Westview Press.

Dukalskis, A., 2011. Interactions in Transition: How Truth Commissions and Trials Complement or Constrain Each Other. *International Studies Review*, 13(3), pp. 432–51.

Elster, J., 2004. *Closing the Books: Transitional Justice in Historical Perspective*, New York: Cambridge University Press.

Engle, K., 2015. Anti-impunity and the Turn to International Criminal Law in Human Rights. *Cornell Law Review*, 100, pp. 1069–127.

Engle, K., Miller, Z. and Davis, D.M., 2016. *Anti-impunity and the Human Rights Agenda*, New York: Cambridge University Press.

Ensalaco, M., 1995. "Truth Commissions for Chile and El Salvador: A Report and Assessment." *Human Rights Quarterly*, 16, pp. 656–75.

Eskridge, William N.J., 2013. The New Textualism and Normative Canons. *Columbia Law Review*, 113(2), pp. 531–92.

Evangelista, M., 1995. The Paradox of State Strength: Transnational Relations, Domestic Structures, and Security Policy in Russia and the Soviet Union. *International Organization*. 49(1), pp. 1–39.

Eyal, G., 2013. For a Sociology of Expertise: The Social Origins of the Autism Epidemic. *American Journal of Sociology*. 118(4), pp. 863–907.

Finnemore, M. and Sikkink, K., 1998. International Norm Dynamics and Political Change. *International Organization*, 52(4), pp. 887–917.

Finnemore, M. and Sikkink, K., 2001. Taking Stock: The Constructivist Research Program in International Relations and Comparative Politics. *Annual Review of Political Science*, 4(1), pp. 391–416.

Fletcher, L.E., Stover, E., Smith, S.P., Koenig, A., Aziz, Z., Kelly, A., Staveteig, S. and Mizoguchi, N., 2008. *Guantánamo and Its Aftermath: US Detention and Interrogation Practices and Their Impact on Former Detainees*, Berkeley, CA: University of California Press.

Fletcher, L., Weinstein, H. and Rowen, J., 2009. Context, Timing and the Dynamics of Transitional Justice: A Historical Perspective. *Human Rights Quarterly*, 31(1), pp. 163–220.

Forsythe, D., 2011. Forum: Transitional Justice: The Quest for Theory to Inform Policy. *International Studies Review*, 13(3), pp. 554–78.

Fourcade, M., 2006. The Construction of a Global Profession: The Transnationalization of Economics. *American Journal of Sociology*, 112(1), pp. 145–94.

Freeden, M., 2006. Ideology and Political Theory. *Journal of Political Ideologies*, 11(1), pp. 3–22.

Freeman, M., 2006. *Truth Commissions and Procedural Fairness*, New York: Cambridge University Press.

Gamson, W.A., 1975. The Social Psychology of Collective Action, in C. M. M. Aldon and D. Norris (eds.), *Frontiers in Social Movement Theory*, New Haven, CT: Yale University Press.

Gardner, J., 1980. *Legal Imperialism: American Lawyers and Foreign Aid in Latin America*. Madison, WI: University of Wisconsin Press.

George, A.L. and Bennett, A., 2005. *Case Studies and Theory Development in the Social Sciences*, Cambridge, MA: MIT Press.

Gibson, J.L., 2002. Truth, Justice, and Reconciliation: Judging the Fairness of Amnesty in South Africa. *American Journal of Political Science*, 46(3), pp. 540–56.

Goffman, E., 1974. *Frame Analysis*, New York: Harper Colophon.

Gomez, M., 2013. Malleable Law: The (Mis)Use of Legal Tools in the Pursuit of a Political Agenda. *ILSA Journal of International and Comparative Law*, 19, pp. 509–54.

Goodale, M. and Merry, S., 2007. *The Practice of Human Rights: Tracking Law between the Global and the Local*, New York: Cambridge University Press.

Grandin, G., 2016. Did Human Rights Watch Sabotage the Colombia Peace Agreement. *The Nation*. October 3.

Gready, P., 2010. *The Era of Transitional Justice: The Aftermath of the Truth and Reconciliation Commission in South Africa and Beyond*, Abingdon, UK: Taylor & Francis.

Gready, P. and Robins, S., 2014. From Transitional to Transformative Justice: A New Agenda for Practice. *International Journal of Transitional Justice*, 8(3), pp. 339–61.

Gupta, A. and Ferguson, J., 1997. *Culture, Power, Place: Explorations in Critical Anthropology*, Raleigh, NC: Duke University Press.

Haas, P., 2013. "Epistemic Communities," in Joel Krieger (ed.), *The Oxford Companion to Comparative Politics*, New York: Oxford University Press, pp. 351–59.

2014. "Ideas, Experts, and Governance," in M. Ambrus, K. Arts, E. Hey, and H. Raulus (eds.), *The Role of "Experts" in International and European Decision Making Processes: Advisors, Decision Makers or Irrelevant Actors*. New York: Cambridge University Press, pp. 19–43.

Hayner, P.B., 1994. Fifteen Truth Commissions – 1974 to 1994: A Comparative Study. *Human Rights Quarterly*, 16(4), pp. 597–655.

2002. *Unspeakable Truths: Facing the Challenge of Truth Commissions*, 1st ed. New York: Routledge.

2010. *Unspeakable Truths: Facing the Challenge of Truth Commissions*, 2nd ed. New York: Routledge.

Henkin, L., 2000. Human Rights: Ideology and Aspiration, Reality and Prospect. In S. Power and G. Allison (eds.), *Realizing Human Rights*, New York: Palgrave Macmillan, pp. 3–38.

Hinton, A.L. (ed.), 2010. *Transitional Justice: Global Mechanisms and Local Realities after Genocide and Mass Violence*, New Brunswick, NJ: Rutgers University Press.

Horne, C.M., 2014. Reconstructing Traditional Justice from the Outside In: Transitional Justice in Aceh and East Timor. *Journal of Peacebuilding and Development*, 9(2), pp. 17–32.

Huyse, L., 1995. Justice after Transition: On the Choices Successor Elites Make in Dealing with the Past. *Law and Social Inquiry*, 20(1), pp. 51–78.

Ingram, P. and Clay, K., 2000. The Choice-Within-Constraints New Institutionalism and Implications for Sociology. *Annual Review of Sociology*, 26(1), pp. 525–46.

Iverson, J., 2013. Transitional Justice, Jus Post Bellum and International Criminal Law: Differentiating the Usages, History and Dynamics. *International Journal of Transitional Justice*, 7(3), pp. 413–33.

Ivković, S.K. and Hagan, J., 2006. The Politics of Punishment and the Siege of Sarajevo: Toward a Conflict Theory of Perceived International (In)Justice. *Law and Society Review*, 40(2), pp. 369–410.

Jacoby, W., 2006. Inspiration, Coalition, and Substitution: External Influences on Postcommunist Transformations. *World Politics*, 58(4), pp. 623–51.

Jenkins, J.C. and Eckert, C.M., 1986. Channeling Black Insurgency: Elite Patronage and Professional Social Movement Organizations in the Development of the Black Movement. *American Sociological Review*, 51(6), pp. 812–29.

Jouhanneau, C., 2008. Si vous avez un problème que vous ne voulez pas régler, créez une commission: Les commissions d'enquête locales dans la Bosnie-Herzégovine d'après-guerre. *Mouvements*, 1, pp. 166–74.

Keck, M. and Sikkink, K., 1998. *Activists beyond Borders: Advocacy Networks in International Networks*, Ithaca, NY: Cornell University Press.

Kelsall, T., 2009. *Culture under Cross-Examination: International Justice and the Special Court for Sierra Leone*, New York: Cambridge University Press.

Khagram, S., Riker, J.V. and Sikkink, K., 2002. *Restructuring World Politics: Transnational Social Movements, Networks and Norms*, Minneapolis: University of Minnesota Press.

Kim, H.J., 2012. Local, National, and International Determinants of Truth Commission: The South Korean Experience. *Human Rights Quarterly*, 34(3), pp. 726–50.

Koenig, A. and Smith, S.C., forthcoming. Procedural Justice in Transitional Contexts.
Korey, W., 2007. *Taking on the World's Repressive Regimes: The Ford Foundation's International Human Rights Policies and Practices*, New York: Palgrave Macmillan.
Kritz, N., 2009. Policy Implications of Empirical Research on Transitional Justice. In Hugo van der Merwe, Victoria Baxter, and Audrey R. Chapman (eds.), *Assessing the Impact of Transitional Justice Challenges for Empirical Research*, Washington, DC: United States Institute of Peace, pp. 13–21.
Kritz, N. and Finci, J., 2001. A Truth and Reconciliation Commission in Bosnia and Herzegovina: An Idea Whose Time Has Come. *International Law FORUM du droit international*, 3(1), pp. 5–58.
Kurzman, C., 2008. Introduction: Meaning-Making in Social Movements. *Anthropological Quarterly*, 81(1), pp. 5–15.
Laplante, L.J., 2008. Transitional Justice and Peace Building: Diagnosing and Addressing the Socioeconomic Roots of Violence through a Human Rights Framework. *International Journal of Transitional Justice*, 2(3), pp. 331–55.
Laplante, L.J. and Theidon, K., 2006. Transitional Justice in Times of Conflict: Colombia's Ley de Justicia y Paz. *Chicago Journal of International Law*, 2(1), pp. 1–34.
Lefranc, S., 2008. La justice transitionnelle n'est pas un concept. *Mouvements*, 1, pp. 61–69.
2010. La professionnalisation d'un militantisme réformateur du droit: L'invention de la justice transitionnelle. *Droit et Société*, 3, pp. 561–89.
Lefranc, S. and Mouralis, G., 2014. De quel(s) droit(s) la justice internationale est-elle faite? Deux moments de la constitution hésitante d'une justice de l'après-conflit. In *Chercheurs à la barre, Socio*, 3, pp. 209–45.
Lemaitre Ripoll, J., 2009. *El derecho como conjuro: Fetichismo legal, violencia y movemientos sociales*. Bogotá, Colombia: Siglo del Hombre Editores, Universidad de los Andes.
Levitt, P. and Merry, S., 2009. Vernacularization on the Ground: Local Uses of Global Women's Rights in Peru, China, India and the United States. *Global Networks*, 9(4), 441–61.
Luttwak, E.N., 1999. Give War a Chance. *Foreign Affairs*, 78(4) [Web].
Lutz, E. and Sikkink, K., 2001. The Justice Cascade: The Evolution and Impact of Foreign Human Rights Trials in Latin America. *Chicago Journal of International Law*, 2, pp. 1–34.
MacCoun, R., 2005. Voice, Control, and Belonging: The Double-Edged Sword of Procedural Fairness. *Annual Review of Law and Social Science*, 1, pp. 171–201.
Madlingozi, T., 2010. On Transitional Justice Entrepreneurs and the Production of Victims. *Journal of Human Rights Practice*, 2(2), pp. 208–28.
Mahoney, J., 2012. The Logic of Process Tracing Tests in the Social Sciences. *Sociological Methods and Research*, 41(4), pp. 570–97.
Mamdani, M., 2002. *When Victims Become Killers: Colonialism, Nativism, and the Genocide in Rwanda*. Princeton, NJ: Princeton University Press.
Massoud, M., 2011. Do Victims of War Need International Law? Human Rights Education Programs in Authoritarian Sudan. *Law and Society Review*, 45(1), pp. 1–32.
2013. *Law's Fragile State: Colonial, Authoritarian, and Humanitarian Legacies in Sudan*. New York: Cambridge University Press.
Mattei, U. and Nader, L., 2008. *Plunder: When the Rule of Law Is Illegal*. Malden, MA: Blackwell Publishing.
Mayer, J. 2009. *The Dark Side: The Inside Story of How the War on Terror Turned into a War on American Ideals*. New York: Doubleday.

McAdam, D., McCarthy, J. and Zald, M.N., 1996. *Comparative Perspectives on Social Movements: Political Opportunities, Mobilizing Structures and Cultural Framings*, Cambridge, UK: Cambridge University Press.

McAdam, D. and Scott, W.R., 2005. Organizations and Movements, in G. Davis, D. McAdam, W.R. Scott, and M.N. Zald (eds.), *Social Movements and Organization Theory*, Cambridge, UK: Cambridge University Press, pp. 4–40.

McCann, M., 2006. Law and Social Movements: Contemporary Perspectives, *Annual Review of Law and Social Science*, 2, pp. 17–38.

McCarthy, J.D. and Zald, M.N., 1973. *The Trend of Social Movements in America: Professionalization and Resource Mobilization*, Morristown, NJ: General Learning Press.

McEvoy, K., 2007. Beyond Legalism: Towards a Thicker Understanding of Transitional Justice. *Journal of Law and Society*, 34(4), pp. 411–40.

Merry, S.E., 1990. *Getting Justice and Getting Even: Legal Consciousness among Working-Class Americans*, Chicago: University of Chicago Press.

2005. Anthropology and Activism: Researching Human Rights across Porous Boundaries. *PoLAR: Political and Legal Anthropology Review*, 28(2), pp. 240–57.

2006. New Legal Realism and the Ethnography of Transnational Law. *Law and Social Inquiry*, 31(4), pp. 975–95.

2013. The Discourses of Mediation and the Power of Naming. *Yale Journal of Law and the Humanities*, 2(1), pp. 1–36.

Merry, S.E. and Stern, R.E., 2005. The Female Inheritance Movement in Hong Kong Theorizing the Local/Global Interface. *Current Anthropology*, 46(3), pp. 387–409.

Meyer, J.W. and Rowan, B., 1977. Institutionalized Organizations: Formal Structure as Myth and Ceremony. *American Journal of Sociology*, 83(2), 340–63.

Meyerstein, A., 2007. Between Law and Culture: Rwanda's Gacaca and Postcolonial Legality. *Law and Social Inquiry*, 32(2), pp. 1–42.

Minow, M., 1998. In Practice Between Vengeance and Forgiveness: South Africa's Truth and Reconciliation Commission. *Negotiation Journal*, 14(4), (October), pp. 319–55.

Minow, M. and Chayes, A., 2003. *Imagine Coexistence: Restoring Humanity after Ethnic Conflict*, San Francisco: Jossey-Bass.

Moore, A., 2013. *Peacebuilding in Practice: Local Experience in Two Bosnian Towns*, Ithaca, NY: Cornell University Press.

Moore, F., 1973. Law and Social Change: The Semi-autonomous Social Field as an Appropriate Subject of Study. *Law and Society Review*, 7(4), pp. 719–46.

Mouralis, G., 2013. The Invention of Transitional Justice in the 1990s, in L. Israel and G. Mouralis (eds.), *Dealing with Wars and Dictatorships: Legal Concepts and Categories in Action*, The Hague: TMC Asser Press, pp. 81–97.

Moyn, S., 2010. *The Last Utopia: Human Rights in History*, Cambridge, MA: Belknap Press of Harvard University Press.

Musila, G.M., 2009. Options for Transitional Justice in Kenya: Autonomy and the Challenge of External Prescriptions. *International Journal of Transitional Justice*, 3(3), pp. 445–64.

Nader, L., 1991. *Harmony Ideology: Justice and Control in a Zapotec Mountain Village*, Palo Alto, CA: Stanford University Press.

1999. Globalization of Law: ADR as Soft Technology. *American Society of International Law Proceedings*, 93, pp. 24–27.

Nader, L. and Grande, E., 2002. Current Illusions and Delusions about Conflict Management in Africa and Elsewhere. *Law and Social Inquiry*, 27(3), pp. 573–91.

Nadery, A.N., 2007. Peace or Justice? Transitional Justice in Afghanistan. *International Journal of Transitional Justice*, 1(1), pp. 173–79.

Naftali, P., 2015. Politics of Truth: On Legal Fetishism and the Rhetoric of Complementarity. *Revue quebecoise de droit international* (December), pp. 121–28.

2016. Crafting a "Right to Truth" in International Law: Converging Mobilizations, Diverging Agendas? *Champ penal*, 13, available at http://champpenal.revues.org/9245.

Nagy, R., 2008. "Transitional Justice as Global Project: Critical Reflections." *Third World Quarterly*, 29, pp. 275–89.

2009. Transitional Justice from Below: Grassroots Activism and the Struggle for Change. *Law and Society Review*, 43(3), pp. 707–09.

2013. The Scope and Bounds of Transitional Justice and the Canadian Truth and Reconciliation Commission. *International Journal of Transitional Justice*, 7(1), pp. 52–73.

2014. The Truth and Reconciliation Commission of Canada: Genesis and Design. *Law and Society Review*, 29(2), pp. 199–217.

Neier, A., 2012. *The International Human Rights Movement: A History*, Princeton, NJ: Princeton University Press.

Nettelfield, L.J., 2010. *Courting Democracy in Bosnia and Herzegovina: The Hague Tribunal's Impact in a Postwar State*, New York: Cambridge University Press.

O'Donnell, G. and Schmitter, P.C., 1986. *Transitions from Authoritarian Rule: Tentative Conclusions about Uncertain Democracies*. Baltimore, MD: Johns Hopkins University Press.

Okello, M.C., 2012. *Where Law Meets Reality: Forging African Transitional Justice*, Cape Town, South Africa: Pambazuka Press.

Olsen, T.D., Payne, L.A. and Reiter, A.G., 2010. *Transitional Justice in Balance: Comparing Processes, Weighing Efficacy*, Washington, DC: United States Institute of Peace Press.

Olsen, T.D., Payne, L.A., Reiter, A.G., and Wiebelhaus-Brahm, E. 2010. When Truth Commissions Improve Human Rights. *International Journal of Transitional Justice* 4(3), pp. 457–76.

Oomen, B., 2005. Donor-Driven Justice and Its Discontents: The Case of Rwanda. *Development and Change*, 36(5), pp. 887–910.

Orozco, I., 2003. La Postguerra Colombiana: Divagaciones Sobre la Venganza, la Justicia y la Reconciliación, Working Paper 306, Kellogg Institute, available at https://kellogg.nd.edu/publications/workingpapers/WPS/306.pdf, accessed February 16, 2017.

Peskin, V., 2008. *International Justice in Rwanda and the Balkans: Virtual Trials and the Struggle for State Cooperation*, New York: Cambridge University Press.

Phillips, T., 2008. Justice in Times of Conflict, in C. Stout (ed.), *The New Humanitarians*, Santa Barbara, CA: Praeger Press.

Popkin, M. and Roht-Arriaza, N., 1995. Truth as Justice: Investigatory Commissions in Latin America. *Law and Social Inquiry*, 20(1), pp. 79–116.

Popovic, D., 2009. *Transitional Justice Guidebook for Bosnia and Herzegovina*, Sarajevo, Bosnia and Herzegovina: United Nations Development Program.

Posner, R., 1998. Professionalisms. *Arizona Law Review* 40, pp. 1–15.

Quinn, J.R. and Freeman, M., 2003. Lessons Learned: Practical Lessons Gleaned from inside the Truth Commissions of Guatemala and South Africa. *Human Rights Quarterly*, 25(4), pp. 1117–49.

Ragin, C.C., 1989. *The Comparative Method: Moving beyond Qualitative and Quantitative Strategies*, Berkeley, CA: University of California Press.

Resnick, D., 2009. The Benefits of Frame Resonance Disputes for Transnational Movements: The Case of Botswana's Central Kalahari Game Reserve. *Social Movement Studies: Journal of Social, Cultural and Political Protest*, 8(1), 55–72.

Risse-Kappen, T., 1995. *Bringing Transnational Relations Back In: Non-state Actors, Domestic Structures, and International Institutions*, New York: Cambridge University Press.

Robins, S., 2012. Transitional Justice as an Elite Discourse. *Critical Asian Studies*, 44(1), pp. 3–30.

Roht-Arriaza, N., 2006. The New Landscape of Transitional Justice, in N. Roht-Arriaza and J. Mariezcurrena (eds.), *Beyond Truth vs. Justice: Transitional Justice in the 21st Century*, New York: Cambridge University Press, pp. 1–16.

Roht-Arriaza, N., and Mariezcurrena, J. (eds.), 2006. *Beyond Truth vs. Justice: Transitional Justice in the 21st Century*, New York: Cambridge University Press.

Roper, S.D. and Barria, L.A., 2009. Why Do States Commission the Truth? Political Considerations in the Establishment of African Truth and Reconciliation Commissions. *Human Rights Review*, 10(3), pp. 373–91.

Rotberg, R.I. and Thompson, D.F., 2000. *Truth v. Justice: The Morality of Truth Commissions*, Princeton, NJ: Princeton University Press.

Rowen, J., 2012. Mobilizing Truth: Agenda Setting in a Transnational Social Movement. *Law and Social Inquiry*, 37(3), pp. 686–718.

Rowen, J., forthcoming. "We Don't Believe in Transitional Justice": Peace and the Politics of Legal Ideas in Colombia. *Law and Social Inquiry*.

Sajjad, T., 2013. *Transitional Justice in South Asia: A Study of Afghanistan and Nepal*, London and New York: Routledge.

Sanchez, N.C. and Ibáñez, C.I. 2014. La justicia transicional como categoría constitucional, in K. Ambos (ed.), *Justicia de transición y constitución: Análisis de la sentencia C-579 de 2013 de la Corte Constitucional*. Bogotá, Colombia: Temis, CEDPAL, Konrad Adenauer Stiftung, pp. 107–54.

Santos, B., 1996. *Towards a Multicultural Conception of Human Rights*, Madison, WI: University of Wisconsin Press.

Sarat, A. (ed.), 2012. *Transitions: Legal Change, Legal Meanings*. Tuscaloosa, AL: University of Alabama Press.

Sharp, D.N., 2013. Beyond the Post-conflict Checklist: Linking Peacebuilding and Transitional Justice through the Lens of Critique. *Chicago Journal of International Law*, 14(1), pp. 165–96.

Shaw, R., 2005. *Rethinking Truth and Reconciliation Commissions: Lessons from Sierra Leone*, Washington, DC: United States Institute of Peace Press, pp. 1–12.

2007. Memory Frictions: Localizing the Truth and Reconciliation Commission in Sierra Leone. *International Journal of Transitional Justice*, 1(2), pp. 183–207.

Shaw, R., Waldorf, L. and Hazan, P., 2010. *Localizing Transitional Justice: Interventions and Priorities after Mass Violence*, Palo Alto, CA: Stanford University Press.

Simmons, B. and Danner, A., 2010. Credible Commitments and the International Criminal Court. *International Organization*, 64(2), pp. 225–56.

Simpson, G., Hodžić, E. and Bickford, L., 2012. *Looking Back, Looking Forward: Promoting Dialogue through Truth Seeking in Bosnia and Herzegovina*, Sarajevo, Bosnia and Herzegovina: United Nations Development Program.

Slyomovics, S., 2005. *The Performance of Human Rights in Morocco*. Philadelphia, PA: University of Pennsylvania Press.

Smith, J., 2008. *Social Movements for Global Democracy*. Baltimore, MD: Johns Hopkins Unviersity Press.

Snow, D.A., Soule, S.A. and Kriesi, H., 2008. *The Blackwell Companion to Social Movements*, Oxford: Blackwell.

Sperling, V., Ferree, M.M. and Risman, B., 2001. Constructing Global Feminism: Transnational Advocacy Networks and Russian Women's Activism. *Signs: Journal of Women in Culture and Society*, 26(4), pp. 1155–86.
Staggenborg, S., 1988. The Consequences of Professionalization and Formalization in the Pro-choice Movement. *American Sociological Review*, 53(4), pp. 585–605.
Steinberg, J., 2011. A *Truth Commission Goes Abroad: Liberian Transitional Justice in New York*. *African Affairs*, 110(438), pp. 35–53.
Stern, C., 1999. The Evolution of Social–Movement Organizations: Niche Competition in Social Space. *European Sociological Review*, 15(1), pp. 91–105.
Stern, N., 2013. Preparing: The Sixth Task of Crisis Leadership. *Journal of Leadership Studies* 7(3), pp. 51–69.
Stover, E., Megally, H. and Mufti, H., 2005. Bremer's "Gordian Knot": Transitional Justice and the US Occupation of Iraq. *Human Rights Quarterly*, 27(3), pp. 830–57.
Strang, D. and Soule, S., 1998. Diffusion in Organizations and Social Movements: From Hybrid Corn to Poison Pills. *Annual Review of Sociology*, 24, 265–90.
Subotić, J., 2009. The Paradox of International Justice Compliance. *International Journal of Transitional Justice*, 3(3), pp. 362–83.
2012. The Transformation of International Transitional Justice Advocacy. *International Journal of Transitional Justice*, 6(1), pp. 106–25.
Suddaby, R. and Viale, T., 2011. Professionals and Field-Level Change: Institutional Work and the Professional Project. *Current Sociology*, 59(4), pp. 423–42.
Sunstein, C.R., 1996. Social Norms and Social Roles. *Columbia Law Review*, 96(4), pp. 903–68.
Sutil, J.C., 1992. Dealing with Past Human Rights Violations: The Chilean Case After Dictatorship, *Notre Dame Law Review*, 67, pp. 1455–85.
Tarrow, S., 1994. *Power in Movement: Social Movements, Collective Action and Politics*, New York: Cambridge University Press.
Tarrow, S., 2001. Transnational Politics: Contention and Institutions in International Politics. *Annual Review of Political Science*, 4(1), pp. 1–20.
Tate, W., 2007. *Counting the Dead: The Culture and Politics of Human Rights Activism in Colombia*. Berkeley, CA: University of California Press.
Taylor, L.K. and Dukalskis, A., 2012. Old Truths and New Politics: Does Truth Commission "Publicness" Impact Democratization? *Journal of Peace Research*, 49(5), pp. 671–84.
Teitel, R., 2002. *Transitional Justice*. New York: Oxford University Press.
2003. Transitional Justice Genealogy. *Harvard Human Rights Journal*, 16, pp. 69–94.
2005. The Law and Politics of Contemporary Transitional Justice. *Cornell International Law Journal*, 38(10), pp. 837–63.
2008. Editorial Note – Transitional Justice Globalized. *International Journal of Transitional Justice*, 2(1), pp. 1–4.
2011. *Humanity's Law*, New York: Oxford University Press.
2014. *Globalizing Transitional Justice: Contemporary Essays*, New York: Oxford Univeristy Press.
Tepperman, J., 2002. Truth and Consequences. *Foreign Affairs*, 81(2), pp. 128–45.
Tilly, C. and Tarrow, S., 2007. *Contentious Politics*. Boulder, CO: Paradigm Publishers.
Theidon, K., 2009. Editorial Note. *International Journal of Transitional Justice*, 3(3), 295–300.
Trubek, D.M. and Galanter, M., 1974. Scholars in Self-Estrangement: Some Reflections on the Crisis in Law and Development Studies in the United States. *Wisconsin Law Review*, 4, pp. 1062–101.

Tsing, A.L., 2005. *Friction: An Ethnography of Global Connection*. Princeton, NJ: Princeton University Press.

Turner, C., 2013. Deconstructing Transitional Justice. *Law and Critique*, 24(2), pp. 193–209.

Uprimny, R. and Saffon, M.P., 2008. Usos y abusos de la justicia transicional en Colombia. *Anuario de derechos humanos*, pp. 165–95.

Vinck, P. and Pham, P.N., 2010. Outreach Evaluation: The International Criminal Court in the Central African Republic. *International Journal of Transitional Justice*, 4(3), pp. 421–42.

Vinjamuri, L. and Snyder, J., 2004. Advocacy and Scholarship in the Study of International War Crime Tribunals and Transitional Justice. *Annual Review of Political Science*, 7, pp. 245–362.

Weinstein, H. and Van der Merwe, H., 2008. Editorial Note. *International Journal of Transitional Justice*, 2(2), pp. 123–25.

Wilensky, H.L., 1964. The Professionalization of Everyone? *American Journal of Sociology*, 70(2), pp. 137–58.

Wilson, R., 2001. *The Politics of Truth and Reconciliation in South Africa*, New York: Cambridge University Press.

De Ycaza, C., 2013. A Search for Truth: A Critical Analysis of the Liberian Truth and Reconciliation Commission. *Human Rights Review*, 14(3), pp. 189–212.

Zalaquett, J., 1994. Balancing Ethical Imperatives and Political Constraints: The Dilemmas of New Democracies Facing Past Human RIghts Violations. *Hastings Law Journal*, 43, pp. 1425–38.

Zald, M.N. and McCarthy, J., 1987. *Social Movements in an Organizational Society*, New Brunswick, NJ: Transaction Publishers.

Žižek, S., 2005. Against Human Rights. *New Left Review*, (34), pp. 115–31.

Index